THE SECOND WORLD WAR IN LITERATURE

THE SECOND WORLD WAR IN LITERATURE

Eight Essays

EDITED BY

IAN HIGGINS

SCOTTISH ACADEMIC PRESS
EDINBURGH AND LONDON

Reprinted, with additional text and corrections, from
FORUM FOR MODERN LANGUAGE STUDIES
Volume XXI No. 1

Published by
Scottish Academic Press Ltd.
33 Montgomery Street, Edinburgh EH7 5JX

SBN 7073 0427 X

This edition first published 1986

© Forum for Modern Language Studies 1986

All rights reserved. No part of this publication may be reproduced, stored in a retrieval system, or transmitted, in any form, or by any means, electronic, mechanical, photocopying, recording or otherwise, without the prior permission of the Scottish Academic Press Ltd., 33 Montgomery Street, Edinburgh EH7 5JX.

British Library Cataloguing in Publication Data

The Second World War in Literature
1. Literature, Modern–20th century–History and criticism.
2. World War, 1939-45–Literature and the war.
I. Higgins, Ian.
809′.93358 PN56.W/

ISBN 0-7073-0427-X

Printed in Great Britain by
ALLEN LITHO, Kirkcaldy

FOREWORD

Forty years after the Second World War, its representation in literature is arousing a lot of interest in criticism. As the war's history and literature (especially novels) come more and more to be written not just by its active participants or by those who lived through it as children, but by people born after 1945, it becomes ever clearer how writing about those who made history between 1939 and 1945 may itself be a way of making history. So, *a fortiori*, may writing about writing. The essays collected here all exemplify these questions, and some focus directly on them.

The present volume originated as an issue of *Forum for Modern Language Studies*, to which three new contributions have been added. Contributors were left free to decide whether to study single writers or small groups of writers, to survey whole periods, or to discuss theoretical or methodological problems implied in the subject. They were, however, asked not to lose from sight the relation between history and the literature examined. Each of these approaches is to be found in the volume, singly or in combination.

H. M. Klein compares the contents of Tambimuttu's 1942 anthology, *Poetry in Wartime*, with those of others published then and since. (Appendix I gives a complete index of authors and first lines.) These specific data enable Klein to compare conceptions of war poetry with one another, and to suggest changes in taste since 1945. The essay shows clearly that these problems can only be fully explored if historical and sociological considerations are allowed to partner textual ones.

Arnold McMillin's survey of literary representation of the war in Russian fiction outlines the heroic mythology of the earliest Soviet war novels, the reaction against it in the late fifties and early sixties, and the subsequent reassertion of orthodoxy. In addition, *samizdat* and *tamizdat* writing are considered alongside legal and illegal Soviet writing, so that the problems of truthfulness and realism are always in the foreground.

The question of myth, in the sense of a "transcendent proposition" shared by all Americans, is central to Eric Homberger's essay: the unquestioningly and unquestionedly patriotic good guy G.I. of fiction in the 1940s dominates the figure of the liberal, both in fiction and outside it. While these war novels in several ways mirrored society, an implied question is that of how far society mirrored the novels. Such interaction is in part the subject of Alan Morris' essay on the elaboration of a Gaullist view of the French Resistance and the widespread literary attacks on it since the late 1960s: where history, whether written or oral, is deficient to the point of becoming myth, literature may take it upon itself to supply the deficiency. A. F. Bance, on the other hand, shows how West German historians have only very recently faced up to the *Wehrmacht*'s involvement in atrocities on the Eastern Front, and that novelists have hitherto also subscribed to the historical myth of a "gentlemanly" German army.

Comparing Bloch's *L'étrange défaite* with Claude Simon's *La route des Flandres*, Anthony Cheal Pugh shows that "encoding" – and therefore, perhaps, some kind of myth-making – is essential to historiography and novel-writing alike. In Appendix II, however, Pugh queries the narrow concept of reference implied in the notion of "referential illusion", and illustrates his argument with previously unpublished autobiographical material supplied by Simon.

Ian Higgins discusses French Resistance poetry in a dual function: the poem voices a collective aspiration and, as a linguistic act, contributes – often deliberately – to the making of history and its transformation into myth. Without using these terms, J. M. Ritchie shows that exiled anti-Nazi German playwrights, including those writing in the Soviet Union about the Eastern Front, could only solve the problem posed by foreign prejudice or ignorance with a stylisation and simplification reminiscent of myth in each of the definitions suggested above.

This book is not comprehensive in coverage, and the essays vary in method. Coverage in such collections depends on how much space there is and what contributors can be found. The inevitable omissions in this volume are naturally a matter of regret. Adopting different methods, however, was deliberate. Taken together, the essays exemplify different approaches to the problem not only of what war literature is, or of what the war was (and is), but of what literature and history are; and the variety of approaches is an essential part of the problem.

I would like to thank Jeff Ashcroft, Ann Cottrell, Douglas Grant, Roy Owen and the patient staff of Allen Litho Ltd. for their help with the production of this book.

I.H.

CONTENTS

CONTRIBUTORS

H. M. KLEIN lectures on English and Comparative Literature at the University of East Anglia. His publications include translations into German and studies of English literature. He has edited and co-edited volumes of essays on the First and Second World Wars in fiction.

ARNOLD McMILLIN is Bowes Professor of Russian in the University of Liverpool. His publications include a history of Byelorussian literature and many articles on war-related topics in modern Russian and Byelorussian literature.

ERIC HOMBERGER lectures on American Studies at the University of East Anglia. He has published books on English and American poetry and on American literature and radical politics, as well as co-editing (with H. M. Klein) a set of essays on the Second World War in fiction.

IAN HIGGINS lectures on French at the University of St Andrews. His publications include studies of Francis Ponge and an anthology of Second World War French poetry.

ANTHONY CHEAL PUGH lectures on French at the University of Durham. His publications include articles on Claude Simon, Robert Pinget, literary theory and a monograph on Simon's novel *Histoire*.

ALAN MORRIS lectures on French at the Huddersfield Polytechnic. He has just completed a Ph.D. thesis on the German Occupation in modern French fiction.

J. M. RITCHIE is Professor of German at the University of Sheffield. His publications include editions, literary histories, translations and a recent book on German literature under National Socialism.

A. F. BANCE is Professor of German at the University of Southampton. Among his books is one on the post-war German novel, and he has edited a volume on writers and politics in Weimar Germany. He contributed the German section to the book on the Second World War in fiction edited by H. M. Klein *et al.*

TAMBIMUTTU'S *POETRY IN WARTIME*

A great deal of European literature since Homer deals with war, but, owing to circumstances and developments that have by now been widely enough discussed, the concept of "War Literature" along with terms like "War Writers" and "War Poets" only emerged with the First World War.[1] Emerged – and became so firmly associated with war itself as to form part of the public horizon of expectation when the Second World War broke out. Hence the question "Where are the war poets?" was voiced fairly soon after 1939 and found many diverging replies.

By 1942 at the latest there existed a large and variegated body of poetry which corresponded to this description, at any rate in some ways. In other ways, again for historical, social and political reasons that have been frequently expounded, it did not. For this public question was, as Vernon Scannell neatly recapitulated,[2] really a demand for new Rupert Brookes or, with others, new Wilfred Owens; and they were not to be had, or at least not in the same quality. Moreover the "total" nature of this war soon made the distinction between soldiers and civilians, and the differences in their war experience much less acute than in 1914-1918.[3]

This development in turn accentuates the problem of delimitation: who is a war poet, or rather: what may be considered as war poetry? The question found many answers at the time and later. An extremely narrow and clear-cut circumscription was fiercely propounded by Keith Douglas: you cannot write war poetry unless you have experienced battle.[4] This corresponds to Mildred Davidson's (occasional) use of the term "fighter poets".[5] A wider concept defines war poets as members of the Services, a principle governing, for example, the two anthologies compiled by Keidrych Rhys, *Poems from the Forces* (1941) and *More Poems from the Forces* (1943),[6] and much later Ian Hamilton's *The Poetry of War 1939-45.*[7] Its neatness is obvious, and the potential "educational value" of service experience, especially, Roy Fuller underlines, for middle-class intellectuals,[8] is a consideration perhaps. Both tend to wear thin when the principle allows Rhys to include, for example, Patricia Ledward in his second collection as an "A.T.C. Driver". At any rate, this delimitation is convenient and underlies the critical surveys of R. N. Currey and A. Banerjee,[9] as well as Scannell.

Much more extended scope was advocated by Julian Symons. Introducing his (diachronous) *Anthology of War Poetry* (1942) he writes:

> War poetry is not a specialised department of poetry; it is . . . quite simply the poetry, comic or tragic, cynical or heroic, joyful, embittered or disillusioned, of people affected by the reality of war.[10]

This conception, not widely taken up in criticism, was to be reflected much later by Brian Gardner's anthology *The Terrible Rain.*[11] A still more open notion surfaces in G. S. Fraser's introduction to the New Apocalypse anthology *The White Horseman* (1941): "to have social value, poetry does not have to show immediate political relevance."[12] One may or may not accept Fraser's claim that "the obscurity of our poetry" is the result "of disintegration, not in ourselves, but in society" (p.30). Taken to its logical conclusion, however, Fraser's thesis could be used to claim that all and every poetic utterance between 1939 and 1945 must count as war poetry.

It is doubtful whether anyone could remain unaffected by the Second World War. However, Symons' formula for "War Poetry" could be used to strike a balance between the particular and the general if one interprets "affected by the reality of war" as this being affected finding tangible expression in the poetry. The narrower area staked out in most criticism might be more usefully designated as "Soldier Poetry". The larger field, a specific period's poetry in its entirety – discussed in our case by, for example, Stephen Spender in 1946 as *Poetry Since 1939*[13] and thirty years later by Eric Homberger in "The 1940s"[14] – is adroitly embraced in Tambimuttu's choice of title, *Poetry in Wartime.*

These considerations relate to what might be called "horizontal" selection. Concurrently, critics and anthologists have of necessity applied "vertical" selection, guided by their respective notions of quality. There can be, as we know only too well, no one answer to the question: what is "good" poetry? The most we can hope for is intersubjective agreement, as when, for example, L. A. G. Strong approvingly formulates C. Day Lewis' three demands as "passion, music, and precision".[15] For past periods, such approval can be gauged in two principal ways, as Robin Skelton has pointed out.[16] Either one accepts guidance from what was commonly thought good at the time (if that can be established) or one is guided by a congruence of opinions as to what still strikes as good from a later point of vantage. And of course one can, in varying proportions, combine both criteria. Quite naturally, most modern criticism in the field works, beyond the individual's personal judgment, with persisting relevance and success as the main points of reference.

Less obviously perhaps, albeit usefully, the bulk of these studies (for example, Currey, Banerjee, Scannell) are heavily poet-centred, often approaching a concatenation of little monographs. Ian Hamilton varies between a discussion of the poets he deems most important: Douglas, Lewis and Fuller as well as "Minor Talents", and a consideration of groups and movements.[17] So does, again on a correspondingly smaller scale, John Press.[18] Davidson (note 5) takes up an overall ordering principle developed by Spender (note 13): that of three generations. Homberger's method is different, in that he foregrounds Louis MacNeice and W. H. Auden while projecting a larger picture of intellectual currents and poetic developments. The canvas itself is the main concern of Robert Hewison's *Under Siege*[19] as well as, on the required smaller scale, of Angus Calder.[20]

The analysis of one particular anthology is a much more limited project than those pursued by the critics I have mentioned. Moreover, perspectives, emphases and methods will necessarily differ. In general terms, the present contribution can be placed with those occupying the middle ground between a "poet-by-poet" approach and an approach illustrating "the state of literature". It is guided by the conviction that studies of this kind may, complementing existing criticism, usefully add to our knowledge and appreciation of poetry in the Second World War.

One thing is certain: a truly astounding amount of poetry was written during the 1939-45 war. Let us take just one witness: Cyril Connolly. In June 1940 he remarked that *Horizon* was being "inundated with poems". In principle he shared the view that war has adverse effects on art; but at that time he drew two interesting conclusions from his observation: "Poetry is still the natural national form of self-expression, the one to which we take most readily" (p.389); and "English poetry was never more interesting or thriving" (p.391). In November 1941 Connolly still noted the same profusion, but in less optimistic terms: most of the hundred poems a week he received "should never have been written" because they were bad – so bad that in that particular issue he printed no poetry at all.[21]

There was, as Hewison shows (pp.76-116), great interest on the part of the public. And, despite severe difficulties of production (disruption and destruction by German bombing, personnel problems due to conscription, swingeing paper rationing, etc.) no dearth of publications to try and answer the demand. There can hardly have been many periods, one is led to think, in which more poetry was printed and read by more people. Whatever one may think of the poetry, and giving due consideration to situational and economic factors then favourable to the genre, this phenomenon still calls for admiration. Among the major organs through which poetry was disseminated we must count, alongside the individual volumes of poets produced by many small firms and the large ones, notably by Routledge (Herbert Read) and Faber (T. S. Eliot),

John Lehmann's various *New Writing* enterprises, *Horizon* itself, C. Wrey Gardiner's *Poetry Quarterly*[22] – and M. [eary] J. [ames] or Thurairajah Tambimuttu's *Poetry London* (henceforth *PL*).[23]

If Connolly among others had fairly firm standards, Tambimuttu (1915-1983) or "Tambi", as he was affectionately called, apparently had not. Indeed, his programme as set out when he launched *PL* (February 1939) seems to advocate general encouragement of poetic creativity, welcoming it in almost any guise as a manifestation of "Life". Such radical, somewhat anarchic enthusiasm, or alternatively simplistic and mystically tinged naïveté can easily be torn to critical shreds. How easily was shown by D. J. Enright whose blistering attack (1947)[24] still reverberated in the *TLS* review of the *PL* reprint in 1971.[25] Another *TLS* review in 1956 took a different stand, calling *PL* "the best produced and most exciting British magazine of new verse",[26] and the *Times* obituary notice stressed that Tambimuttu's *PL* had managed to publish, "in the course of its fifteen issues, almost every British poet of note".[27]

One should not in any case make too much of a distinction between *PL* and other magazines. Those influencing the course of poetry in the forties stand – or, as the following decade made out – fall together, by and large. It is a question of degrees and emphases. If there was a debasement of the critical faculties, Tambimuttu may have been the worst offender, but he was not the only one. And matters were far less clear-cut than Enright suggests. Excepting the *PL* "bumper" issue 3, No. 10 (December 1944) into which Tambimuttu packed everything he had not found space for previously, priding himself on the mass of unknowns among them, there is a sizeable measure of overlap regarding the poets published in various periodicals.[28] Nor should one underestimate the generosity displayed by many sides at the time. Hewison mentions that Eliot and Read, favouring different tendencies, sent each other offered manuscripts (op.cit., p.98). And Symons, to take a very precise example, who had been the object of one of Tambimuttu's rare excursions into critical demolition,[29] later both published in and reviewed for *PL*.[30] Finally, the impression, variously propagated, of a cosy, mutually congratulatory clique[31] cannot stand unchallenged. One is on the contrary surprised at the vivacity, indeed fierceness with which work was on occasion criticised.[32]

This is not the place, however, to discuss the magazine as such or to follow the colourful career of its creator beyond noting that he was himself a poet,[33] was some time after his arrival in London from Ceylon (1937) encouraged by Eliot,[34] and held during the war years a literally unique position in London's literary world. The key note we need to retain is Tambimuttu's preference for "catholicity" over "critical dogma" (Hewison).[35] For this is the fundamental characteristic also of *Poetry in Wartime* (henceforth *PWT*), the anthology of verse which Faber published in July 1942, announcing it as a collection of "the best poems written since the beginning of the war – some of which are also 'war poems'" (wrapper).[36] The nature of Eliot's involvement with this volume, if any, cannot apparently be ascertained. It is hardly conceivable, however, that he should not at least have generally approved of it.[37] The *TLS* on the other hand, while finding quite a number of poems to praise, attacked the anthology's. prevailing mood.[38] Tambimuttu himself, calling it "the strain of sadness running throughout", had already distanced himself from it. In the reviewer's opinion this was hardly the stuff to give the nation at that juncture. The public was not deterred: at 6*s*. a copy, *PWT* sold about 4,000 copies within a year; not bad, though not exactly stunning as a commercial success.[39]

Tambimuttu's "Prefatory Note" to *PWT* is very brief. Apart from the disclaimer he states that most poems were written after the outbreak of war, and that the younger poets had been allotted more space. A letter to Fraser, published in *PL* (December 1944), slightly enlarges on both points, calling *PWT* "a cross-section of verse written between September 1939 and September 1941" and defining its aim as "chiefly [to] introduce some interesting new poets without sacrificing its representativeness".[40]

Representativeness (a more positive term than catholicity) is the decisive notion. In broad terms, this has led to an assemblage of forty-nine poets (originally fifty, see below), of whom the oldest are Richard Church and Read (both born 1893), the youngest probably Keyes (born 1922) and Francis King (born 1923). The range of poetic tendencies is indicated by the presence of Auden as well as Dylan Thomas. In the reader's immediate experience, Tambimuttu's principle can produce extraordinary juxtapositions, like the one, on facing pages, of Desmond Hawkins' "Night Raid" which ends with:

> She was shivering and laughing and throwing her head back.
> On the pavement men looked up thoughtfully,
> Making plausible conjectures. The night sky
> Throbbed under the cool bandage of the searchlights.

and J. F. Hendry's "London Before Invasion, 1940", ending:

> Flood-tides, returning, may bring with them blood and fire,
> Blenching with wet panic spirit that must be rock.
> May bring a future tossed and torn, as slippery as wrack.
> All time adrift in torrents of blind war.

On about 190 pages, representativeness could possibly mean pieces by most that were significant or promising at the time. It does *not*, one misses many voices: among the soldier poets whom later critics accorded special importance, first and foremost Douglas,[41] also Campbell, Causley and Ross;[42] curiously and significantly, Fuller (who had originally been included with one poem) was quietly dropped in the 1943 reprint (cf. note 36). As regards other poets, Tambimuttu's (silly) claim stung the reviewer for the *New Statesman and Nation* into exclaiming: "The best poems? 'East Coker' isn't there, and there are gaps all along the line from Binyon to Betjeman."[44] Extending that line a little, one would in particular add Edith Sitwell. And even among those included one might question specific decisions, wondering, for example, whether, if only one poem by Spender was to be there, "To Poets and Airmen" was the most felicitous choice.

However imperfect its execution, the aim of representativeness is noteworthy and distinguishes *PWT* from many other anthologies – those that united poets of common educational background, or converging aesthetic notions, from the services-only anthologies and the younger/new poets-only ones. Indeed, its scope really renders *PWT* unique in its time. Its degree of representativeness can be further gauged by overlaps in various directions. Keyes only from the *Eight Oxford Poets* (1941),[45] five (Stephen Coates, Alexander Comfort, Nicholas Moore, George Scurfield and Terence Tiller) of the eleven *Poets of Tomorrow* (1940),[46] Gascoyne only of the *Poets of Tomorrow* (1942);[47] four poets (Hendry, Moore, Dylan Thomas and Henry Treece) out of seven in *The New Apocalypse* (1940),[48] again Hendry, Moore and Treece from *The White Horseman*, additionally: Fraser, Tom Scott and Vernon Watkins;[49] among thirty-one poets assembled by Rhys in *Poems from the Forces* (1941), originally ten, then nine (Gavin Ewart, Fraser, [Fuller], Hendry, Alun Lewis, Mervyn Peake, Alan Rook, Tom Scott, Scurfield, John Waller) are also found in *PWT*, as are eight (Comfort, Gascoyne, J. C. Hall, King, Moore, Norman Nicholson, Rook and Waller) from thirty-six in *Poems of this War By Younger Poets*, edited by Patricia Ledward and Colin Strang (1942)[50] and nine (Comfort, Fraser, Hall, Moore, Nicholson, Ridler, Scarfe, Treece and Watkins) from the twenty-five poets in *Lyra*, edited by Comfort and Robert Greacen (1942).[51]

These are principally, under one guise or another, young poets' anthologies, and one notices several overlaps they have amongst each other irrespective of *PWT*. For the element of continuity in the genre, which forms part of Tambimuttu's intention to be representative, one needs to look at a different type of collection. Thus, Day Lewis and Strong, covering 1920-1940 (note 15) include ninety-eight poets, and only thirteen of them recur in *PWT*; Ridler's much more selective *Little Book of Modern Verse* (1942),[52] though ranging from Hopkins to Ruthven Todd, contains work by only thirty-nine poets, and fifteen of them one also finds in *PWT*. The most interesting comparison in this direction is perhaps Geoffrey Grigson's parting shot (fittingly published in August 1939): *New Verse: An Anthology*,[53] which unites twenty-six poets from the magazine's successive issues; ten of them reappear in Tambimuttu's volume.

The value of such "head-counting" is limited. Yet it should not be dismissed. There is a point at which a quantitative aspect assumes other dimensions. The emphasis in *PWT* lies clearly on the "neo-romantic" tendency, others are given a small share only. The most striking contrast is that one finds one poem by Auden as opposed to six by Scarfe (of *Auden and After* notoriety). This consideration invites a look at Lehmann's preferences, though one cannot strictly compare the one-off anthology with the long sequence of various *New Writing* issues.[54] Both Lehmann and Tambimuttu give generous space to Barker, Gascoyne, and Nicholson. Otherwise their policies differ markedly: as a rule one finds that the poets frequently appearing in *New Writing* are of small account in *PWT* or altogether absent, and conversely, of those most amply represented in *PWT* there are no poems at all in Lehmann's publications (Fraser, Alfred Marnau,[55] Kathleen Raine, Rook, Watkins) or very few (Lawrence Durrell, Alun Lewis, Moore, Ridler, Lynette Roberts). This need not in all cases express critical, let alone ideological disagreements; various factors, perhaps even trivial, purely external ones, will have contributed. Moreover, an analysis of *PL* itself might yield a modified picture. The one emerging from this comparison with *PWT* helps, all provisos notwithstanding, to round off this consideration of the anthology's general composition. The *New Statesman and Nation* concluded that *PWT* is "varied, talented, uneven and on the whole representative of the generation 'since Auden'" (note 44). H. B. Mallalieu, reviewing the volume for *Poetry Quarterly*, went much further. While making several other reservations, he confirmed that Tambimuttu achieved what he set out to do – to give "a representative picture of the three years since war became active again over the whole of Europe".[56] This seems over-generous, where the other appears niggardly; the facts point to somewhere in between the two, probably a little nearer to Mallalieu.

Tambimuttu's assembling of *PWT* was determined, alongside of his overall aims, by availability; and that, under the circumstances, means to some extent chance. He took what he thought good (or "best") wherever he could find it, from manuscripts submitted to printed sources. For thirty-nine poems he resorted to *PL* issues, for five more to Reginald Moore's *Selected Writing* (1941), for which he had also himself chosen the poetry.[57]

I have been unable to make a complete check, but even so the element of doubling is interesting. Thus, for example, Ewart's sonnet "The point where beauty and intelligence meet" had already appeared in *Horizon* (1, No. 12, Dec. 1940), Lewis' "All day it has rained" in *Horizon* (2, No. 13, Jan. 1941), and Waller's "Aldershot" in *Horizon* (2, No. 17, May 1941) – and all three had been included by Rhys in *Poems from the Forces* (1941). So had Rook's "Retreat", which was also chosen by Ledward and Strang for *Poems of this War* (like *PWT*, July 1942; p. 24f.). This piece and another one of Rook's, "London, 1940" (p. 33) are the only overlaps in poems (as opposed to poets) between *PWT* and *Poems of this War*. Together with Hall, Ledward was partly involved by Tambimuttu in his selection process (cf. "Prefatory Note"), and she would naturally have sought to avoid having many parallels. Tambimuttu also had contacts with Comfort, which may explain that only one poem appeared in both *Lyra* and *PWT*. It is a particularly significant one: Ridler's "Now as Then" which seems to pre-empt[58] Dorothy Sayers' stridently confident "The English War"[59] – to say nothing of Siegfried Sassoon's "Silent Service"[60] – with a questioning variety of the attitude that found much more bitter expression in Day Lewis' famous "Where are the War Poets?"[61]

Laurie Lee's poems "Larch Tree", "Juniper", and "Look into wombs and factories and behold" Tambimuttu took from Lehmann's *Folios of New Writing*.[62] In all, I have noticed 24 double or multiple printings of poems; probably there are still more. For some poets there were individual volumes available, most obviously for the older poets like Michael Roberts (born 1902), whose two poems in *PWT* came from *Orion Marches* (Sept. 1939). What makes the doublings with preceding and simultaneous other selections so important is, however, that they indicate a degree of congruent critical judgment.

Of Tambimuttu's florid, meandering existence and activities at the centre of London's wartime *bohème* there exist graphic descriptions, mostly more warm-hearted than Derek Stanford's,[63] Julian Maclaren-Ross being rather cooler.[64] In general, while thrilled and delighted by all this, an outsider need not be a philistine to wonder how Tambimuttu could ever have achieved anything as an editor. And yet he unquestionably did achieve a great deal. *PL* itself looks beautifully produced; so does the plainer, unadorned anthology. Nevertheless, with stories in mind like the one about a new Dylan Thomas poem in the chamber-pot (Stanford, p. 157), one may reasonably look with some apprehension at the editing in *PWT*. A thorough assessment would in itself be a major, fascinating job of bibliography and textual criticism. Here a glance must suffice. The main impression is one of unevenness, with intriguing puzzles unresolved.

Breathtaking accidents occurred. Thus Auden's "September 1, 1939" appears here as "September 1, 1941"; l. 15 "That has driven a culture mad" is truncated to "That culture mad", etc.[65] Strange little words disturb Church's "Something Private".[66] Gascoyne's last section of "Miserere" is headed "Miserere" instead of "Ecce Homo".[67] Choosing poems by Rook, an eye must have slipped: what both "Contents" and the actual title of one piece announce is "Poem near Béthune", but the text is that of "Poem from H.Q.".[68] On the other hand, many poems are carefully reproduced.

There are many interesting examples in which the poets themselves at some later point in time effected changes, for example Ridler[69] and Lynette Roberts,[70] most remarkably Dylan Thomas. His "On a Wedding Anniversary", correctly carried over into *PWT* from *PL* (Jan./Feb. 1941)[71] was completely dismantled and rebuilt by Thomas for inclusion in *Deaths and Entrances* (1946).[72] Serious questions arise, however, with variations in *PWT* that look like deliberate improvements,[73] and most of all with heavy conceptual, even structural as well as verbal discrepancies between closely preceding or following separate printings and *PWT*. This applies especially to poems by Comfort,[74] Alun Lewis[75] and Scarfe.[76] The lack of critical editions renders it impossible at the moment to pursue this whole question further; one must be content with having shown that such problems exist.

As opposed to Ledward and Strang, who group their *Poems of this War* under thematic headings, Tambimuttu adopts (like most others) the alphabetical sequence – his runs from Auden to George Woodcock, with one dramatic exception: Empson's "Aubade" is placed at the very end in the manner of an (anticlimactic) epilogue. Hawkins' and Hendry's London poems chance to touch; there are others, notably Peake's "London, 1941" and Raine's "London Revisited". Closely allied in theme, many poems focus on the bombings, for example, Scarfe's "Ballad of the Safe Area" and Thomas' "Deaths and Entrances" – a striking contrast in mood, execution and, one must add, success (dare-devilry sits uneasily on bardic shoulders, something evident also from Treece's "Ballad of the Ranting Lad"). Lee's "Larch Tree" also belongs here, as does Lynette Roberts' "Lamentation" and, among still others, Michael Roberts' "The Castle", although it precedes the war.

Poems talking to specific people – other poets, friends, relations – like Rook's "For Christopher" and Todd's "Personal History. For my Son",[72] Barker's "To David Gill" and Durrell's "Letter to Seferis the Greek", Barker's "To my Mother" and Ridler's "To Robin and Kirstie" (both favourite anthology pieces) could have formed a large section conveying a multi-faceted, moving picture of war's effects on human lives and relationships, just as the numerous love poems like Fraser's "Poem for M.J." and Lewis' "Postscript for Gweno". In others, for example Church's "Something Private" and "Gascoyne's "A Wartime Dawn", the effect on the creative individual is central.

These themes and others would presumably fall under Tambimuttu's (conventional) concept of wartime as opposed to war poetry. The latter, in the sense of soldiers and fighting, is hardly present in *PWT*, the principal voice (and a tenuous one at that) being Rook, though there are others. "Advice for a Journey" by Keyes (with Herbert Corby's "Poem on Joining the Royal Air Force, 1941" as a feeble parallel) relates to Read's "To a Conscript of 1940". Among poems of Army life Lewis' "All day it has rained", Waller's "Aldershot" and Scarfe's "Sunday Leave" could have formed, together with some others, an interesting group into which Ewart's "Officer's Mess", had it been available, would have nicely fitted.[78]

Neither in *PWT* nor in its approximate parallels, Ledward and Strang's *Poems of this War* and Comfort and Greacen's *Lyra*, does one find many pieces displaying enthusiastic patriotism, combative spirit, ardour for the cause and defiance of fate; and the same might be said with almost equal justice (as one would expect, given the degree of overlap in poets with *PWT* and the others) about Rhys' *Poems from the Forces*.[79] In that anthology a different tone is more noticeable (to be discussed below), but this relates to different issues and does little to bridge the distance of all four anthologies to, say, J. C. Squire's *Poems of Two Wars*,[80] or Lord Dunsany's *War Poems*,[81] let alone Gordon Boshell's *My Pen My Sword* and A. P. Herbert's *A.T.I.*[82]

Reviewers were not slow to spot and reprove this lack; but it is hard to see why the *TLS* should have kept its attack oblique and muted with *Poems of this War* but openly pounced on *PWT*.[83] Ridler's "Now as Then" does, after all, end with:

> And since of two evils our victory would be the less,
> And coming soon, leave some strength for peace,
> Hopeful like Minot, and the rest, we pray:
> "Lord, turn [to?] us again, confer on us victory".

And Audrey Beecham goes much further; her "Norway" should nearly have pleased a George Rostrevor Hamilton.[84]

If the cause is scarcely proclaimed, the enemy is not much present either, certainly qua enemy; rarely named or defined, he is, on the other hand, omnipresent as a threat, as bombers in the air, as shattered houses and lives left behind; as violence suffered or, in Day Lewis' phrase ("The Stand-To", l.17), "a cold wind from Europe". However, the enemy is unmistakable, even if starkly described only by Gascoyne:

See, the centurions wear riding-boots,
Black shirts and badges and peaked caps,
Greet one another with raised-arm salutes:
They have cold eyes, unsmiling lips;
Yet these his brothers know not what they do. (lines 125-29)

The "Christ of Revolution and of Poetry" darkly appealed to at the end of "Miserere",

That man's long journey through the night
May not have been in vain,

would be expected to sweep away other things besides the German National Socialist Reich; but that is a different story.

On balance, *PWT* does show a marked emphasis on detachment, on withdrawn preoccupation with nature or the self, the private sphere, and a wary, at times ironic eye on particulars in the world outside. This bent, which it shares with much poetry during those years, is remarkable, especially as it contrasts with the spirit prevailing in contemporary (popular) fiction.[85] To explain these poets' or budding poets' temper, Comfort, reviewing Rhys, advanced an interesting argument: that the activities of waging a war, ultimately of killing, and of writing poetry are at heart incompatible, and that a deep-seated malaise results from attempts to combining them.[86] This is a doubtful proposition; examples to the contrary abound in both World Wars. The literary as well as material situation at the time, and the history of the preceding decades furnish more convincing explanations if applied to this question along the lines of Spender and Robert Graves.[87] Tambimuttu, who must have been possessed of a rare blend of innocence and shrewdness, obviously anticipated criticism. He was astute in disclaiming responsibility, having been true to his critical lights in selecting. A good deal about them, as reflected in his choices, has already become visible. More will emerge from aspects of *PWT* that remain to be treated.

One of the things immediately noticeable is the interest shown in longer poems.[88] One-fifth (twenty-eight of 141) exceed forty lines, up to Gascoyne's "Miserere" with 147 and W. R. Rodger's "Summer Holidays" with 172 lines. This trait is stronger in *PWT* than in *Lyra*, as well as in *Poems of this War* and *Poems from the Forces*. The great variety of forms, on the other hand, it shares with them. From strict sonnets and regular four-line stanzas to extremely free verse one finds innumerable intermediaries and variations, with regard to metre as well as rhyme. Among them is a richness in pararhyme or half-rhyme (so memorably used in the First World War by Wilfred Owen).[89] Yet it is rarely wrought to the hardness of, for example, Fuller's "August 1940"[90] or Laurence Whistler's "It will not last"[91] or indeed John Bayliss' "Sermon from History",[92] to take conspicuous examples from the other three collections. This is clearly not a question of sound alone, but of tone, texture and mood. For all the overlaps, there is in *PWT* more hesitancy, more questioning – yes, "sadness", or rather mutedness, as opposed to starkness and sinew, although those are not altogether lacking. As Rhys' *Poems from the Forces* is somewhat more consistently different from *PWT*, one might pursue this aspect with particular reference to this anthology.

Trying to characterise the preponderant atmosphere, the "feel" one retains from two masses of heterogenous poems, is no easy matter. Looking at pieces which occur in both anthologies is a helpful step: they seem to own a different timbre in the two environments; good examples of this are Lewis' "All Day it has Rained" and the (identical) extract from Hendry's "Four Seasons of War". Fairly similar poems provide another line of approach. Durrell's "Epitaph" ("Here lies Michael of the small bone"), on the "periphery" of *PWT*, as it were, would not be particularly noticed in *Poems from the Forces*; Fuller's "Epitaph on a Bombing Victim" would strongly strike one in *PWT*. Within *PWT* alone the hardness, the subordinate tone, is for example most strongly perceptible in closely touching poems, as the two by Michael Roberts:

> Suburbs creep up the hill, and the trams are running,
> Children find ghostly playmates in the ruins;
> The sun glares on the emptiness, and vanished walls
> Burn with a bitter death and unfulfilled perfection.
> ("The Castle", lines 13-16)

> Between the factory hooter and the snub-nosed bullet,
> Under the shadow of the guns, the corn ripens,
> And folly cannot die, but cannot grow for ever.
> ("In Our Time", lines 13-15)

Keith Douglas is not included in either anthology; that was to come later in *PL* (note 41) and in *More Poems from the Forces* (note 6). Trying to imagine him in *PWT* or in *Poems from the Forces*, one would see him more easily not in Tambimuttu's collection but in that of Rhys – not because he would have been "eligible" for Rhys, but because in *Poems from the Forces* one sees more of an energy akin to his, however crudely exercised in this hypothetical context. This has nothing to do with overall quality; in that respect many disappointments await the reader in both anthologies.

Reviewing *Poems from the Forces* in *PL*, Francis King distinguishes between "Poets" and "Journalists", and finds too many of the latter sort for his liking.[93] If "reporting", however, means reproducing experience in poetry with little or no transmutation, one can turn this reproach against *PWT* as well – there, too, much "reporting" is being done, though the matter reported may more often be the poets' thoughts and feelings than the world around them. Moore's "The Ruin and the Sun" (beginning: "Do I make my disasters clear?") and Tom

Scott's "Poem in Time of Search" are blatant examples; they could be multiplied.

Tambimuttu (who had, incidentally, unlike all the others, the grace not to anthologise himself)[94] was in fact over-generous; he, as well as his fellow-compilers of anthologies, should have exercised greater selectivity among the works of his "interesting new poets". And not only with them. Some already more established poets, for example Barker, Durrell and Raine,[95] elided several pieces he had included, when they came to assemble their work later on; and one tends to agree with their tacit self-judgment. What distinguishes *PWT* from the collections mainly adduced for comparison here, is that even with the younger contributors Tambimuttu showed a flair, or a predilection, for literary, or even more generally speaking, artistic minds.

The Listener found some of Rhys' poets interesting and promising (not surprisingly, Lewis; one wonders why not Fuller). On the whole, however, this review is most unfavourable, suspecting that the vast majority of Rhys' "soldiers, airmen and sailors" would "probably stop writing when the war ends, but while the war lasts it is an inoffensive and sensible activity" – but should preferably not be made public.[96] One is bound to add that for too many, for example, Timothy Corsellis and Bertram Warr (whom Ledward and Strang also included) the choice did not arise. They were killed.

Not all of Tambimuttu's younger contributors continued largely with poetry, though many did. Others developed further as novelists, critics, writers of travel books etc.; and James Forsyth, for example, had already been writing plays anyway. Uniting so many people of literary or (thinking especially of Peake and Brenda Chamberlain)[97] multiply art-oriented talents between two covers is thus another characteristic of *PWT*. It certainly struck *The Listener*:

> Most wartime anthologies of poetry will survive, if they survive at all, merely as historical or sociological documents; their poetic interest will be negligible. Mr. Tambimuttu's *Poetry in Wartime* is a brilliant exception; it would have been equally timely if we were now at peace, and one imagines that it will retain its value after the war. Reading it, one is satisfyingly conscious of being among poets writing poems, not of being somewhere in the neighbourhood of a vague depression called, by reason of association, poetry.[98]

He means *Poems from the Forces*; and in the review of *PWT* he includes one of *Poets of this War*, not lambasting it as he had Rhys, but also dismissing Ledward and Strang in favour of Tambimuttu. To balance this, one remembers Mallalieu's reservations (note 56), those of the *New Statesman and Nation* (note 44), and in particular the *TLS*'s complaint not only about the prevailing mood, but also specifically: "It is remarkable how little music there is in this verse" (note 38).

The Listener seems, in retrospect, to exaggerate the differences, slightly unjust to all sides. Laying this question apart, however, the bold prediction about *PWT*'s future invites a glance at the subsequent fortunes of Tambimuttu's choices. Three anthologies of war poetry, published in the middle 1960s, can serve as a first point of reference. Hamilton's *The Poetry of War 1939-1945* (note 7) is the most exclusive, concentrating, as his critical work in the field (note 17) already demonstrates, on those poets who continued the "thirties" tradition. No surprise therefore, that only five (six) of the forty-nine (fifty) poets represented in *PWT* find admittance, though the recurrence of four of its poems is noteworthy.[99] Charles Hamblett, on the other hand, whose gruff, soldierlike Introduction reminds of Rhys and would seem to bode ill for Tambimuttu's poets, includes no less than thirty-nine (forty) of them in *I Burn for England*, and, what is more amazing, fifty-three of their poems. Indeed it appears that Hamblett was guided by *PWT* for stretches of his vast collection.[100] Brian Gardner's *The Terrible Rain* (note 11), more broadly based than the other two, has twenty-five of the *PWT* poets, though only eleven of their poems.

A second group for comparison are war period anthologies such as Maurice Wollman's *Poems of the War Years* (1950)[101] and Ronald Blythe's *Writing in a War* (1966/82).[102] Sixteen years apart, these two selections show fairly constant agreement from our point of view: both include twenty (twenty-one) of Tambimuttu's forty-nine (fifty) poets (thirteen (fourteen) are the same ones),[103] Wollman giving ten, Blythe eleven of the poems. If one remembers that *PWT* appeared in the middle of the war, while these later anthologies all had to consider the entire period, with many more poets coming to the fore, the congruence of assessment (excepting Hamilton), already sizeable, increases in weight.

Extending the frame of reference, a dramatic contrast is seen between Robin Skelton's *Poetry of the Forties* (1968; see note 16) with thirty (thirty-one) poets, ten poems from *PWT*, and David Wright's *English Poetry 1940-1960* (1965) with only nine (ten) poets and one poem found in Tambimuttu's volume.[104] Even allowing for each critic's subjective judgment, this contrast highlights the difference in poetic temper between the two decades. Branching out even more widely, one notices again a fair degree of consistency: Kenneth Allott's *Contemporary Verse* (1950),[105] with twenty-four (twenty-five) *PWT* poets, and seven poems, is roughly on a par with the 1951 Michael Roberts/Anne Ridler *Faber Book of Modern Verse*: twenty-one (twenty-two) *PWT* poets, though only one poem.[106] This consistency of judgment is confirmed by Philip Larkin (1972), who includes nineteen (twenty) poets and three poems Tambimuttu had chosen.[107]

Two things are vital here: firstly, one doubts whether any of these later anthologists except Hamblett (and possibly Allott and Ridler) had *PWT* in mind when setting about their work, or paid particular attention to it. In that sense Tambimuttu's collection does not seem to have "survived". Secondly: anyone can think of a dozen or a score of poets without whom none of these anthologies would have been viable, each within its chosen scope. These findings cannot really surprise, therefore. That proves Tambimuttu's point, however – he aimed precisely at a "cross-section" of poetry written roughly within the space of three years. The low incidence of actual poems rather than poets taken up in later selections is far too complex an issue to allow of a cursory glance. For poets whose work is contained in *PWT* it is essential, however, to complement the criterion hitherto employed, that of presence in later anthologies, by its opposite, absence. It turns out that four poets do not recur in any of the later collections consulted: Audrey Beecham, Brenda Chamberlain, Stephen Coates and, a special case, Marnau (cf. note 55); and six others appealed to Hamblett only: Forsyth, D. S. Savage, Tom Scott, Scurfield, Lynette Roberts (that really causes regret and surprise) and Woodcock. The remaining thirty-nine (forty) poets Tambimuttu had selected were chosen by at least two later anthologists as well. This criterion also proves, as far as it goes, Tambimuttu's point.

English poetry of the Second World War represents a vast field, and an uncommonly interesting one in many respects. Much work, including much elementary spadework, remains to be done, and the wartime anthologies offer a particularly promising entry. If one were given the chance to reprint one, and only one of them, *PWT* would seem the obvious choice. Contrary to what *The Listener* imagined, and the many interesting and beautiful poems it contains notwithstanding, it would primarily serve the purpose of documentation; but there is nothing wrong, one must argue, with historical and sociological work on poetry. On the contrary, there is a great deal to be said for it.

H. M. KLEIN

East Anglia

NOTES

[1]Cf. e.g. M. Howard, "Military Experience in Literature", *Essays by Divers Hands*, NS 41 (1980), 29-39; M. Davidson (see note 5), Ch.1; Bernard Bergonzi, *Heroes' Twilight* (London: Macmillan, 1965), Paul Fussell, *The Great War and Modern Memory* (London et al.: Oxford UP, 1975); Maurice Bowra, *Poetry and the First World War* (Oxford: Blackwell, 1961), and my Introduction to *The First World War in Fiction* (London: Macmillan, 1976).

[2]V. Scannell, *Not without Glory: Poets of the Second World War* (London: The Woburn Press, 1976), p.16.

[3]Cf. e.g. A. J. P. Taylor, *The Second World War* (London: Hamish Hamilton, 1975, repr. Harmondsworth: Penguin Books, 1976), p.21. Cf. also Michael Hamburger, *The Truth of Poetry* (London: Weidenfeld & Nicholson, 1969, repr. Harmondsworth: Penguin Books, 1972), pp.164, 192.

[4]"Poets in this War", an undated MS (probably 1943), first published in *TLS*, 23 April 1971, p.478. Douglas is one of the few poets of the Second World War on whom serious scholarly work has already been done, cf. Desmond Graham, *Keith Douglas 1920-1944: A Biography* (London et. al.: Oxford UP, 1974).

[5]M. Davidson, *The Poetry is in the Pity* (London: Chatto & Windus, 1972).

[6]*Poems from the Forces: A Collection of Verses by Serving Members of the Navy, Army, and Air Force*, ed. K. Rhys (London: Routledge, 1941); *More Poems from the Forces* . . . , ed. K. Rhys (London: Routledge, 1943), a much larger collection, assembling 75 poets.

[7]*The Poetry of War 1939-45*, ed. Ian Hamilton (London: Alan Ross Ltd., 1965).

[8]R. Fuller, "English Poetry of the Two World Wars" in: *Professors and Gods* (London: Deutsch, 1973), pp.117-35; here: p.118. Cf. also Fuller, "Poetry in My Time", *Essays by Divers Hands* 35 (1969), 67-84.

[9] R. N. Currey, *Poets of the 1939-1945 War* (London: Longmans, Green & Co. for the British Council and the National Book League, 1960); A. Banerjee, *Spirit Above Wars: A Study of the English Poetry of the Two World Wars* (London: Macmillan, 1976).

[10] *An Anthology of War Poetry*, compiled by Julian Symons (Harmondsworth: Penguin Books, 1942), p.VIII. Cf. Cyril Connolly in *Horizon* 3, No.13 (Jan.1941), 5. I was unable to obtain a copy of Symons' earlier anthology: *Some Poems in War-Time* (London: Diener and Reynolds, 1940).

[11] *The Terrible Rain: The War Poets 1939-1945*, ed. B. Gardner (London: Methuen, 1966, repr.1968).

[12] *The white horseman: prose and verse of the new apocalypse*, ed. J. F. Hendry and Henry Treece (London: Routledge, 1941), "introduction", p.28.

[13] First published separately as a British Council pamphlet in 1946, then united with three others in the volume *Since 1939, Drama, The Novel, Poetry, Prose Literature*, by Robert Speaight et. al. (London: Phoenix House, 1949); cf. pp.103-69.

[14] E. Homberger, *The Art of the Real: Poetry in England and America since 1939* (London et. al.: Dent; Totowa, N.J.: Rowman and Littlefield, 1977), pp.1-59.

[15] *A New Anthology of Modern Verse 1920-1940*, ed. C. Day Lewis and L. A. G. Strong (London: Methuen, 1941), p.XIV.

[16] *Poetry of the Forties*, ed. R. Skelton (Harmondsworth: Penguin Books, 1968), p.15.

[17] I. Hamilton, "Poetry: The Forties", *The London Magazine* NS 4, No.1 (April 1964), 81-89; No.3 (June 1964), 67-72; No.5 (August 1964), 75-79; and No.10 (January 1965), 83-86.

[18] J. Press, *A Map of Modern English Verse* (London et. al.: Oxford UP, 1969).

[19] R. Hewison, *Under Siege: Literary Life in London 1939-45* (London: Weidenfeld and Nicolson, 1977, repr. Quartet Books, 1979).

[20] A. Calder, *The People's War: Britain 1939-1945* (London: Jonathan Cape, 1969, repr. Granada, 1971, 1982), cf. esp. pp.578-604.

[21] C. Connolly, "Comment", *Horizon* 1, No.6 (June 1940), 389-93; "Comment", *Horizon* 4, No.23 (Nov.1941), 299-302; for more detail and Connolly's wavering on the issue, see Hewison (note 19), Ch.1, 8.

[22] At first he was only assistant editor (1939); from Spring 1940 onwards co-editor; by Spring 1941 he was sole editor, the war conditions presumably having made the necessary degree of collaboration impossible across the Atlantic.

[23] There appeared 16 numbers between February 1939 and September 1949. I have used the reprint, London: Frank Cass and Co., 1971, in 4 vols.

[24] D. J. Enright, "The Significance of *Poetry London*", *The Critic* 1, No.1 (Spring 1947), 3-10.

[25] "Interment of the intellectual", *TLS*, 19 Feb.1971, p.206 (by Hamilton. Thanks are due for this information (and that in note 38) to the current editor of the *TLS*). There followed a lively correspondence.

[26] On the occasion of Tambimuttu's attempt at a new start with *Poetry London-New York*, cf. *TLS*, 7 Sept. 1956, p.530.

[27] "Tambimuttu", *The Times*, 24 June 1983, p.14.

[28] I have checked *Horizon*, *Poetry Quarterly* and the *New Writing* series; I doubt whether looking further afield would produce very different results.

[29] *PL* No.2 (April 1939), "Mr. Symons in his Nursery", reviewing *Confusions about X*.

[30] The first Symons poem in *PL* was "The Intellectuals" in No.7 (Oct.-Nov.1942), 41-42, i.e. after *PWT*. For a review cf. No.10 (Dec.1944), 244-45 "The Quiet Voice" (G. Grigson's *Under the Cliff*).

[31] Cf. e.g. Rhys (note 6) and still Hamblett (note 100); esp. Naomi Ryde Smith, quoted by Hewison (note 19), p.100. Rhys, the husband of Lynette Roberts, cannot have aimed at Tambimuttu in particular; he was a good friend.

[32] E.g. Kathleen Raine on Francis Scarfe's *Auden and After* (London: Routledge, 1942) in *PL* No.8 (Nov.-Dec.1942), 120-22; George Woodcock ibid., 124-27, reviewing *Poets of Tomorrow* (1942), among them David Gascoyne; J. C. Hall in *Poetry Quarterly* 4, No.1 (Spring 1942), 36-37 attacking the New Apocalypse, and Henry Treece answering back in *Poetry Quarterly* 4, No.2 (Summer 1942), 66-67.

[33] Not a prolific one, it appears. See *Out of this War* (London: Fortune Press, 1941) and *Natarajah. A Poem for Mr T. S. Eliot's Sixtieth Birthday* (London: Editions Poetry London, 1948); and the collection *Indian Love Songs* (Mount Vernon, 1954). There are pieces by Tambimuttu in *PL*, e.g. in No.4 (Jan.-Feb.1941), 102-105. His great gift was for organising (or getting organised) poetry publications and literary wreaths to poets, such as his famous *Symposium* for T. S. Eliot (1948) and *Festschrift* for Marianne Moore (1964); cf. Selwyn Kittredge, "Mr Tambimuttu's Birthday Books", *PBSA* 67 (1973), 188-92.

[34]Cf. Kittredge (note 33), 191; Anthony Dickins, "Tambimuttu and *Poetry London*", *The London Magazine* 5, No.9 (Dec.1965), 53-57, here: 56; and ibid. Gavin Ewart, "Tambi the Great", 57-60, here: 58. I could not find a single book about Eliot in which this acquaintance and help is mentioned.

[35]Hewison, op.cit., p.99; Tambimuttu used "catholic" himself in this connection, cf. *PL* No.9 (no month given), p.3.

[36]This formulation shows Tambimuttu's delimitation between "wartime" and "war" poetry very clearly. I have used the reprint, London: Faber, July 1943. It is an exact reproduction of the original 1942 edition, *except* that on pp.66-67 Fraser's "To a Scottish Poet" was fitted into the space originally occupied by Fuller's "So many rivers . . . ". The reasons for this regrettable but symptomatic suppression of Fuller are not known.

[37]There is no information preserved, and if there were, it might not be communicated, I was told by the Faber archivist, Mrs C. Cruickshank, whom I warmly thank for her help with several points relating to *PWT*.

[38]"War-Time poets: Sense of Frustration", *TLS*, 5 Sept. 1942, p.440, by Hugh L'Anson Fausset (cf. note 25).

[39]Thanks are due to Mr John Kimber (University of East Anglia Library) and Mr David McKitterick (Cambridge University Library) for their help in arriving at this conclusion.

[40]*PL* No.10 (Dec.1944), 219. Tambimuttu also mentions *PWT* in *PL* 9, p.3.

[41]The first printing of Douglas in *PL* was No.7 (Oct.-Nov.1942), 19-22. Thereafter regularly. Cf. also Tambimuttu's generous, long "Tenth Letter. In Memory of Keith Douglas", *PL* No.10 (Dec.1944).

[42]Poems by Ross are included in *PL* No.10 (Dec.1944), cf.138-42; also a review of Durrell's *A Private Country*, p.236-38.

[43]*New Statesman and Nation*, 12 September 1942, p.175-76 in "New Anthologies"; cf. esp. p.176.

[44]One feels less sure about Betjeman; Binyon's "The Burning of the Leaves" however would have been a very valuable addition.

[45]*Eight Oxford Poets*, selected by Michael Meyer and Sidney Keyes (London: Routledge, 1941).

[46]*Poets of Tomorrow. Second Selection. Cambridge Poetry 1940* (London: The Hogarth Press, 1940).

[47]*Poets of Tomorrow. Third Selection. Cambridge Poetry 1942* (London: The Hogarth Press, 1942).

[48]*The New Apocalypse: an anthology of criticism, poems and stories* (London: The Fortune Press, 1940).

[49]*The white horseman* (cf. note 12).

[50]*Poems of this War by Younger Poets*, ed. Patricia Ledward and Colin Strang. With an Introduction by Edmund Blunden (Cambridge UP, 1942). I am grateful to Mr M. H. Black of CUP for kindly answering my queries about this anthology. It seems that Frank Kendon may have suggested both the anthology and the Introduction. Mr Black estimates the initial issue at about 1,500 copies. There was a reprint in November 1942, which I have used.

[51]*Lyra: an anthology of new lyric*, ed. Alex Comfort and Robert Greacen (Billericay: The Grey Walls Press (i.e. Wrey Gardiner), 1942).

[52]*A Little Book of Modern Verse*, chosen by Anne Ridler, with a preface by T. S. Eliot (London: Faber, 1941; repr.1942).

[53]*New Verse. An anthology of poems which have appeared in the first thirty numbers of "New Verse"*, compiled by Geoffrey Grigson (London: Faber, 1939).

[54]Such a systematic check would have been most laborious without *New Writing: Author and Subject Index*, comp. Fred H. Higginson (London: Nether Press, 1968). One would wish that more work were undertaken in this direction.

[55]Alfred Marnau was a young, German-speaking Czech refugee whose work was translated by Ernst O. Sigler. A collection, *Poems*, appeared in 1944.

[56]H. B. Mallalieu in *Poetry Quarterly* 4, No.3 (Autumn 1942), 112-13.

[57]*Selected Writing*, ed. Reginald Moore (London: Nicholson & Watson, 1941). This firm also published *PL* for most of its span. I have only seen this issue of *Selected Writing* (Autumn 1941); there may have been others, previous to *PWT*.

[58]In *Nine Bright Shiners* (London: Faber, 1943), p.21, the poem bears the subtitle: "September 1939", suppressed by both Rhys and Tambimuttu. I take it to refer to the time of writing.

[59]*TLS* 7. Sept. 1940, p.445; repr. e.g. by Gardner (note 11), p.45.

[60] S. Sassoon, *The Collected Poems 1908-1956* (London: Faber, 1961, repr.1971), p.257. The poem is dated "May 23, 1940".

[61] For this poem, cf. Hewison, op.cit., p.183. First published by Lehmann in *Penguin New Writing* 3 (Feb.1941), p.114; repr. a.o. by R. Blythe (note 102), p.172 and P. Larkin (note 107), p.353.

[62] J. Lehmann, ed., *Folios of New Writing* (London: The Hogarth Press) 3 (Spring 1941), pp.18-22, Laurie Lee, "Four Poems".

[63] D. Stanford, *Inside the Forties: Literary Memoirs 1937-1957* (London: Sidgwick & Jackson, 1977), cf. esp. pp.74-75, 94-95, 154-58. More affectionate are the reports by Dickins and Ewart (note 34) and those by Durrell (*Sunday Times*, 26 June 1983, p.43) and Raine (*The Times*, 29 June 1983, p.12).

[64] J. Maclaren-Ross, *Memoirs of the Forties* (London: Alan Ross, 1965), "Tambimuttu and the Progress of *Poetry London*", pp.135-52. More on Tambimuttu also in Hewison (note 19), p.95ff., esp. pp.100, 113.

[65] Further errors: l.19, "O" instead of "I"; l.83, a superfluous "in", plus some smaller fry. The poem first appeared in *New Republic*, 18 Oct. 1939, p.297; cf. *The English Auden: Poems, Essays and Dramatic Writings 1927-1939*, ed. E. Mendelson (London: Faber, 1977), pp.245-47.

[66] *The Solitary Man and other poems* (London: Dent, 1941), p.17 shows exact agreement with *The Collected Poems* of Church (London: Heinemann, 1948), pp.205-206, against Tambimuttu's erratic (?) readings.

[67] Cf. *Poems 1937-1942* (London: Editions Poetry London, 1943, repr.1948), p.5; and *Collected Poems*, ed. R. Skelton (London: Oxford UP, 1965), p.44. The typography suggests that this portion of the poem was carried over from *PL* No.3 (Nov.1940), pp.72-73, where it is printed singly – and indeed headed "Miserere".

[68] Cf. *Soldiers, This Solitude* (London: Routledge, 1942), p.35ff. as opposed to 29ff. An intriguing case: Tambimuttu prints the last 5 poems of this volume, though not in the same order; as *Soldiers, This Solitude* likewise appeared in July, it cannot have been the copy text.

[69] A. Ridler, *Nine Bright Shiners* (cf. note 58). Cf. "Before Sleep", p.12 (*PWT*, p.124) and esp. "Zennor", p.34 (*PWT*, p.125f.).

[70] L. Roberts, *Poems* (London: Faber, 1944), p.7 "Poem from Llanybri" (*PWT*, p.129f.), p.12-13 "The Circle of C" (*PWT*, p.130f.) and p.43 "Xaquixaguana" (*PWT*, p.131).

[71] *PL* No.4 (Jan.-Feb.1941), 91; *PWT*, p.170f.

[72] Cf. *Collected Poems 1934-1952* (London: Dent, 1952, repr.1962), p.124. Daniel Jones, editing *The Poems* (London: Dent, 1971), grossly understates the case in saying "the poem underwent some revision" (p.161).

[73] E.g. Moore, "The Ruin and the Sun", *PWT*, p.108, lines 31-32 seem better than in *the white horseman* (note 12), p.102; Watkins, "The Shooting of Werfel", *PWT*, p.181, l.7 better than *Selected Poems* (Montreal: The Christian Brothers, 1948) p.18 which reproduces the *The Ballad of the Mari Lwyd* (London: Faber, 1941) version. In Nicholson's "The Blackberry", l.6 "red rust" of *PWT* (p.112) is superior to "red dust" of *Five Rivers* (London: Faber, 1944), p.37. In Allott's "Ode in Wartime", *PWT*, p.15, l.12 "in every ear" makes much more sense than "in every year" of *Collected Poems* (London: Secker & Warburg, 1975), p.60, but I could not obtain an earlier Allott volume to check; *The Ventriloquist's Doll* (London, 1943) is extremely rare. There are several other examples of doubt.

[74] Comfort, "Stylites", *PWT*, pp.35-37, as opposed to his volume *A Wreath for the Living* (London: Routledge, October 1942), pp.13-16.

[75] Lewis, "To Edward Thomas", *PWT*, pp.94-95, as opposed to *Raiders' Dawn* (London: Allen & Unwin, March 1942), pp.21-23; *Selected Poetry and Prose*, ed. I. Hamilton (London: Allen & Unwin, 1966), pp.75-76 reproduces *Raiders' Dawn* without any elucidation, not even mentioning that this other version exists.

[76] Scarfe, "Icarus: Poem for an Aviator", *PWT*, pp.151-52, as opposed to *Forty Poems and Ballads* (London: Fortune Press, 1941), p.20.

[77] For a moving prose analogy cf. Stephen Haggard, *I'll Go To Bed At Noon: A Soldier's Letter to his Sons* (London: Faber, 1944). He was killed in action.

[78] Cf. *The Collected Ewart 1933-1980: Poems* (London: Hutchinson, 1980), p.73f.; included e.g. by Gardner (note 11), p.129f. He dates it 1942, it was thus probably too late for *PWT*.

[79] The subtitle (see note 6) might however have inhibited criticism. Introducing the anthology, Col. The Rt. Hon. Walter Elliott has some troubles, admitting that readers coming to the volume with traditional expectations "would be very greatly taken aback". And he has to quote from someone Rhys did not include, Nathaniel Gubbins, in order to show the kind of spirit these poets will, he trusts, soon acquire.

[80] Squire, *Poems of Two Wars* (London: Hutchinson, 1940), cf. p.39ff. Dedicated to the Prime Minister, by then Churchill.

[81] Lord Dunsany, *War Poems* (London: Hutchinson, 1941).

[82] Boshell, *My Pen My Sword* (London: Hodder and Stoughton, 1941); rather wittier, if that is the word, than Herbert's later *A.T.I. "There is no need for alarm"* (London: Ornum Press, 1944), with its A-Z of pep poems. He should have stuck to prose: *The Secret Battle* (London: Methuen, 1919, repr., most deservedly, London: Oxford UP, 1982) remains an early important novel of 1914-1918.

[83] Cf. note 76. Perhaps Blunden's association with *Poems of this War* had some restraining effect. Blunden's Introduction shows that he himself was somewhat ill at ease with these poems, however. For the *TLS* on *PWT* see note 38.

[84] A summary of his views is contained in his "Letter on Interpreting the War" which Connolly printed in *Horizon* 6, No.31 (July 1942), p.73, a reply to Comfort in *Horizon* 5, No.29 (May 1942), 358-62.

[85] Cf. "Britain" in *The Second World War in Fiction*, ed. H. M. Klein with J. E. Flower and E. Homberger (London: Macmillan, 1984), pp.1-47.

[86] *Poetry Quarterly* 4, No.1 (Spring, 1942), 33f.

[87] Spender, "War Poetry in this War", *The Listener*, 16 Oct. 1941, 539-40; Graves, "War Poetry in this War", *The Listener*, 23 Oct. 1941, 566-67.

[88] One notices that Tambimuttu's *Out of this War* (cf. note 33) is itself a long poem, long enough to print separately in fact. It did not much impress the *TLS* (cf. "Iron Moments", 13 Sept. 1941, p.456); one cannot disagree.

[89] On the whole, there are few elements in *PWT* directly traceable to First World War poetry. To be sure, there is Alun Lewis; but despite the poem "To Edward Thomas" his influence on Lewis seems more limited than is often argued, e.g. by Scannell (note 2), p.59. (For this poem cf. also note 75.) Another example is Herbert Corby, whose "Sonnet, August 1940" recalls Brooke's "The Soldier" from *1914*, cf. *The Poetical Works*, ed. Geoffrey Keynes (London: Faber, 1960), p.23.

[90] *Poems from the Forces* (note 6), pp.35-37. Half-rhyme mingled with full rhyme.

[91] *Poems of this War* (note 50), p.87f. Again mingled.

[92] *Lyra* (note 51), p.17f. Half-rhyme throughout.

[93] *PL*, No.8 (Nov.-Dec. 1942), "Poets and Journalists", 123f.

[94] He was, on the other hand, included by Comfort and Greacen in *Lyra*, with "The Spreading Cross" (p.58f.). Tambimuttu did print poems of his own in *PL* of course; for examples see note 33.

[95] Barker, *Collected Poems 1930-1955* (London: Faber, 1957) does not contain "To L.B." ("When the mask, when the mask, my darling, my darling"); Durrell, *Collected Poems 1931-1974*, ed. J. A. Brigham (London: Faber, 3rd rev.edn., 1980), lacks "Epitaph" and "Island Fugue"; Raine, *Collected Poems 1935-1980* (London: Allen & Unwin, 1981), misses out "Envoi to A.M." and "London Revisited".

[96] *The Listener*, 12 Feb. 1942, p.216f.

[97] Cf. e.g. her *Poems with Drawings* (London: Enitharmon Press, 1969; Peake is well known anyway, but cf. the stimulating selection *Peake's Progress: Selected Writings and Drawings*, ed. Maeve Gilman (London: Allen Lane, 1978).

[98] *The Listener*, 10 Sept. 1942, p.344.

[99] Hamilton includes: Corby, Ewart, [Fuller], Keyes, Alun Lewis, and Spender. The 4 poems are all by Lewis. With the other poets, Hamilton's choices differ from *PWT*.

[100] *I Burn for England: An anthology of the poetry of World War II* (London: Leslie Frewin, 1966). With 139 poets and 297 poems the largest I have seen.

[101] *Poems of the War Years: An Anthology*, compiled by Francis Wollman (London: Macmillan, 1950).

[102] Published in 1966 as *The Components of the Scene*; I have only seen the rev.edn. under the title *Writing in a War: Stories, Poems, and Essays of the Second World War*, which Blythe dedicated to John Heath-Stubbs (Harmondsworth: Penguin Books, 1982).

[103] Auden, Barker, Corby, Fraser, [Fuller], Gascoyne, Alun Lewis, C. Day Lewis, MacNeice, Michael Roberts, Rook, Spender, Dylan Thomas, and Watkins. It is interesting to compare Wollman and Blythe here with the miniature anthology Press (note 18) appends to his Chapter "Poets of the Second World War and of the 1940s". There are 12 poets in all; 7 (8) of them: Barker, Durrell, [Fuller], Gascoyne, Alun Lewis, Nicholson, Treece, and Watkins belong to Tambimuttu's choices.

[104] *The Mid-Century: English Poetry 1940-1960*, ed. David Wright (Harmondsworth: Penguin Books, 1965). The poets are: Auden, Barker, Durrell, Empson, [Fuller], Gascoyne, Keyes, MacNeice, Dylan Thomas, and Watkins; the poem is "Ecce Homo" from "Miserere".

[105] *The Penguin Book of Contemporary Verse* (Harmondsworth, 1950, repr.1959).

[106] *The Faber Book of Modern Verse*. Originally published in 1936. The 2nd, rev.edn. (London, 1951, 1960) has a supplement chosen by Ridler; the bulk of the 21 (22) poets also found in *PWT* corresponds to this supplement.

[107] *The Oxford Book of Twentieth-Century English Verse* (Oxford: Clarendon Press, 1973, repr.1974).

THE SECOND WORLD WAR IN OFFICIAL AND UNOFFICIAL RUSSIAN PROSE

The aim of this article is to survey some of the ways in which the last War has been described, not only in official Soviet prose of various periods but also in works of *samizdat* and *tamizdat*,[1] as well as in literature written outside the Soviet Union.[2] Both synchronic and diachronic comparison will be attempted, but on the basis of a limited number of specific themes and approaches, and with no pretension to comprehensiveness in chronology or themes, be it in official or unofficial prose.[3] None the less a brief historical outline may serve as a useful introduction in terms both of periodisation and of changing thematic emphasis.

Tadeusz Konwicki, in a recent unofficial Polish novel, *Wschody i zachody księżyca* (*Moonrises, Moonsets*), has written of his mixed reactions to the multiplicity of wars which he experienced as a thirteen-year-old schoolboy in Lithuania ("Wars break out. My wars"), beginning with the German bombardment of Vilna, the outbreak of the Soviet-Polish war on 17 September 1939, the several weeks of Soviet occupation, the Lithuanian invasion of Vilna, the Polish-Lithuanian war, the Soviet-Lithuanian war, the German-Soviet war, and finally the Home Army-NKVD war.[4] For Russians, of course, the situation was quite different, for when they were invaded in June 1941, after years of Stalinist repression and, from 1939, a pact with Nazi Germany which many citizens must have found bewildering, the nature of the war and the enemy quickly became apparent, even though in some regions, particularly the Ukraine, the Germans were at first welcomed as liberators. The confusion, demoralisation, and, indeed, terror of the purges was replaced by a much more comprehensible external threat which united rather than divided the nation. This change of atmosphere brought about by Hitler's attack is well described by Boris Pasternak in *Doktor Zhivago*: "And when war broke out, its real horrors, the real danger and menace of real death, were a blessing compared with the inhuman power of the lie, a relief because it broke the spell of the dead letter."[5] During this first period of the war literature was, as might be expected, aimed almost exclusively at raising morale, the commonest genres being short stories, sketches, and poems. Like the Germans,[6] Russian writers had no hesitation in declaring the war to be "sacred",[7] and they concentrated on building up a national mythology, based on a heroic reconstruction of past military feats and oversimplified but – at a time of heavy losses – affecting and necessary morale-boosting triumphs; perhaps not surprisingly, little of the fiction of this period was concerned with individual soldiers or with any but the most unambiguous moral issues. Amongst the best examples of this kind of schematic propaganda writing were stories like Valentin Kataev's *Flag* (*The Flag*), Vasily Grossman's *Narod bessmerten* (*The People are Immortal*) and Mikhail Sholokhov's

Nauka nenavisti (*The Science of Hate*), all written in 1942. The aim of such works was to present the strongest possible contrast between the bestially cruel and destructive Fascist enemy and, on the other hand, the valiant, humane, and noble Russians, whose conduct was, in the literal sense of the word, exemplary: it was not, for instance, unknown for inspiring texts to be read to Soviet troops before they went into battle. Such inspirational war literature, often crudely melodramatic, is now of historical interest only.

As the tide gradually turned, particularly after the battle of Stalingrad, Soviet war writing became less concerned with abstract heroics and more inclined to show the horrendous realities of total conflict, although it was only slowly that the plight and experiences of individual soldiers began to figure in literature. This period, which lasted for about five years until 1947, is marked by a turning away from stylisation and a parallel reduction in ideological tendentiousness. The main forms now used were long short stories, novellas, novels, and plays, amongst the best examples being Konstantin Simonov's novel *Dni i nochi* (*Days and Nights*, 1944) and Aleksandr Bek's *Volokolamskoe shosse* (*The Volokolamsk Highway*) of the same year. Formulaic and propagandistic elements were still prominent by Western standards, but the works of Bek and Simonov marked a distinct improvement on what had gone before, and stand out amongst the greyly schematic war writing of the period.

The Red Army's increasing successes and ultimate victory undoubtedly eased some of the pressure on writers, and in the immediate post-war period it was occasionally possible for strongly realistic novels like Viktor Nekrasov's celebrated *V okopakh Stalingrada* (*In the Trenches of Stalingrad*, 1945) to show fighting in a small context, revealing the psychological and physical problems of credible, individual soldiers, whilst paying little attention to overall strategy and eschewing most of the obligatory large-scale clichés, such as the myth of a wise and skilful higher leadership, clichés which had been *de rigueur* before this brief period of relatively unvarnished realism and were, indeed, to return with renewed vigour after it.

Nekrasov received the Stalin prize in 1946, but in the years that followed he, like other prominent writers, was subjected to harsh Party criticism with the renewed hardening of official cultural policy. Now the war's early disasters were to be glossed over, Soviet feats of arms glorified, and the country's "historic mission" under the wise guidance of the Party and, of course, its Leader, revealed in its heroic "reality".[8] During this period many of the best writers simply avoided the theme of war, but for those who continued, all negative phenomena such as fear, cowardice, lack of patriotism, and treachery became taboo, whilst authors accused of paying insufficient attention to the supposedly leading role of Party officials were expected to correct their oversight. Some, not necessarily the most cynical, were able to make these adjustments with a moderate degree of success; others, like Aleksandr Fadeev, struggled desperately to re-write their novels in an acceptable manner, but failed to over-simplify already fairly conventional works to a degree which could satisfy the political censors. Fadeev's struggles with his *magnum opus Molodaya gvardiya* (*The Young Guard*, 1945), his subsequent decline into alcoholism, and suicide at the dawn of a new era in 1956 is a vivid, though not paradigmatic, cautionary tale, for the majority of hack writers, mostly now well forgotten, adapted themselves readily to every whim of their capricious and repressive Leader.

The twentieth Party Congress in 1956, when Khrushchev attempted to dispel the Stalin myth, led to, amongst other things, rapid developments in Soviet literature. War again became a topic which serious writers could tackle, and a strong trend developed for young ex-combatants to re-create their first-hand experiences, usually setting their works in very small crisis-ridden environments, and providing little or no strategic or other overall perspective. It is with the post-Stalin period and its extension into the present day that this survey will be principally concerned. War literature written outside the Soviet Union, however, belongs mainly to the immediate post-war years.

There is a degree of irony in the fact that Russian émigrés living in Europe could see Hitler's threat to Russia and to civilisation in general much more clearly than could Stalin in the years leading up to 1941. But despite the latter's moral support for Hitler's various campaigns, including the invasion of France,[9] most émigrés rallied to support of the Soviet side when they saw their former fatherland threatened; indeed, at this period émigré sentiment was closer to that of Soviet Russia than at any other period. It was, however, the second wave of emigration, coinciding with the end of the war, that provided the first examples of war prose, often in the form of reminiscences or fictionalised accounts of the authors' own experiences. Some of the themes introduced at this time were taboo in Soviet writing of the same period; some, indeed, still are. For example, of the two novels about the siege of Leningrad entitled *Blokada* (*The Blockade*) – one by émigré Anatoly Darov (see note 5), the other written between 1968 and 1973 by the ultra-conventional Soviet writer Aleksandr Chakovsky – Darov's, whilst hardly rising above the low literary level of the later epic, is much more realistic in its portrayal of the mixed feelings of confusion and panic at the start of the war, treachery, the welcoming of Hitler by some sections of the population, and, indeed, some of the really unmentionable horrors of the blockade such as the eating of human flesh.[10] Chakovsky's novel, like most Soviet-printed works, ignores these elements and is remarkable mainly for unimpeachable political conservatism, and an attempt to reintroduce Stalin into literature. However, a recent imaginative and honest documentary by two gifted Soviet writers (one Byelorussian, the other Russian) gives the fullest and most realistic account of this appalling period yet published: Ales' Adamovich and Daniil Granin, *Blokadnaya kniga* (*A Book of the Blockade*, Moscow, 1982).

The beginning of the war is also important in Vasily Alekseev's *Rossiya soldatskaya* (*Soldiering Russia*, New York, 1954), a fresh and uninhibited account of a period that has suffered much falsification, although it remains on the unambitious level of most émigré prose of the Second Wave. Much more important in purely cognitive terms was historian Aleksandr Nekrich's *1941, 22 iyunya* (*22 June 1941*), published in 1965. A serious attempt to portray Soviet unpreparedness at the start of the war, it has been translated into many languages. In Russia, however, it was within six months restricted to special library collections, and in August 1967 removed altogether. Nekrich himself was obliged to emigrate in 1976. The latter fact serves as a simple reminder that in the present day the distinction between Soviet and émigré writers is no longer a straightforward one in view of the emigration or expatriation of so many writers; another relevant example is that of Viktor Nekrasov, one of the best Soviet war novelists, who now lives in Paris. Nor should the fact that a book about the war is written outside the Soviet Union be assumed to indicate outspokenness or an unorthodox point of view. Aron Abramovich's study of the active role of Jews in the struggle against Hitler, *V reshayushchey voine. Uchastie i rol' evreev v voine protiv natsizma* (*In the Decisive War. The Participation and Role of Jews in the War against Nazism*, Tel-Aviv, 1983) is remarkable for its closeness to orthodox Soviet positions. However, the title of a recent *samizdat* prose fragment, "Voina bez prikras" ("Unvarnished War")[11] points to much of the difference between official, that is, censored, and unofficial writing. There is nothing sensational in this rare example of *samizdat* writing on a theme that is more usually ignored, but the full horror of war is depicted, including the concomitant breakdown of social morality: indeed, the depiction of naked selfishness would seem to be one of the themes that precluded this story from official publication.

Censorship, endemic in Russian literary life since long before the Revolution, has ever been especially alert to slights on the military; amongst celebrated examples may be cited the reception given to Kuprin's account of turn-of-the-century army life *Poedinok* (*The Duel*, 1905) or Babel''s colourful pageant of Cossacks at war *Konarmiya* (*Red Cavalry*, 1926). A particularly interesting example of censorship in action may be found in Anatoly Kuznetsov's *Babiy yar*, a heavily cut version of which was published in the journal *Yunost'* in 1966. The author defected to Britain in 1969 and brought with him a microfilm of his original uncensored version, which first appeared in book form in 1970 and in English translation in 1971, in each case printed in such a way as to make the censor's excisions clearly visible.[12] At once comic and tragic, the extensive cut passages relate to absolutely anything that could be deemed discreditable to the Red Army or civilian population. These include accounts of genuine horrors like cannibalism and the active support for the Nazi death squads by anti-semitic Kievans, as well as a wide range of political taboo-breaking such as a humorous view of the Ribbentrop-Molotov pact as seen by children in cinema newsreels, a frank picture of the positive welcome given to the German invaders/liberators by most of the local population, and, perhaps most heinous of all, liberal parallels drawn between Hitler and Stalin, the SS and the KGB. As an illustration of comprehensive taboo-breaking and demonstration of the realities of censorship, Kuznetsov's novel has few, if any rivals.

The pre-war friendship between Hitler and Stalin is treated with heavy irony in several pieces of satirical prose published outside the Soviet Union, most recently by Vladimir Voinovich, who was forced to emigrate in 1980. In *Pretendent na prestol* (*Pretender to the Throne*, Paris, 1979) and "V krugu druzey" ("In a Circle of Friends", in *Putyom vzaimnoy perepiski*, Paris, 1969) Stalin and his henchmen are depicted as totally unprepared, not least because the Soviet Leader regards Hitler as his true friend. Kuznetsov and Voinovich both lay emphasis on their similarities and affinities, as also on those between the chief organs of their power. An important serious, as opposed to satirical, treatment of the same question is to be found in the last and most significant novel of Vasily Grossman, who has already been mentioned as the author of a highly successful propaganda work in 1942. Grossman's unfinished *Zhizn' i sud'ba* (*Life and Fate*, 1960) is a major contribution to Russian war prose. Almost all manuscript copies were confiscated by the KGB in 1961, but the work survived in one copy which was smuggled to the West and partially published in the mid-1970s, a "full" edition appearing only in 1980. In this wide-ranging philosophical novel the author not only depicts the cruelty and meaninglessness of war with appallingly vivid realism, but reflects with deep pessimism on Soviet as well as German anti-semitism, portraying the two sides in the brutal death struggle as on an equally abysmal moral level. For Grossman in his last work (he died in 1964) Leninism-Stalinism and Nazism are equated; hardly ever can a writer have undergone such a fundamental and desperate evolution of belief.[13]

Any consideration of Russian literature about the war, or, indeed, about anything else, must take account of the concept of truth, and in particular its various Soviet forms. It is a word that was frequently used in critical writing during the Thaw by liberal and conservative critics alike.[14] At the height of *Novyy mir*'s richest period in the 1960s when war literature found its most sophisticated and realistic expression in translations of the novels of the Soviet Byelorussian writer Vasil Bykaŭ, the watchword for all writers was "truth". Not "the great truth", which could all too easily become simply what a given critic or writer would have liked to have happened, that is, a form of idealisation, but the truth of personal experience, the truth of concrete facts, sometimes, in appropriate contexts, known as the truth of the trenches (*okopnaya pravda*). If Solzhenitsyn was perhaps the ultimate representative of the type of new realism associated with *Novyy mir* in its heyday, then Bykaŭ and Okudzhava, who had also experienced the war as young men, came, particularly in Bykaŭ's case, to personify harsh realism and unheroic truthfulness in their treatment of a topic which has all too often been distorted, and was in the pre-1956 period widely discredited.[15] In the Brezhnev era strenuous efforts were made to challenge the new realism of the Thaw, some typical examples being found in the critical statements of Ivan Stadnyuk, a mediocre war writer and apologist for Stalin, whose novel *Voina* (*War*, 1974-80) amazed literary opinion inside and outside the Soviet Union by being awarded the State Prize for Literature in 1983, an event with perhaps more serious implications and certainly less anecdotal possibilities than the earlier award of the even more prestigious Lenin Prize to a war epic by Mr Brezhnev himself.[16] Writing in the highly orthodox journal *Molodaya gvardiya* in 1970, Stadnyuk declared: "Some writers have begun to replace the great and shining truth by the little truth (*pravdochka*) of the petty fact."[17] The same line is adopted by his biographer Boris Leonov,[18] who refers to liberals "fussing about truth" (*pod shumok "pravde"*)[19] in contrast to whom Stadnyuk aims "to establish truth and to oppose as strongly as possible existing 'objective' distortions of the truth of the heroic 1940s".[20] Despite his mediocrity as a writer, it may be worth quoting Stadnyuk's views at some length, since they reflect much of current official thinking about the war and how it should be depicted in literature. Describing the period of the Thaw, he writes:

> The creative streams which bore the main truth about the last War began to dry up, the truth of the genuine heroic feat, the truth of the greatness of Soviet man, the truth of the unbendingness of the Communists and the main generalising truth, the sense of which lies in the fact that the Soviet state, the Soviet people and its Armed Forces bore the main burden of the Second World War and played a decisive role in the smashing of a powerful enemy. On the sea of literature here and there rose up the crests of rather murky, ill-smelling waves. There began to appear works whose authors conducted their creative search not in the heroic principles of the past years of disaster but in negative phenomena which, of course, also took place on the different fronts stretching over many thousands of kilometres during four years of heavy fighting. Of course all sorts of things happened in the War. Alongside inevitable casualties there were also unjustified sacrifices, in the War bad commanders were to be found and cases of cowardice, treachery, gullibility occurred. And although all this existed, it in no measure, even to a thousandth degree, reflected the great and principal truth about Soviet man in the War.[21]

It may be noted that whilst Stadnyuk, having attacked those who approach history from positions of "a certain philosophical-historical Daltonism", concludes, "To the great good fortune of history the powers which defend truth cannot be overcome",[22] Anatoly Kuznetsov expresses the same message from a completely different viewpoint when he writes (in one of the many passages to which the censor took exception), "However much you burn and disperse, cover over, and trample down, human memory still remains."[23]

War writing during the Thaw had a number of characteristic features in addition to the harshness of its unvarnished realism now so unacceptable to writers of Stadnyuk's ilk. These features distinguish it equally from earlier war writing and from the works of the new conservatives, since the latter's demands in several ways imply a return to the principles of Stalinist literature. Although convincing generalisations are impossible, the new writers of the early 1960s characteristically set their stories and novels in the disastrous early months of the war, presenting young soldiers in situations of a desperate or even hopeless kind. Smallness of scale and narrowness of context naturally precluded any broad overview, any attempt to present what Stadnyuk called "the main, generalising truth", and little or no insight is given into overall policy or command. Instead of idealisation or exaggerated heroism there is to be found in many writers of the Thaw a very strong moral sense, often rich in contemporary implications. Entirely typical in the latter respect is Vasil Bykaŭ, whose works represent war writing of this period at its best.[24] None of the above generalisations represents more than a tendency, however, and exceptions can be found at every hand. For example, Bykaŭ's harshest and most searching work, the highly controversial *Miortvym nie balić* (*The Dead Feel No Pain*, 1965) is on a considerably larger scale than his other stories hitherto. Another exception of a quite different kind is to be found in the fact that whilst the liberal, truth-seeking writers of the Thaw very frequently turned to the early months of the war, depicting (indirectly, of course) the disastrous results of the Molotov-Ribbentrop pact and Stalin's decimation of the officer corps in terms of inadequate preparation and weak or sometimes cynical leadership, the selfsame period is portrayed by Stadnyuk in his novel *Voina*, where no indication is given of the unpreparedness and ubiquitous suspicion which so facilitated Hitler's early successes, but where, on the contrary, Stalin is portrayed as a wise and far-sighted leader, conducting policies which would inevitably lead to victory. The restoration of such myths has little appeal, let alone credibility, for the great majority of Soviet or Western readers, and novels like Bykaŭ's, or Konstantin Simonov's *Zhivye i mertvye* (*The Living and the Dead*, 1959) and *Soldatami ne rozhdayutsya* (*Soldiers Are Made, Not Born*, 1963-64), and Grigory Baklanov's *Iyul' 41-ogo goda* (*July 1941*, 1965) continue to represent the most honest and absorbing Soviet literary treatments of the beginning of the war.

Kuznetsov's portrayal of this period in Kiev is something of a case apart, since he combines harrowing descriptions of atrocities with a light-hearted, ironic view of many features of Soviet reality of the time. Though less strongly so, the same may be said of the early parts of Anatoly Darov's New York-published *Blokada*. Josephine Woll is essentially right, however, when she says in her commentary to a bibliography of Soviet dissident literature, "the reality of life in the Stalin years . . . was far too horrific to be treated humorously, and with very few exceptions the tone of fiction treating the Stalin era is far more realistic, flatter, with less authorial comment."[25] There are some major exceptions, of course, such as Bulgakov's *Master i Margarita* (1929-40) or *Sandro iz Chegema* (*Sandro from Chegem*) by Fazil' Iskander (in the full, American-published version).[26] Something may be said at this point about humour in Russian war literature. Although a highly untypical phenomenon, it cannot be entirely ignored, for one of the great comic novels of the century, Vladimir Voinovich's *tamizdat Zhizn' i neobychaynye priklyucheniya soldata Ivana Chonkina* (*The Life and Extraordinary Adventures of Private Chonkin*, 1963-70) is set precisely in the immediate pre-war and early war period. Bearing some superficial resemblances to Jaroslav Hašek's classic anti-war novel, Voinovich's book is not so much against war, which is essentially only in the background, as a satire on myriad different aspects of Stalinism, exposed by the naïvely honest hero Ivan Chonkin, whose simple view of life takes no account of the cunning, falsity, and double-think endemic in Soviet society under Stalin. This latterday Ivan the Fool (*Ivanushka-durachok*) has, in fact, little in common with the good soldier Švejk, representing not so much an interesting psychological phenomenon in himself as a catalyst for the self-exposure of an absurd and corrupt world.[27] Belonging to the tradition of Gogol′, Bulgakov, and Zoshchenko,[28] Voinovich's novel does not so much continue, as some critics have suggested,[29] a Švejkian anti-militarist tradition, as the broader stream of Russian political and social satirical comedy. Far closer to the spirit of Hašek is an interesting earlier "war" novel recently republished: Sergey Klychkov, *Sakharnyy nemets* (*The Sugar German*, first published Moscow, 1929; reprinted Paris, 1983). Finally may be mentioned in this connection the humorous quasi-documentary reminiscences of life in the Red Army by Lev Larsky, who now lives in Israel, *Memuary rotnogo pridurka* (*Memoirs of a Company Fool*, 1979-82).

Returning to the main features of Russian writing about the war in the 1960s, the choice of young heroes is very characteristic of Bykaŭ, who himself entered the war at the age of eighteen. It is also reflected in many powerful stories by such contemporaries as Vladimir Bogomolov in *Ivan* (1958) and *Zosya* (1965), or in Viktor Nekrasov's characteristically unflinching *Vtoraya noch′* (*The Second Night*, 1960), but it is nowhere more affecting than in Bulat Okudzhava's excellent novella *Bud′ zdorov, shkolyar* (*Good Luck, Schoolboy*), a frank but low-key and entirely unsensational story of callow youth facing a dangerous and unknown future, which has not been republished in the Soviet Union since it first appeared in the historic "provincial" literary collection, *Tarusskie stranitsy* (*Pages from Tarusa*, Kaluga, 1961). Whilst Bykaŭ, whose works consistently feature young heroes, had "no wish to read, let alone write during the War and for some time after it",[30] it is perhaps worth noting that Stadnyuk, the would-be depicter of higher truth, became a writer during the war years, and, in his own words, "in the first half of the sixties . . . began to think seriously about a theme which had been in my mind during the first postwar years. I considered how a real military leader is born".[31] In this respect he was making a specific attempt to correct the "false" impression of what another apologist for Stalin, P. E. Glinkin, called "the most total unpreparedness for war, whose beginning was presented in . . . studies and literary works as complete chaos, shame, and catastrophe". The greyness of this picture is seen by Glinkin as typical of distortions in some interpretations of the past as a result of the "overcoming of the results of the cult of personality".[32]

The range of characters in Bykaŭ's stories includes heroes, as well as demagogues, cowards, and traitors, his heroes being specifically those, usually very young, "who came face to face with the enemy".[33] This is individual heroism without pomp and circumstance, the bravery born of necessity which often remained unsung. Some writers of the new realism went even further in this direction, and the narrator of Okudzhava's *Bud' zdorov, shkolyar* is in the author's eyes less a hero than an anti-hero.[34] False heroics were an essential part of Stalinist war literature, and so it is not surprising to find many war writers of the 1960s, and with them *Novyy mir* critics like Lakshin, rejecting anything that could be associated with earlier idealisations and distortions. This tendency was described by Boris Leonov in typically intemperate language when he wrote, "for a certain time there floated to the surface the poisonous little theory of deheroicisation".[35] Since as early as 1959 the tendency to portray apparently insignificant figures in war literature has attracted steady fire from orthodox critics, including the dreaded accusation of Remarquism, a term of abuse, drawn, ironically, from the name of one of the great war writers of the century.

The breadth or narrowness of context in Russian prose about the Second World War is far from unconnected with the question of heroics and idealisation. The same writers who had turned to unheroic young individuals for their depictions of war also characteristically avoided any broad overview such as was painfully characteristic of panoramic Stalinist war novels, and also of such later works as Chakovsky's *Blokada* and, in less epic form, Stadnyuk's *Voina*. The effect of small contexts, clearly understood by conservative ideologists, has been well described by Karl Eimermacher:

> The smaller the section of reality depicted the less we are aware of any bias, of a conscious historical perspective. Mass heroism becomes individual heroism; the presentation becomes more realistic, sometimes naturalistic; the Russian soldiers can scarcely be distinguished from those of other armies. The portrayal of the Germans and attitudes towards them become less and less generalised. The Germans are no longer seen simply as fascists or the enemy, but as human beings with problems akin to those of the Russians.[36]

A further feature of small contexts, also noted by Eimermacher, is that "the often hopeless battles and confrontations with cruelty, terror and death permit both positive and negative characteristics to emerge with greater intensity and clarity".[37] In this respect the works of Grigory Baklanov such as *Yuzhnee glavnogo udara* (*South of the Main Thrust*, 1958), *Pyad' zemli* (*A Patch of Earth*, 1959), and *Mertvye sramu ne imut* (*The Dead Feel No Shame*, 1961) are typical, as are such harrowing and often criticised works of Vasil Bykaŭ as *Kruhlanski most* (*The Bridge at Kruhlany*, 1969) and *Miortvym nie balić*.[38]

As has been stressed, the atmosphere of truthfulness and realism that was born in 1956 did not last. Already in 1959 critical attacks on the new or in some case re-born writers were increasing in intensity. By 1968 many of the old taboos, which had been broken, at least in part, during the Thaw, were being vigorously restored, and a major ideological transformation in the treatment of war in literature was being imposed. Not only were completely negative features ignored (phenomena like cannibalism and willing co-operation with the enemy had, after all, always been the exclusive domain of émigré and *tamizdat* writing) but such fundamental questions as cowardice, desertion, treachery, bad leadership, meaningless sacrifices, and the position of those who had been taken prisoner or surrounded by the enemy (*ipso facto* traitors in Stalinist terms) had also become again unacceptable in literature. In the present day Soviet war prose is once more close to being entirely discredited[39] (the awarding of official prizes has nothing to do with the development of serious and lasting literature), as writers of little talent, and critics with more ideological instinct than literary acumen try to foster what at worst seems akin to a war psychosis, by presenting the Second World War as a source of inspiration. Eimermacher has noted a not entirely dissimilar switch in East German literature when in 1959 a literary anthology *Nimm das Gewehr* appeared, with the apparent aim of inspiring the young to enthusiasm for the craft of soldiery and the art of war.[40] Such parallels are problematical, however, for although the coming together of supposedly opposed ideological positions may present itself with depressing clarity to deeply disillusioned writers like the Jew Grossman or the Christian Koryakov, and although it provides material for much black humour in Kuznetsov's quasi-autobiographical novel or the all-embracing satire of Voinovich, it is none the less alien to the great majority of Soviet writers, orthodox and liberal, critics, and readers alike. The terrible devastation and cruelty of the German invasion of Russia, unique in the totality of its horror, cannot be forgotten.[41] The best writers have sought through an unflinchingly honest and realistic reappraisal of what happened in the war to remove this important sphere of literature from the realm of idealised, politically guided fantasy, and through their harsh realism not only to record the undoubted horrors of the past, but also to cast light on the complex moral problems of the present day. Perhaps only in Germany itself, West and East, does war literature carry such a strong political, philosophical, social, and moral resonance as it does in modern Russian prose.[42]

ARNOLD McMILLIN

Liverpool

NOTES

* The author is indebted to the British Academy for a grant which facilitated the preparatory research for this article.

[1] *Samizdat* (literally "self-publishing") refers to the circulation of unpublishable material; its derivative *tamizdat* (literally "publishing there") describes illegal publication of literature abroad.

[2] The shift in cultural balance produced by the emigration or expatriation of many outstanding Russian writers in the 1970s has rendered the term émigré literature no longer appropriate. For an analysis of this phenomenon see Carl R. Proffer, "The Remarkable Decade that Destroyed Russian Emigre Literature", *Russia*, 1981, vol. 3, pp.33-35. The point is further illustrated by the fact that an excellent recent survey of contemporary Russian prose treats official and unofficial writing together, although the latter predominates: Petr Vail' and Aleksandr Genis, *Sovremennaya russkaya proza* (Ann Arbor, 1982). A study of this branch of Russian literature, currently being written by the present author with Gerald Stanton Smith, also avoids the limiting term émigré in its working title: "Russian Literature outside Soviet Russia: 1917 to the Present Day."

[3]Although unofficial Russian war literature has received little critical attention, its mainstream, official counterpart forms the subject of an incessant flood of Soviet books and articles as well as a number of English-language publications. See, for example, S. Lochtin, "The War in the Soviet Novel. From the Heroic to the Prosaic", *Soviet Survey*, 1960, vol.33, pp.62-69, and Karl Eimermacher, "War Literature", in C. D. Kernig (ed.) *Marxism, Communism and Western Society: A Comparative Encyclopedia*, New York, 1973, vol.7, pp.328-40, both of which include bibliographical information, and, amongst Soviet surveys, L. A. Plotkin, *Literatura i voina. Velikaya Otechestvennaya voina v russkoy proze*, Leningrad, 1967. Also of interest is the very individual analysis of several major Soviet war novelists by Grigorij Svirskij: "Voennaya proza i proza militaristskaya", *Revue des Etudes Slaves*, 1982, vol.54, no.3, pp.355-85.

[4]Tadeusz Konwicki, "Polish Dreams and Delusions", *Index on Censorship*, 1983, no.2, pp.18-21.

[5]Boris Pasternak, *Doktor Zhivago*, Milan, 1957, p.519. Similar feelings are described by A. Dar [Anatoly Darov] in his short novel about the siege of Leningrad *Blokada* (*The Blockade*, New York, 1964), p.39. This work, printed separately only in 1964, first appeared in a rotaprint version in Munich in 1945, after which the second edition was published in the Frankfurt-based journal *Grani*, 1953-1955.

[6]See A. von Cibulka, "Die Aufgabe unserer Kriegsdichtung", *Propyläen*, 1942-1943, vol.40, pp.33-34.

[7]See Eimermacher, op.cit., p.335.

[8]It is difficult not to see in such abstractions certain parallels with some of the German ideologists of a few years earlier: for example, "We shall have to go beyond the basic demand of an ethical espousal of war and enquire of the writer whether he recognises the revolutionary event of our spiritual awakening and is capable of making it the ideological foundation of his book" (H. W. Hagen, "Gedanken zum kommenden Kriegsbuch", *Weltliteratur*, 1940, new series, vol.15, no.12, pp.230-31).

It may also be noted that the Soviet name for the Second World War (1941-45) in the Great Patriotic War (Velikaya Otechestvennaya voina) parallelling the "Greater German War of Liberation". See Eimermacher, op.cit., p.330. A further angle on this theme is the comment of the popular Soviet balladeer and novelist Bulat Okudzhava, himself the author of an outstandingly truthful war novella of the post-Stalin period, that "It was not a Great, but a Terrible War. A Loathsome War. It ravaged our souls and made us cruel" (Aleksandr Gershkovich, "Neobychnoe interv'yu Bulata Okudzhavy", *Obozrenie*, 1984, no.8, p.24).

[9]See for example the telegram from Ambassador Schulenburg to the German Foreign Ministry reporting the Soviet government's congratulations on the brilliant success of the German armed forces: Yu. Fel'shtinsky, *SSR – Germaniya 1939-1941*, New York, 1983, pp.55-56.

[10]Darov, *Blokada*, pp.39-40 et ff., 201. Harrison Salisbury is said to have found Darov's novel useful for his own studies of the war.

[11]D. Aksel'rod, "Voina bez prikras", *Novyy zhurnal*, 1983, vol.153, pp.28-45. The author, without whose permission or knowledge this fragment was published, has been in detention since November 1982.

[12]A. Anatoly (Kuznetsov), *Babiy yar*, Frankfurt/a/Main, 1970; A. Anatoli, *Baby Yar*, London, 1971. An English translation of the censored, *Yunost'*, version appeared in New York in 1967.

[13]This equation is doubtless why Efim Etkind cites Grossman's novel as a prime example of taboo-breaking. See "Sovetskie tabu", *Sintaksis*, 1981, no.9, p.20. A very similar conviction to Grossman's is expressed in the highly individual, spiritual, even religious, war novel by Mikhail Koryakov who left the Soviet Union in 1945: *Osvobozhdenie dushi* (*Liberation of the Soul*, New York, 1952).

[14]See, for example, three articles on the outstanding Soviet Byelorussian war novelist Vasil Bykaŭ: A. Viarcinski, "Hałoŭnaje – praŭda ... ", *Litaratura i mastactva*, 9 October 1964; Je. Hiercovič, "Dźviuch praŭd nie byvaje", *Źviazda*, 1 February 1966; V. Sevruk, "Pravda o velikoy voine", *Pravda*, 17 April 1966.

[15]Although a Byelorussian, Bykaŭ has, through translations into Russian, played an important role in the development of not only Byelorussian but, indeed, also Soviet Russian literature, and he has often been linked with the best Russian writers of the 1960s. See, for example, Marc Slonim, *Soviet Russian Literature: Writers and Problems, 1917-1977*, 2nd edition, New York, 1977, p.406, where he is linked with Belov, Bitov, Trifonov, Voinovich, Shukshin, Rasputin, and Aitmatov. Vail' and Genis (op.cit., p.149) specifically link him with the new realism of the Thaw: "*Novyy mir*, with Shukshin, Dudintsev, Tendryakov, Mozhaev, Abramov, Trifonov, Bykov, Lakshin, and, above all, Solzhenitsyn, was the tribune of a new direction in Soviet literature: 'the truth about everything'."

Solzhenitsyn's own contributions to literature about the Second World War were, predictably, not printable under Soviet conditions. More surprisingly, perhaps, they are not in prose, comprising a narrative poem of 1954 *Prusskie nochi* (*Prussian Nights*, Paris 1974) and the verse play about the behaviour of the Red Army as conquerors which it was intended to precede, *Pir pobediteley* (*The Victors' Feast*). Solzhenitsyn has since repudiated all his early poetry.

At this point may be mentioned another unofficial work dealing with the end of the war, although it is mostly concerned with the post-war occupation of Berlin: Grigory Klimov, *Berlinskiy kreml'* (*The Berlin Kremlin*, Frankfurt/a/Main, 1953).

[16] It should be noted that both the theme of war itself and Stadnyuk's attempt to rehabilitate Stalin as a military leader are very typical of certain strong trends in the Soviet Union today. For further thoughts on war psychosis see Gershkovich, op.cit., p.23.

[17] Ivan Stadnyuk, "Vesna pobednaya", *Molodaya gvardiya*, 1970, no.5, p.312.

[18] Leonov has also written on Vsevolod Kochetov, an ideologically similar, albeit more talented, writer.

[19] Boris Leonov, *Glavnyy ob''ekt. Ocherk tvorchestva Ivana Stadnyuka*, Moscow, 1978, p.154.

[20] Leonov, op.cit., p.158. The author of these lines has himself been accused by Soviet critics of writing in the spirit of "bourgeois objectivism": *Polymia*, 1980, no.5, p.312 et ff.

[21] Stadnyuk, "Vesna pobednaya", p.312.

[22] Quoted in Leonov, op.cit., p.159.

[23] Kuznetsov, op.cit., (Frankfurt edition), p.484. This position is very close to Bulgakov's celebrated "manuscripts do not burn" in *Master i Margarita*: Mikhail Bulgakov, *Tri romana*, Moscow, 1973, p.703.

[24] On the contemporary significance of this writer's work see Arnold McMillin, "War and Peace in the Prose of Vasil Bykaŭ", *Die Welt der Slawen*, 1983, no.1, pp.110-21.

[25] Josephine Woll, *Soviet Dissident Literature: A Critical Guide*, Boston, 1983, p.xxx.

[26] For a depiction of Stalin and his henchmen at play see, for instance, the chapter "Piry Valtasara" ("Belshazzar's Feasts") in Fazil' Iskander, *Sandro iz Chegema*, Ann Arbor, 1979, pp.187-229.

[27] For more detailed analysis of the relationship between Chonkin and Švejk see Arnold McMillin, "Individuals against the System: Chonkin and Švejk", *Westslavische Beiträge*, vol.1, forthcoming.

[28] Voinovich has traced the roots of his own work in "an old Russian tradition from Gogol, Chekhov, Bulgakov". See "An Interview with Vladimir Voinovich", *Quarto*, April 1981, nos.7-8, p.7. It may be noted that the sequel to *Chonkin, Pretendent na prestol*, is harsher in tone, being written when Voinovich had no chance or expectation of being able to publish in the Soviet Union.

[29] See, for instance, Peter Petro, "Hašek, Voinovich, and the Tradition of Anti-Militarist Satire", *Canadian Slavonic Papers*, 1980, vol.22, pp.116-21. In another article devoted entirely to scatalogical details in Voinovich's novel Serge Lecomte suggests that in his depiction of Chonkin receiving news of the German invasion whilst in the lavatory the author "is making the act of defecation into a sort of war protest" ("Scatalogical Details in Vojnovič's *Žizn' i neobyčajnye priključenija soldata Ivana Čonkina*", *Russian Language Journal*, 1980, vol.117, p.146).

[30] Vasil Bykov, "On Behalf of My Generation", *Soviet Literature*, 1980, no.10, p.22.

[31] Ivan Stadnyuk, "Loyalty to a Theme", ibid., p.3.

[32] P. E. Glinkin, *Muza v pokhodnoy shineli*, Leningrad, 1970, pp.102-3.

[33] Bykov, "On Behalf of My Generation", p.124.

[34] Gershkovich, op.cit., p.23.

[35] Leonov, op.cit., p.154.

[36] Eimermacher, op.cit., p.338. Amongst the many clear examples of this phenomenon may be mentioned N. M. Gribachev's *Kto umret segodnya?* (*Who Will Die Today?*, Moscow, 1960), and Bykaŭ's highly controversial short story *Adna noč* (*One Night*, Minsk, 1961) in which a German and a Soviet Byelorussian soldier, both carpenters by trade, are trapped together in a ruined building for the night. The Soviet soldier's feeling of helplessness before immense and incomprehensible elements also finds some echo in German war literature. See, for instance, H. Günther, "Die neue deutsche Kriegsdichtung und die Schule", *Schulwarte*, 1953, vol.6, no.10, p.579. Also of interest in this connection is Daniil Granin's short story "Plennye" ("Prisoners"), *Znamya*, 1964, no.12, pp.167-74.

As an exception to several of the many generalisations made in this article may be mentioned an excellent recent story by a hitherto unknown writer who describes a genuinely heroic character but in a situation of the gravest danger and in a small temporal context (three days): Vyacheslav Kondrat'ev, "Sashka", *Druzhba narodov*, 1979, no.2, pp.5-88.

[37] Eimermacher, op.cit., p.338.

[38] See note 24.

[39] Vasil Bykaŭ is in this, as in so much else, an important exception, and his latest work, *Znak biady* (*The Sign of Misfortune*), is one of the best works of Soviet literature to be published in recent years: see *Polymia*, 1982, no.8, pp.18-167.

[40] Eimermacher, op.cit., p.332.

[41] One of the best recent accounts of the horror of Hitler's war in Eastern Europe is to be found in Ales' Adamovich's *Karateli* (*The Punishers*, Moscow, 1981).

[42] The Soviet Union's more recent military conflicts have yet to be reflected in serious official literature, although the Soviet-Chinese border dispute and the war in Afghanistan have not infrequently figured in popular quasi-documentary stories, particularly in newspapers such as the specifically army-orientated *Krasnaya zvezda*. However, there have appeared several interesting *tamizdat* works by a talented young writer, Vladimir Rybakov, which present an unvarnished picture of the life of soldiers serving on the Chinese border in the 1960s. See, for instance, his novel *Tyazhest'* (*The Burden*, Frankfurt/a/Main, 1977), currently being translated into English, and the story "Zheltoe i krasnoe" ("The Yellow and the Red", 1979).

THE AMERICAN WAR NOVEL AND THE DEFEATED LIBERAL

The American "war novel" of the late 1940s has more than one kind of warfare taking place within its pages. There was the war against the enemy, German or Japanese; there was also a struggle taking place in the war novels between liberals and reactionaries. This latter warfare, especially virulent within the US Army, and which often resulted in the death or disillusionment of the liberals, reflected what were basically post-war concerns. It is well-known that most of the war novels in America were written after the war. It is a less familiar point that war novels, especially those which appeared soon after the war, were often the vehicle for political and social tensions which found expressions in the first Cold War presidential election in 1948.

During World War II the war correspondent occupied a position of prestige and influence which his First World War counterpart, struggling against conditions of strict censorship and news management, would have envied. Journalists became the eyes and ears, and sometimes the conscience, of the American people. Their first hand accounts of invasions and battles brought home, in broadcasts, articles, books and, less successfully, newsreels, the reality of war:

> Curran was dead all right. . . . At the bottom and on one side of the gully there was a pile of grey shredded fabric. It had no shape and it was not very big. The whole bottom of the gully was coated evenly with a grey powder and you would not have noticed the pile of grey shredded fabric except for a foot and a shoe with no body attached to it. This object lay by the edge of the pile.
>
> There was no blood whatever. All the blood had been blown out of the man who had worn this shoe. He was shredded and the pile of shreds was coated with the grey dust of pulverised rock.[1]

This kind of detail – not simply death in battle, but utter obliteration – seldom appears in First World War journalism. "But our troops passed on steadily," wrote Philip Gibbs of the second day of the Somme offensive in 1916,

> with fixed bayonets at parade step, not turning their heads when comrades dropped to right and left of them. They took the first line of German trenches, which were blown to dustheaps with the bodies of the men who had held them. In the second line there were men still living, and still resolute enough to defend themselves. They were bombed out of this position, and our men went on to the third line still under machine-gun fire.[2]

Gibbs was not a dishonest writer, but his wartime dispatches belong to a patriotic ideological discourse designed to hide the truth of war from his readers, and to sustain their morale. No American war correspondent wanted to lower morale on the home front, but they were operating in a cultural climate which was, to some extent, more open and frank about war casualties and death. The gain in openness may owe something to the realistic descriptions of battle in the war fiction and memoirs which appeared after 1918.[3] Journalists learned from novelists that gung-ho bravery was, in representations of war, only a small part of the story. "Human interest" journalism, as practised by Ernie Pyle; battle diaries, in which the correspondent shared the combatant's danger (Ira Wolfert's *Battle for the Solomons* and Richard Tregaskis' *Guadalcanal Diary*, both 1943); and the powerful descriptions by Martha Gellhorn of a hospital ship during the Normandy invasions, and of an English burns hospital, took the journalist to the heart of the experience of war.[4]

Young journalists like Hersey, Wolfert and Tregaskis were themselves aspiring novelists; the great figures in American fiction of the 1930s – Hemingway, Steinbeck and Dos Passos – became war correspondents.[5] War journalism increasingly showed "literary" qualities; a journalistic element characterised the first phase of war fiction. In part it was a way of dealing with the question of topicality. As the conditions of warfare changed, and as the locations altered, certain "placing" devices were needed to establish the authenticity of a scene, a piece of dialogue. Details of the 1941 Nomura-Hull talks appear in William Martin Camp's *Retreat, Hell!* (1943). Albert Maltz in *The Cross and the Arrow* (1944) attempted to recreate the German mood of the Summer of 1941 by comparing it to events later in the war: "The bombings had not begun; the German armies were knifing into Russia without serious opposition; the factory was still in Düsseldorf, running smoothly."[6] Both novels are exercises in re-creation, in the historical imagination. There were few novels which could dispense with such devices; those which did, like Harry Brown's *A Walk in the Sun* (1944), had the isolated, timeless quality of a fable in which war, and the army, were unchanging conditions which everyman endured.

The intertwining of journalism and fiction shaped representations of the experience of war, nowhere more clearly than in the problem of the anxious liberal and the disengaged G.I. Few liberals relished an unthinking, flag-waving patriotism. They preferred to think about the nation's commitment to the war in personal, individualistic and essentially rational terms. Before pursuing the liberal case, it might be appropriate to consider an illiberal war novel, a book steeped in military pride and patriotism: Camp's *Retreat, Hell!* Unlike most of the post-war novels about the Marine Corps, like Leon Uris' *Battle Cry* (1953) and Anton Myrer's *The Big War* (1959), Camp's novel was written from the viewpoint of the regular soldier – the "thirty year man" which Prewitt hopes to become in Jones' *From Here to Eternity* (1952). Camp reminds us of the long involvement of the Marines on the Philippines, and that they had observed the Japanese way of war in Shanghai in 1937. *Retreat, Hell!*, despite its title, is a novel about military defeat. As in so many other accounts of defeat, victory, at least *moral* victory and honour, are retrieved from disaster. Central to the idea of moral victory is the assumption that "we" were the good guys, and that the enemy were vicious, cruel and dehumanised.

> Holding their rifles over their heads, they leaped into the water like so many little brown beetles and swarmed toward the shore. Suddenly the defending artillery opened up just as the foaming white surf turned to waves of brown.[7]

The second fundamental belief is that the Filippinos and Americans were resolute allies, and that only traitors among them sympathised with the Japanese and hoped for the defeat of the white man:

> Filippino and American alike, they stood shoulder to shoulder, as stout-hearted a crew as I had ever seen, fighting day and night, eating cold rice, weak vegetable-broth, and hard-tack, but light hearted and optimistic in the face of it.
> (p.263)

The third assumption was that at the end of their resistance on the Bataan peninsula, despite the secret departure of "the General" (MacArthur) for Australia, the Marines kept up their hope, faith and fighting spirit. The three points are not really at issue in *Retreat, Hell!* for they function as transcendent propositions or myths which all Americans share. Only once does morale crack, when a Harvard-educated soldier, Witherspoon, loses his nerve and blames the lack of ammunition, food and reinforcements on the indifference of those back home. Their patriotism was no more than a cloak for financial self-interest:

> "What do you think all this stuff about duty and honour and ... and ... patriotism is for? Do you know? Can you tell me?" he cried, glaring at me from red-rimmed eyes.
>
> Here's where I should have let him have it right between the eyes. But I couldn't. It would be murder, and they wouldn't believe me when I told them why.
>
> "Well, I'll tell you what it's for. It's to hoodwink us into believing a lot of stuff so we'll stand up an' fight to protect their factories and their investments and their positions ... Do you know why the Marines were in China at all? Do you?"
>
> "To protect American lives and property," I said, waiting for him to turn his head so I could get it over quick. I was going to kill him and hide his body. They'd never know he was a traitor and talked that way ...
>
> "Property, eh? What th' hell are Americans doing with property in China? Ain't they got enough property at home, back in the States?"
> (pp.280-1)

When Witherspoon angrily threw down his rifle, the narrator, Private Bancroft, felt it "was like seeing Old Glory torn down and trampled upon". But the crisis passed, Witherspoon calmed down and apologised. We last see him before the final Japanese attack, getting a haircut and shave, wanting to die fighting like a proud Marine. His "treason" and his criticism of America have been purged. In Camp's eyes there was no question of motivation for the good G.I. Patriotism and service pride were everywhere a sufficient guarantee.

Liberals, as they observed the conduct of the war, did not share Camp's simple-minded conservative beliefs.[8] They feared that because the country came so late into the conflict, and because the war was so remote from personal experience, most Americans remained indifferent to its deeper meanings. "We suffer some minor inconveniences," wrote Quentin Reynolds, "but actually the war hasn't touched us yet. It hasn't touched us as it has touched the people of Britain or Russia. I am sure that if we were called upon to make the sacrifrces they have made we, as a people, would be quite equal to our destiny."[9] Liberals by profession had to be optimistic, but there were many dismaying indications to worry them. Ralph Ingersoll, for example, wrote that "the spiritual commitment has been made in the name of the American people by its leaders but the great body of public opinion has not committed itself and the majority of the individuals in the army have not committed themselves."[10] John Hersey's Major Joppolo in *A Bell for Adano* (1944) was equally concerned: "I just don't know whether our soldiers think much about causes. That's one thing that worries me about this war."[11]

A surprisingly high number of war novels feature liberal-minded characters, of whom Major Joppolo was perhaps the most celebrated. For the most part they are viewed with suspicion and dislike by the men under them, and with distrust by those above them. It is no doubt a tendentious portrait, but one which is firmly rooted in the changing political atmosphere in the United States. Before considering the relationship between text and society, some examples of liberals in war novels, and their fate, will highlight their tenuous position. Joseph, the narrator of Saul Bellow's *Dangling Man* (1944), is a humane victim of a world in which the human perspective no longer seems to matter. As much a casualty as a symptom of the process, his conscience is a millstone:

> "I'm a chopped and shredded man."
> "Easily exasperated."
> "You know how it is. I'm harried, pushed, badgered, worried, nagged, heckled ... "
> "By what? Conscience?"
> "Well, it's a kind of conscience. I don't respect it as I do my own. It's the public part of me. It goes deep. It's the world internalised, in short."
> "What does it want?"
> "It wants me to stop living this way"[12]

The liberal was the inner-directed man, the one with the conscience and the over-sized super-ego; thus Lieutenant Doug Roberts:

> "I guess the minimum thing I'd say now is that the war seems to me – or should I say seemed – immensely worth while (positively and consciously and inherently, that is – not accidentally, as you say), and that I feel a hell of a compulsion to be in it."[13]

But the liberal-idealist like Lt. Roberts gave way after the war to novels in which a bitter anti-army feeling dominates. PFC Joe Hammond in Robert Lowry's *Casualty* (1946) despises the meaningless work he does in an Army Public Relations office near Foggia. Surrounded by sycophants and cynics, he is clearly an heir of Saul Bellow's Joseph, a man who would like to be energised by ideals but who only feels nausea at the lies and "poor-spirited" men which the Army protected and encouraged. On impulse Hammond took a guard detail for a drunken friend who had just received a "dear John" letter. Inevitably he was caught, broken to ranks and punished. His thoughts about the war and the Army are poignant in that Hammond was not an indifferent G.I. but a frustrated liberal:

> He felt that he was on neither side of this war. It was *their* war. How could he take active part in anything that helped men he despised . . . rise and glorify themselves? . . . The enemy out there, hundreds of miles away, was an unknown quantity, something Joe had never seen. But he saw these fools, these great men of the American Army, in action. He hated them. He hated what they were, what they stood for, what they wanted in life. He hated them clean through to the soles of their shoes.[14]

He concludes that "the army is a Fascist institution itself". Similar attitudes appear in Vance Bourjaily's *The End of My Life* (1947), in which four American volunteer Ambulance Drivers with the Red Cross are exposed to the calculated sadistic brutality of a British Army Field Punishment Camp in Syria:

> "You think, perhaps, that this is only the British Army talking? No, honey. This is every army in the world. The British, Russian, Armenian, German, French, Scandinavian, Mongolian and Congolian armies. And the American army. The nice, clean, right-thinking democratic American Army, which, with its smug pretense that it runs things differently, is the most vicious of all."[15]

Sgt. "Fatso" Judson and the stockade scenes in *From Here to Eternity* (1952), and Sgt. Ransome, who severely beats up the hero of Myrer's *The Big War* (1957), suggest the enduring force of Bourjaily's passage. The positive emotions of a Major Harris or Lt. Roberts have been replaced by profoundly negative emotions, of hatred and fear, which typify liberal attitudes towards the Army after the war.

As their views of the army began to change, liberals were in turn perceived in a harsher and more hostile light. John Cobb's *The Gesture* (1948) describes a Harvard Law School and State Department liberal, Major Gregory Harris, who attempts to integrate a racially-segregated air base in England. The narrator, Whipple, an AAF bombardier, shares Harris' social background (he has been to Yale) but none of his idealism. Whipple despises Harris' "aura of rigidity", his lack of knowledge of the men in his command:

> I studied his face. His lips were pressed together. His eyes seemed to focus on some spot about twenty miles away. Oh, there sat the fanatic, all right . . . The amazing thing was that he seemed to have so little self-knowledge.[16]

Harris is granted none of the stature of a hero, but he manages to defend himself, and his personal and social ideals, with quiet dignity:

> "I may be a consummate coward for all I know. But my point is, if a man can set and live by his own standards in our country, then he should live up to those standards here. It's all right for these others to fly for awhile and then go home. But that doesn't make it all right for me."[17]

The narrator does his best to undermine Harris' authority, and to oppose his plan to billet Negro construction workers in the airfield barracks. Whipple succeeds, and survives the war; Harris, relieved of his command of the bomb group, takes a dangerous mission and dies unmourned.

The longer, and better-known, war novels of 1948 each contain a version of the liberal's dilemma in the army. Stefan Heym's *The Crusaders* contrasts the cynical, amoral opportunists among the Army officers (Major Willoughby and Captain Loomis) with Sergeant Bing, whose parents were German refugees and who tries to infuse some idealism into the propaganda unit's material, and a well-meaning Lt. Yates who would like to do good but who has had a life-time of conformity to train him otherwise. Irwin Shaw's *The Young Lions* gradually draws three major characters (Michael Whitacre, a New York liberal; Noah Ackerman, a Jew; and Christian Diestle, a ruthless Nazi) into a fatal conjuncture. The two Americans here each had to learn that there were limits to their ability to contribute to the cause. Ackerman learned to stop knocking his head against a brick wall. Sergeant Rickett's anti-Semitism would never be dissolved. Col. Pavone coldly dismissed Whitacre's desire to effectively be a part of the war. Only Captain Green, who agreed to a Jewish service being held at a death camp, allows Ackerman a glimpse of humane hope for the postwar world. *The Young Lions* contrasts strikingly with "Act of Faith", Shaw's short story in which a pervasive anti-Semitism in America, and in the armed forces, makes Seager, a Jewish soldier, wonder if he should bring his Luger and bayonet home from the war for self-defence in America. But the "candid and tough and dependable" faces of his two best friends, Olsen and Welch, assuage his anxieties:

> He would have to rely upon them, later on, out of uniform, on their native streets, more than he had ever relied on them on the bullet-swept street and in the dark minefield in France.[18]

Shaw was less able to sustain this optimism across the larger canvas of his novel, but for him the fate of the Jews, and the fate of liberalism, were inextricably linked. James Gould Cozzens' *Guard of Honor* shared few of Shaw's social ideals. The chief representative of liberalism in his novel was a dislikeable lieutenant named Edsell, formerly a contributor to radical magazines, a "sorehead" who was "exultantly dedicated to making all the trouble he could."[19] Like Witherspoon in Camp's *Retreat, Hell!*, Edsell voiced a Marxist critique of American society. Liberals might think in terms of an individual's social obligation, but not Lt. Edsell:

> "The Federal state, the thing that runs the country; the product of class antagonisms and the instrument of class domination. He [the conscientious objector] owes it what? Whatever it calls itself, whatever it is – here, Russia, Germany, Japan – it's nothing but a set-up to keep in power a few people who lied and cheated their way there, and to make everybody else work for them. What he owes it is a kick in the teeth, every time he can give it one without getting himself liquidated." (p.474)

A better-mannered liberalism might sincerely deplore Lt. Edsell. But the conservative "realism" voiced by the novel's central characters, General "Bus" Beal and Col "Judge" Ross, scarcely stooped to such distinctions. The racial issue must be defused, "handled", accepted as reality; solid men like Beal and Ross must look after each other; Edsell must be punished and to be made to feel fear.

The fates of liberals in the war novels of 1948 are instructive. Sgt. Bing died in a tank after making a desperate plea for a large German force in a wood to surrender. "If it happens somewhere, it happens to me. They had killed him, and he had been a good man."[20] Ackerman dies; Whitacre, the "inadequate American", trained to salute and close-order drill, was left to hunt down and kill Ackerman's killer; and Edsell was crushed, frustrated, humiliated; the old guard kept the lid on. In *The Crusaders, The Young Lions,* and *Guard of Honor* the defeat of liberalism is the dramatic hinge upon which the novels turn. The most prominent "defeated" liberal in the major novels of 1948 undoubtedly was Lt. Hearn in Norman Mailer's *The Naked and the Dead*. He too dies in the end, a deceived victim of a ruthless and cunning Sgt. Croft. But of the four principal novels under discussion, Mailer gives the most nuanced picture of the American liberal, and roots his account of Hearn in a social context (money and privileged education – Harvard) and a sexual nature which is more comprehensive than any of the other novels, and more persuasive. It is perhaps not necessary to repeat here an analysis of Hearn made elsewhere.[21] "The guilts he made himself feel, the injustices that angered him were never genuine."[22] His problem was that Gen. Cummings taunted him and Sgt. Croft and the I. & R. platoon disbelieved him: the classic dilemma of the bourgeois liberal. Cummings, an over-drawn Grand Inquisitor, identifies the contradiction within Hearn's liberalism: his immediate personal welfare and self-interest depended upon the structures of injustice, the Army's ladder of fear, which Hearn rejected in principle but was irrevocably committed to in practice:

> "to make an Army work you have to have every man in it fitted into a fear ladder. . . . The Army functions best when you're frightened of the man above you, and contemptuous of your subordinates." (p.176)

Hearn secretly relied upon the General to protect him from his own rash temperament. The Army is, of course, by definition an illiberal institution, and Hearn's fate was to be at the mercy of men whom he despised as bigots and reactionaries. (Gen. Cummings warns him: "'The rights you have as a person depend completely upon my whim'" (p.82).) At the time of his death Hearn was no longer able to think of himself as a liberal. He had been driven to a shocking self-knowledge: "He wanted Cummings to approve of him again . . . Beyond Cummings, deeper now, was his own desire to lead the platoon. It had grown, ignited suddenly, become one of the most satisfactory things he had ever done. He could understand Croft's staring at the mountain through the field glasses, or killing the bird. When he searched himself, he was just another Croft" (p.580).

Mailer's book portrays a liberalism not only defeated but scarcely any longer possessed of identity. The fascists and reactionaries (Gen. Cummings and Sgt. Croft) do not have things all their own way, but they have survived the battle. Hearn, deceived by Sgt. Croft, is a victim sharing the pathos, if not the dignity, of Maj. Harris in *The Gesture*, Lt. Roberts in *Mister Roberts*, Noah Ackerman in *The Young Lions* or Sgt. Bing in *The Crusaders*, liberals who have died in some recognisable sense as liberals. Why is their fate so central to the American novel of the Second World War? To answer that, we must return to the changing political atmosphere within which liberals functioned during and after the war, and in which the novels of defeated liberalism were written.

We are accustomed to regard the war years as a period of recoil and numbed retreat.[23] With the deaths of Joyce and Yeats, and the discrediting of Ezra Pound in Fascist Italy, the Modern Movement seemed to be at an end. The movement to the left on the part of American writers and intellectuals was halted and then reversed. The New Deal lost momentum. The hammer blows of history killed fellow-travelling: the Moscow trials, the Spanish Civil War, the Stalin-Hitler pact, and then the Russian partitioning of Poland and invasion of Finland left the intellectuals pessimistic, demoralised, quiescent. Auden, who settled in New York in 1939, led a general movement of poets away from political or social commitments.[24] Orwell, who in 1940 feared that the autonomous individual was going to be "stamped out of existence," wrote that

> Progress and reaction have both turned out to be swindles. Seemingly there is nothing left but quietism – robbing reality of its terrors by simply submitting to it. Get inside the whale – or rather admit that you are inside the whale (for you *are*, of course). Give yourself over to the world-process, stop fighting against it or pretending that you control it; simply accept it, endure it, record it.[25]

Sidney Hook wrote in 1940 that "all the dogmas of party, church and school seem to be liquefying under the corrosive acids of doubt, self-distrust and panic"; Koestler wrote of those fellow writers who achieved "the journey from the pink decade to the Yogi decade" with "monkey-like" agility; and Hook, a formidable polemicist, identified a "flight from responsibility" and reason in 1943 as key symptoms of "The New Failure of Nerve".[26] Philip Rahv talked of the "moral collapse" of the intellectuals:

> Among them smugness has become the pseudonym of panic, and the more rapidly they abandon the values of culture the more sonorous their speeches in its defence. Everywhere they submit to the accomplished fact, everywhere they place themselves under the surveillance of authority, they rationalise, they explain away.[27]

This inner confusion and decay of liberalism came precisely at the moment when America had finally gone to war against the Fascist powers, and in an alliance with Russia. But the united front certainties were irrecoverable. As the prestige of the Communist Party soared on the coattails of Stalingrad and the triumphs of Zhukov and Koniev, and when the Comintern was dissolved in

April 1943, as a sign of Russian commitment to the alliance with the capitalist powers, and when the Communist Party in May 1944 was replaced by an avowedly "non-partisan" Communist Political Association, the ground was shifting under liberalism and the New Deal. From 1942 Roosevelt accepted the wholesale dismemberment of New Deal programmes, as though that was the sacrifice required to keep conservatives in the war. Despite the defeat of Wilkie in 1940, the mood in Republican circles was emboldened. Henry R. Luce published a celebrated editorial in *Life* magazine of 17 February 1941 titled "The American Century". The new order Luce envisaged was openly capitalist. A "free economic system" would have to expand or die: "Tyrannies may require a large amount of living space. But Freedom requires and will require far more living space than Tyranny. Peace cannot endure unless it prevails over a large part of the world."[28] This was a Darwinian language, of *lebensraum* and continual struggle, out of Mackinder by Spengler. As Luce's biographer, W. A. Swanberg, put it, Luce's vision was of "a century of General Motors, Standard Oil, Pan-Am – and of Time-Life-Fortune – entrenched in Asia and Africa with the protection of American military power."[29] Liberals freely attacked Luce's editorial, correctly estimating its ominous nature. (It is as though Mailer's General Cummings emerged, full-blown, out of Luce's skull.) But it was not until May 1942, six months after America entered the war, that a prominent liberal, Vice-President Henry Wallace, articulated an alternative vision of the future:

> Perhaps it will be America's opportunity to suggest the freedoms and duties by which the common man must live. Everywhere the common man must learn to build his own industries with his own hands in a practical fashion. Everywhere the common man must learn to increase his productivity so that he and his children can eventually pay to the world community all that they have received. No nation will have the God-given right to exploit other nations.[30]

The title of Wallace's speech ("The Price of Free World Victory") was quickly forgotten. It was handier to refer to its meaning as "the century of the common man". It caught the mood of the American people, and directly appealed to their idealism and longing to believe in the nobility of their cause. It made Wallace a symbol of liberal and internationalist hopes for the rest of the war. Luce, too, appealed to American ideals. His notion of a "humanitarian army of Americans" who would administer a generous provision of "all that we cannot eat" to the needy world, anticipates the Marshall Plan and the Peace Corps. But the difference between "The American Century" and "the century of the common man" was clear and decisive. Wallace, who was by no means an enemy of capitalism or uninterested in the foreign markets of American farmers, talked of development, growth, autonomy; he could be chief of the World Bank or of UNESCO today. Luce, on the other hand, was talking about markets and American hegemony. They shared an internationalist perspective which gained ground among the American political elites throughout the war.[31] A sign of the shift in public mood was the immense success of Wendell

Willkie's *One World* in 1943. A half-million copies were sold within the first month of publication. It was not an unopposed viewpoint. In August 1943 the Secretary of State, Cordell Hull, effectively engineered the resignation of his internationalist-minded Under-Secretary, Sumner Welles. And in July 1944 President Roosevelt dumped Wallace in favour of Harry Truman as his running-mate. Wallace and Welles were heroic "sacrifices" towards the creation of a new world order. All those characters in American war novels who hope for "good fellowship and social equality", like the "humanitarian dope", Clevinger, in *Catch-22*, reflect the presence of idealistic, Wallaceite liberalism in American politics.[32] "What has happened in Washington since Pearl Harbour", wrote Malcolm Cowley,

> is the defeat of a whole class of people who went to work for the government, not in the expectation of becoming rich or powerful – though some of them learned to love power – and not in the hope of building up estates that would provide safe incomes for their children, but simply because they wanted to have fruitful careers and get things done. They hoped to be the engineers of American prosperity . . . They are the people who are interested in ideas and are not frightened by new ones.[33]

With the death of Roosevelt, the exodus of New Dealers from government was accelerated. Liberals, led by Henry Wallace, clung to the hope that the wartime alliance against Fascism could be maintained. Throughout 1946 he persisted in advocating Russian-American accord, and attacked those who in his view were pushing America into an arms race which would result in war. Wallace defended the right of the Soviet Union to a political sphere of interest in Eastern Europe, and in an address in Madison Square Garden in September 1946, warned: "The tougher we get, the tougher the Russians will get."[34] He was forced to resign from Truman's cabinet following the outcry against the speech. He again was a hero to liberals, a defender of peace and an opponent of what became the Truman Doctrine in 1947. Wallace's critics, of whom ex-Communists like James Wechsler and ex-Trotskyites like Dwight Macdonald were the most pointed, identified a desperate inadequacy in Wallace's view of the world.[35] He did not face up to the "fact" of Soviet expansionism, nor did he accept the Soviet "threat". He reacted negatively to the Marshall Plan; and seemed to condone the Russian coup in Czechoslovakia in 1948. His campaign as Progressive Party candidate for president was a political shambles and disaster.[36] Wallace failed to win the support of any significant group within the liberal constituency; the left-wing labour unions were unable to mobilise their rank-and-file on his behalf; and those who might have looked to him for leadership concluded that he was naïve about the Russians and a tool in the hand of the American Communists.[37] Those who stayed with Wallace would, in later years, be described as naïve. Among their number was Norman Mailer, who in the last two weeks of the electoral campaign made eighteen speeches for Wallace.[38] The "idealistic" liberals, who clung to the hope that a war with Russia could be avoided, were destroyed as a political force with Wallace's defeat. When Mailer addressed a cultural and scientific congress for world peace held at the Waldorf Astoria Hotel in New York in March 1949, he announced a dramatic break with Stalinism and began an erratic political itinerary which led from revolutionary socialism to "left conservatism". The survivors in 1948 were the realists, the cold-war liberals, for whom a tough anti-communism was the beginning, and sometimes the end, of all political wisdom.[39] The Communists were open to devastating attacks upon their corporate existence; their fellow-travelling supporters reeled under the impact of Taft-Hartley injunctions, House Un-American Activities Committee investigations, and the effects of Executive Order 9835, signed by Truman in March 1947, which established a loyalty check for all federal employees and revived the Attorney General's list of subversive organisations.[40] During Wallace's campaign Whittaker Chambers named Alger Hiss as a Communist; Julius Rosenberg was reported by his brother-in-law, David Greenglass, to have said, "We've got to be like soldiers. It doesn't matter if Stalin is sending his troops to be killed. What difference does it make as long as the victory is ours?"[41] The Cold War was firmly in the saddle, and the defeated liberal idealists were among the most prominent victims. The war novel was, in ways not always understood, an important dimension of the political struggles of the war years and its aftermath. It was at once a mirror in which Americans could view their changing political physiognomy, and a reflection of tensions in a culture in which united front liberalism was confronted by historic defeat.

ERIC HOMBERGER

East Anglia

NOTES

[1]Ralph Ingersoll, *The Battle is the Pay-Off* (Washington: The Infantry Journal, 1943), p.181. Ingersoll resigned as editor of the liberal newspaper *P.M.* to serve in the army. His *Report on England* (1940) was based on his reports to *P.M.* He also published *Action on All Fronts* (1942); a novel, *Wine of Violence* (1951) was set in wartime London.

[2]Sir Philip Gibbs, *The War Dispatches* (London: Anthony Gibbs and Phillips, 1966; reissued London: Tandem Books, 1968), p.49. Gibbs wrote several books on the impact of the Second World War in England: *Battle Within* (1944) and *Through the Storm* (1945).

[3]The standard authority is Stanley Cooperman, *World War I and the American Novel* (Baltimore: Johns Hopkins University Press, 1970). The post-war disillusionment of writers like Hemingway, Dos Passos and Cummings was hardly representative of the generality of Americans who fought in the war. This point is searchingly discussed in David M. Kennedy, *Over Here: The First World War and American Society* (New York: Oxford University Press, 1980).

[4]Pyle (1900-1945), a Scripps-Howard correspondent, published three books during the war: *Ernie Pyle in England* (1941), *Here is Your War* (1943) and *Brave Men* (1944). Wolfert, a correspondent for the North American Newspaper Alliance, won a Pulitzer Prize for his *Battle for the Solomons* (1943). Tragaskis, like Wolfert, was on Guadalcanal throughout the battle. His *Guadalcanal Diary* (1943) was a bestseller; it was made into a film by Twentieth-Century-Fox that same year. Gellhorn was Ernest Hemingway's third wife. His influence on her prose is abundantly evident. Gellhorn was a correspondent for *Collier's* in Europe in 1943-45; her reports are collected in *The Face of War* (1959).

[5] See *By-Line: Ernest Hemingway*, ed. William White (1967); John Steinbeck, *Once There Was a War* (1959); John Dos Passos, *State of the Nation* (1945) and *Tour of Duty* (1946).

[6] Albert Maltz, *The Cross and the Arrow* (London: George Harrap, 1946), p.100. First published New York, 1944.

[7] William Martin Camp, *Retreat, Hell!* (New York: Appleton-Century, 1943; London: Constable, 1944), p.235.

[8] Liberals accepted the abandonment of many social reforms during the war, in the hope that victory would make even greater changes possible. Instead, as Richard Polenberg argues, "the war weakened American liberalism in many ways". See Polenberg, *War and Society: The United States 1941-1945* (Philadelphia: J. B. Lippincott, 1972), ch.3. John Morton Blum lays the responsibility for liberal reverses from 1942 upon the frail shoulders of the President: "Because Roosevelt had not tried, he had built up no reservoir of liberal public and congressional support on which he would call when he needed to." Blum, *V Was for Victory: Politics and American Culture During World War II* (New York: Harcourt, Brace, Jovanovich, 1976), pp.234-45. See also note 39.

[9] Reynolds, *The Curtain Rises* (London: Cassell, 1944), p.299.

[10] Ingersoll, *The Battle is the Pay-Off*, p.204.

[11] John Hersey, *A Bell for Adano* (New York: Knopf, 1944), pp.228-9.

[12] Saul Bellow, *Dangling Man* (Harmondsworth: Penguin Books, 1963), p.137. First published New York, 1944.

[13] Thomas Heggen, *Mister Roberts* (Boston: Houghton Mifflin, 1946), p.163.

[14] Robert Lowry, *Casualty* (New York: New Directions, 1946; reissued Westport, Conn.: Greenwood Press, 1971), p.142.

[15] Vance Bourjaily, *The End of My Life* (New York: Dial Press, 1947; London: W. H. Allen, 1963), pp.83-5.

[16] John Cobb [John C. Cooper, III], *The Gesture* (New York and London: Harper & Brothers, 1948), p.205.

[17] *The Gesture*, p.78. Clevinger in Heller's *Catch-22* is a similarly-motivated man of conscience, perceived incredulously by the narrator, Yossarian, as a dangerous lunatic.

[18] "Act of Faith", *Mixed Company : Collected Short Stories of Irwin Shaw* (London: Jonathan Cape, 1952), p.47.

[19] James Gould Cozzens, *Guard of Honour* (New York: Harcourt, Brace, 1948; London: Longmans, Green, 1949), p.387.

[20] Stefan Heym, *The Crusaders* (Boston: Little, Brown), 1948, p.498.

[21] *The Second World War in Fiction*, ed. Holger Klein with John Flower and Eric Homberger (London: Macmillan, 1984), pp.187-90.

[22] Norman Mailer, *The Naked and the Dead* (New York: Random House, 1948; London: Allen Wingate, 1949), p.169. For Mailer in 1947-48, Hearn's bourgeois liberalism was by its very nature inauthentic. It is revealing, however, that the focus of this comment on Hearn is psychological; the question is no longer *political*.

[23] See the standard work, Chester Eisenberg, *Fiction of the Forties* (Chicago: University of Chicago Press, 1963).

[24] See the present author's *The Art of the Real: Poetry in England and America since 1939* (London: J. M. Dent, 1977), ch.1.

[25] Orwell, *Collected Essays, Journalism and Letters*, ed. Sonia Orwell and Ian Angus. 4 vols. (London; Secker & Warburg, 1968). I,526. "Inside the Whale" was published in New York in *New Directions in Prose and Poetry* (1940).

[26] Hook, "Metaphysics, War and the Intellectuals", *Menorah Journal*, XXVIII (Autumn 1940), pp.326-37; Arthur Koestler, *The Yogi and the Commissar* (London: Jonathan Cape, 1945), the title essay first appearing in *Horizon*, June 1942; and Hook, "The New Failure of Nerve", *Partisan Review*, X (January-February 1943), pp.2-23.

[27] Philip Rahv, "Trials of the Mind," *Partisan Review*, IV (April 1938), pp.3-11; reprinted in Rahv's *Essays on Literature and Politics 1932-1972*, ed. Arabel J. Porter and Andrew J. Dvosin (Boston: Houghton Mifflin, 1978), pp.284-92.

[28] Luce's "The American Century" is conveniently reprinted in Richard Polenberg, ed., *America at War: The Home Front, 1941-1945* (Englewood Cliffs, N.J.: Prentice-Hall, 1968), pp.153-8.

[29] W. A. Swanberg, *Luce and His Empire* (New York: Scribner's, 1972; reissued New York: Dell, 1973), p.260.

[30] Wallace's speech is reprinted in Polenberg, *America at War*, pp.158-63. On Wallace's role, see Norman D. Markowitz, *The Rise and Fall of the People's Century: Henry A. Wallace and American Liberalism, 1941-1948* (New York: The Free Press, 1973).

[31] See Robert A. Divine, *Second Chance: The Triumph of Internationalism in America During World War II* (New York: Atheneum, 1967). It was Divine who described the broken careers of Wendell Willkie, Sumner Welles and Henry Wallace as "sacrifices" towards the creation of a new international order.

[32] Martin Abzug, *Spearhead* (New York: Dial Press, 1946), p.133. The wish for good fellowship was expressed by a timid and unsympathetic liberal, Capt. Hollis, who was opposed in the novel by an anti-fascist sergeant who, because he was an émigré German, knew that the Wehrmacht could not be beaten by those who opposed it with humanitarianism in their hearts.

[33] Malcolm Cowley, "The End of the New Deal", *The New Republic*, CVIII (31 May 1943), pp.729-32.

[34] Wallace quoted by Alonzo Hamby, "Henry A. Wallace, the Liberals and Soviet-American Relations," *Review of Politics*, XXX (April 1968), pp.153-69.

[35] Dwight Macdonald, *Henry Wallace: The Man and the Myth* (New York: Vanguard Press 1948), and James Wechsler, *The Age of Suspicion* (London: André Deutsch, 1954), 218ff. Wechsler travelled with Wallace throughout the campaign in 1949, but was profoundly and consistently sceptical about Wallace, and suspicious of his manipulation by the communists.

[36] See Markowitz, *The Rise and Fall of the People's Century*, ch.8; and Robert A. Divine, "The Cold War and the Election of 1948", *Journal of American History*, LIX (June 1972), pp.90-110.

[37] From the point of view of the Communist Party, the fateful decision to split the CIO and support Wallace in 1948 has always seemed something of a mystery. An analysis published in the Party's *Political Affairs* (July 1953), blamed the decision on "an over-estimation of the radicalisation of the masses and an under-estimation of the deep-seated influence of the labour reformists on the working class". The complex manœuvrings behind the decision are ably described in Joseph R. Starobin, *American Communism in Crisis, 1943-1957* (Cambridge, Mass.: Harvard University Press, 1972). A less sympathetic account by David J. Saposs, *Communism in American Politics* (Washington, D.C.: Public Affairs Press, 1960), pp.154-73, sees more clearly why Wallace wavered about a third-party candidacy, but does not see any wavering on the part of the Communists.

[38] Hilary Mills, *Mailer: A Biography* (New York: Empire Books, 1982), pp.107-15.

[39] See Norman Markowitz, "A View from the Left: From the Popular Front to Cold War Liberalism" in *The Specter: Original Essays on the Cold War and the Origins of McCarthyism*, ed. Robert Griffiths and Athan Theoharis (New York: New Viewpoints, 1974), pp.90-115.

[40] Victor S. Navasky, *Naming Names* (London: John Calder, 1982), p.21.

[41] Allan Weinstein, *Perjury: The Hiss Chambers Case* (London: Hutchinson, 1978), pp.5-7; Ronald Radosh and Joyce Milton, *The Rosenberg File: A Search for the Truth* (London: Weidenfeld & Nicolson, 1983), p.73.

TRADITION AND MYTH IN FRENCH RESISTANCE POETRY: REACTION OR SUBVERSION?

In 1945, Benjamin Péret published *Le déshonneur des poètes*, a violent attack on a sample of Resistance poetry.[1] These are not poems at all, says Péret (p.80). A true poem is by definition subversive (p.75), but these are reactionary in both "forme", most of them reverting to traditional rhyme and alexandrine (p.82),[2] and "contenu", most of them essentially trying to revive the religious myth, for which nationalism and the myths of *patrie* and leader are just modern substitutes (pp.78-9, 82). These moribund myths contrast with the creative ones to which writers have given voice at crucial moments in the past, for example in Year II of the French Revolution (p.80).

Péret does not define *patrie*, nationalism or leader; religion offers a "paradis illusoire" (p.81); and myth is the "exalted" collective urge of a whole people, to which the writer should give voice. From now on, when referring to myth in Péret's sense, I shall use the word *mythe*. Péret's outburst is useful because it reduces to simple terms the criticisms most usually made of Resistance poetry. In this essay, I am going to look at the notions of *patrie* and France as they typically appear in Resistance poetry, to see some ways in which they might be myths, and with what function, and to suggest some ways in which the use of traditional prosodic forms contributes to that function. I shall take it for granted that this poetry is indeed poetry. Because it is a big subject and space is limited, I shall concentrate on a few poets, chosen to combine maximum variety with maximum representativeness.

Péret talks about "nationalisme", not "patriotisme", although the *mythe* he invokes is that of *patrie* and not nation. As he uses the word pejoratively, I take him to mean something like chauvinism – an aggressive, exclusive, blinkered vaunting of *patrie*. He says that true poetry has no *patrie*, being eternal and universal (p.87). *Patrie* and nationalism, in Péret's use, seem to represent the attitudes characteristic of post-1870 revanchism, Barrésianism and Maurrassianism. Certainly, if the modern concept of nation originated in the French Revolution, nationalism and patriotism seem to have changed their meaning in France since then. For Sieyès, the first ideologue of the Revolution, the Third Estate embodied the nation as an ideal, moral entity, an extension of natural law. This is the essence of French Revolutionary nationalism. In so far as it grew out of Enlightenment rationalism, its ideology was a voluntarist liberal humanism which saw the struggle as being for *fraternité* – something universal, not national, a *patrie* of humanity. If patriotism implies willingness to defend the national territory and autonomy, we must recognise that the Revolutionary patriots who sang the *Marseillaise* were defending their soil in the name of ideals originally very different from those of Déroulède, Barrès, Maurras or the Pétain of Montoire.

Not surprisingly, the soil, the physical countryside of France, is a common image in Resistance poetry. Aragon's is a good example. In the retreat to Dunkirk, the land itself shrank (*YE* 39).[3] The "conscrit des cent villages" bids farewell to the whole countryside of France (*DF* 54-8). Elsewhere, Aragon writes: "Ceux qui portent des fleurs ont de la France aux bras" (*EP* 63). Poets as unsentimental as Frénaud and Marcenac can write:

> Vainqueur aride,
> tu n'emportes pas mon sol,
> le poids des morts accroche
> la terre vieille et tendre[4]

and:

> Terre incertaine Terre lourde
> Les meilleurs de tes fils sont étendus sur toi[5]

This topos of "les morts terriens" (Masson, *DM* 39-41) is as common as that of the soil, and closely associated with it. The opening lines of Emmanuel's "Lamentation pour le temps de l'avent" are typical of the association:

> Où es-tu mon pays d'eau vive et de forêts
> pays aimé des morts, terre fidèle et tendre?
> Je tâte en vain du pied le sol, guettant le rythme
> tentant de prolonger mon sang jusqu'à tes morts . . . (*CD* 93)

As Emmanuel's lines show, however, the Occupation and Collaboration make this soil seem alien, or even absent. So he can write in the first of the *Cantos*:

> Qui a perdu sa patrie
> jamais n'en trouve une autre
>
> Mais où est, à moi, ma patrie? (*Can* 9)

Masson writes: "français je suis en France étranger" (*Lum* 11), and Aragon: "nous étions des étrangers en France" (*DF* 64), and again: "En étrange pays dans mon pays lui-même" (*YE* 92), a line he later adopted as the title of a collection of his Resistance poetry. So strong a sense of exile on one's own soil implies a distinction between *patrie* and territory. Emmanuel writes:

> Les hommes, non la terre
> peuvent être asservis (*Can* 52)

Tardieu's "Le paysage" begins: "Non, la terre n'est pas couverte d'arbres, de pierres, de fleuves: elle est couverte d'hommes" (*JP* 93), and his "France retrouvée" ends with a reference to "cette terre et ce ciel qui n'ont jamais trahi" (*JP* 107). This last example is especially clear. The speaker's relief and delight at rediscovering the beauties of the French countryside is not a sentimental identification of France with the soil: treason, like servitude, is something human, and the beauty and the meaning of the countryside is a function of what human beings do in it.

The *patrie*, then, is not so much the soil or what grows in it or is built on it, as a state of mind. In "Lamentation pour le temps de l'avent" Emmanuel writes: "on est seul par millions sans patrie que la peur" (*CD* 94), and he entitled a whole volume of war poems *Tristesse ô ma patrie* (Paris: Fontaine, 1946). Aragon writes: "Ma patrie est la faim la misère et l'amour" (*YE* 87); the condemned man in his "Ballade de celui qui chanta dans les supplices" says:

Je meurs et France demeure
Mon amour et mon refus (*DF* 45)

Most of these images involve a fear of isolation. The *patrie* is more than just a state of mind; it is a determination to overcome isolation by constituting a group living by certain values. It is the future to which the exile looks forward. However, exile by definition implies something that has been lost – that is, the past. The *patrie* envisaged in Resistance poetry is not to be created out of nothing; it will be a certain attitude to the past. An Emmanuel *canto* puts this tension between future and past very clearly:

T'ont-ils si loin défigurée
que notre plus folle espérance
soit la seule mémoire assurée
qui de toi nous demeure ô France? (*Can* 32)

Is our hope the only memory, or is the memory our only hope? The unresolvable ambiguity makes it clear that France is not something given, but something to be hoped for (and willed) in the name of certain values from the past.

Hence the widespread invocation of French history and legend. Among the Resistance poets, Aragon makes the most systematic use of history. What he says about it helps to pinpoint the theme of history in Resistance poetry as a whole. Reference to mediaeval poets and warriors is a common form of *contrebande* in his poetry.[6] One function of it is, as he explains in his vital essay "De l'exactitude historique en poésie", to combat Fascist "mythes de la race" with "les images de la Nation" (*EP* 24) – that is, with something historical. But, as he points out, if this history is shot through with legend and myth, invoking the history does not mean weeding out legend and myth. They are essential parts of the culture, of the history (pp.25-6). Indeed, that history is itself a "légende enivrante" (p.27). A legend, for Aragon, is a story passed on by word of mouth, to which poets may also contribute (pp.26, 28). His poem "Légende de Gabriel Péri" exemplifies the process.[7] Written to mark the second anniversary of Péri's execution, it contains a number of involuntary inaccuracies of fact, as Aragon explains in a note (*DF* 75-6). The truth of the legend lies not in the "historical facts" it recounts, but in the values it conveys. As Aragon writes in this poem:

Redoutez les morts exemplaires
Tyrans qui massacrez en vain
Elles sont un terrible vin
Pour un peuple et pour sa colère (*DF* 74)

So exemplary figures from the past like Joan of Arc, or exemplary events like Valmy, or exemplary songs like the *Marseillaise*, all of which are often referred to in Resistance poetry, become an "intoxicating legend" used as a counter-poison to Nazi and Vichy myth (cf. *EP* 25-7). Joan is a particularly good example of this battle. Used by Vichy as the exemplary enemy of the English, she is used by Resistance poets as the exemplary enemy of the Invader.

A legend would appear to acquire this exemplary value when the very mention of a name, without any supporting narrative, is enough to signify the values which the original story conveyed. This is the sense in which one can call Joan or Valmy myths, although it is a quite different sense from Péret's *mythe*. To denote myth in this sense, and to avoid confusion, I shall henceforth use the phrase "proverbial myth".

Resistance poetry, then, conveys an awareness that if "history is being made", language is essential to the making. The many implicit and explicit parallels between past events and present ones are one way of showing that history is being made. Another is the ready use of a past tense to refer to the present, as if the text were written from the point of view of a future historian. Seghers makes especially effective use of this device (e.g. *TM* 21-2, 23-4, 38, 39-40). A similar device is the widespread use of the future tense. However naïve, sentimental or tragic such accounts of the future may seem today, it is important to realise that they were not so much prophecies as statements of will, a will that the situation should develop, and be recounted, in accordance with one set of values and not another. A quotation from Seghers' "Le carrousel" (1943) helps to illustrate the point:

> Mes amis, on vivait dans la flamme et la guerre
> Le temps blet, l'amour mort et l'attente, l'attente,
> (. . .)
> Une fille de feu d'un poète dira
> 43, feutre étouffant, la préhistoire,
> Les violettes vendues contre deux mots d'espoir
> Et l'épée de l'espoir si pesante à nos bras. (*TM* 39)

This is "préhistoire" – nothing is happening, nothing is said. But hope is carrying a sword (however heavy), and the *words* of hope are going to make history happen – a history, moreover, which will be read in the poetry that was written at the time, and about which poets will also talk once it has happened. The future expression of events is all-important in the minds of those trying to make them happen. "France . . . légendaire tu renaisses", writes Aragon (*DF* 82). Referring to the Santé prison in Paris, Masson writes:

> Comme l'on dit Stalingrad l'on dira un jour La Santé
> vieille vieille bastille où saignent mes héros (*Lum* 14)

Masson's words are a deliberate contribution to turning present events, both inside and outside France, into a universal proverbial myth comparable to those from the past. So, in "Camps de concentration", he writes: "Les temps viendront où l'on enseignera l'Histoire; il faut qu'on l'apprenne à nos enfants" (*Lum* 29); and Seghers writes that the executed Châteaubriant hostages will be resurrected "dans nos écoles. . . . ils entendront . . . d'autres enfants dire leurs noms" (*TM* 19).

History, legend and proverbial myth are linguistic phenomena. With almost all the Resistance poets, language itself is a prominent theme. This is partly because the Nazi and Vichy regimes were based on a perceived abuse of language. Comparing occupied France to an enchanted mediaeval forest, Aragon says that "les sorciers de Vichy et les dragons de Germanie avaient donné à toutes les paroles une valeur incantatoire pervertie, rien ne s'appelait plus de son nom" (*EP* 26). This idea is a commonplace in Resistance poetry. The perversion of language is a particularly important theme in Emmanuel. As he explained after the war: "Ce régime ne pouvait vivre qu'en pervertissant les mots: mais qui blesse le langage, blesse l'homme."[8] Emmanuel's formulation opens out from the question of political regime to the wider question of humanity. This brings us to the heart of the problem of *patrie* in Resistance poetry.

It is indeed striking that when the theme of language arises in Emmanuel's poetry, it is as something of existential as well as national importance. Masson writes: "Ils ont pris mon langage français au lasso" (*Lum* 70), but Emmanuel:

> la Voix déserte et chauve a ravagé
> ton Ame, ô ma patrie (*CD* 94),

or again:

> il y a l'air prostitué au mensonge, et la Voix
> souillant jusqu'au secret de l'âme (*CD* 108)

This voice of destruction is an attack on God and humanity. It is the voice of propaganda and censorship, but it is also the voice of God in humanity and of humanity in God. Human beings have brought destruction on themselves, and their salvation – that is, the realisation of God – is in their own hands. Emmanuel writes as a Christian, albeit a very individual one. Tardieu does not, but in "Incarnation" he evokes a similar struggle between good and evil, and it is similarly experienced as a battle for voice:

> Un être grave et douloureux
> qui vient du fond des âges
> (. . .)
> emprunte ma voix pour parler
> (. . .)
> Comment, comment, puisque c'est moi,
> bâillonner cette bouche affreuse? (*JP* 65, 68)

The very many references to enforced silence and clenched teeth in Resistance poetry are not simply evocations of censorship, they are images of human beings as essentially linguistic creatures. Not to speak is a nightmarish, inhuman paralysis, witness Tardieu:

> Parle un bâillon sur la bouche!
> (. . .)
> peut-être l'homme est-il mort? (*JP* 90)

In Seghers' "Le carrousel", words are like gravel in the mouth, and the silence is suffocating (*TM* 39). All through Emmanuel's poetry, there runs the determination to give humanity back its voice:

> Viens, Esprit Créateur! Rends la Parole au monde,
> que l'homme en soit le feu méridien et le chant. (*CD* 153)

In Seghers' "Octobre 41", the dead hostages will be resurrected "vêtus de feu dans nos écoles" (*TM* 19): *our* history as taught in *our* schools is inseparable from the universal pentecostal gift of tongues.

Propaganda and censorship have therefore debased the French language, and with it the French people as human beings. So silence is as damaging politically as it is existentially. Tardieu puts this subtly in "Vacances":

> Puisque les morts ne peuvent plus se taire,
> est-ce aux vivants à garder leur silence? (*JP* 87)

Better to use the debased language against itself than to keep one's mouth clean in silence. As Aragon writes, "Il faudrait rendre sens aux mots blasphématoires" (*EP* 69), or again:

> (. . .)
> Quand ton pays est amour défendu
> Quand il te faut la voix des faux-prophètes
> Pour redonner vie à l'espoir perdu (*YE* 53)

So what is this hope? We are back with the notion of *patrie* as something virtual, and a value. It has to be talked about, it is history that has to be made. To the extent that it still has to be made, it is a *mythe* in Péret's sense. To the extent that it will be exemplary, it will be an extension of "legend" in Aragon's sense, a proverbial myth. Even the physical countryside of France is *essentially* linguistic in Resistance poetry. This is the central idea in Aragon's "Le conscrit des cent villages", as I will suggest below. The list of villages is an intoxicating draught "où flambe et tremble la patrie" (*DF* 56). A similar idea occurs in Emmanuel's much more cosmic "Lamentation pour le temps de l'avent":

> Et tes villes aux noms comme des noms de femme
> (que de fois de leurs noms je me suis enivré) (*CD* 93)

In Eluard's "Gabriel Péri", we read that

> Il y a des mots qui font vivre
> Et ce sont des mots innocents
> Le mot chaleur le mot confiance
> Amour justice et le mot liberté
> (. . .)
> Et certains noms de pays de villages
> Et certains noms de femmes et d'amis
> Ajoutons-y Péri (*OC* I 1262)

Not specifying the names has the same effect as specifying a hundred: a general idea elbows out parochial loyalties. The names and the nouns (*nom* means both) are all values, to be cherished, fought for and realised. Péri's name-noun is to become a "mot", something like a proverb, a dictionary entry alongside the others. Eluard is urging in effect that the legend should become a proverbial myth, that the very name Péri should henceforth symbolise uncompromising resistance to the enemies of freedom and *fraternité*. In other words, he will be able to be invoked in the future in the same way as figures like Joan have been invoked in the Resistance.[9] It is significant that Eluard should be talking about *words* here. What gives life is the *word* justice, the *word* freedom, and so on.

Similarly, every stanza of "Liberté" ends "J'écris ton *nom*", until the poem finishes:

> Et par le pouvoir d'un *mot*
> Je recommence ma vie
> Je suis né pour te connaître
> Pour te *nommer*
>
> Liberté. (*OC* I 1107; my italics)

Clearly, then, if France is a *patrie*, it is more than soil or history. In one of Masson's poems, the speaker says that his "voyageuse patrie" is "Ma Mère Révolution" (*Lum* 22, 21). This combination of Communism and Christianity is something supra-national. In another poem, Masson writes that the war is opening up a land "où l'homme enfin va régner" (*Lum* 65), and elsewhere:

> Il n'y a pas que cette patrie à délivrer
> il y mille patries à faire, tout un puissant kilométrage
> de liens à briser (*Lum* 90)

Aragon's "Prélude à la diane française" begins with a reference not to France, but to humanity:

> L'homme où est l'homme l'homme L'homme
> Floué roué troué meurtri
> Avec le mépris pour patrie (*DF* 19)

In very many of these poems, France is the France whose Revolutionary citizens, again in Masson's words,

> portaient l'arbre de la liberté entre les épaules
> aux matins de l'Europe (*PDI* 21)

Throughout Emmanuel's Resistance poems, too, this universalist liberalism is symbolised by the tree. And in France, he writes, there lived "la plus humaine race d'hommes" (*CD* 96). French territorial integrity, for the majority of the Resistance poets, is not an end in itself, but a mediation for *l'homme* – humanity, not as an essence to be preserved, but as an ideal *fraternité* requiring ever-renewed realisation.

To return to Péret's criticisms. The Resistance poets often do hark back to the past. But to what past? The *patrie* they invoke is not that of Déroulède, Barrès, Maurras or the ministries of the Third Republic.[10] It is typical that in 1939 Seghers should have launched his soldiers' poetry magazine, *Poètes casqués*, with a feature on Péguy and an editorial refusing any *bourrage de crâne*. Péguy's *mystique républicaine* was a belief in the universal freedom which in his view was represented by Joan and the French Revolution. His militarism, if that is the right word, was a militant willingness to defend that freedom. It was this Péguy – and not Déroulède, Barrès or Maurras – who was honoured alongside Gabriel Péri by the clandestine Editions de Minuit.[11]

The essence of Péret's criticism is that the Resistance poets put themselves at the service of a dogma instead of giving voice to the collective aspiration of the people, to a *mythe*. The poets themselves certainly did not see it that way. They may have been wrong, of course, but Seghers spoke for them all: "Le chant du poète répond à une attente. . . . Il chante et c'est son pays qui chante, ce sont des hommes et des femmes qui se retrouvent dans son chant. . . . Il est dans le bronze de cloches qu'on a fondues, dans la ville qui pleure ses morts, dans la ténacité de celui qui espère. Il est, le poète, la voix d'un peuple."[12]

Péret also saw the reversion to traditional prosodic forms as reactionary, and inseparable from the reactionary themes. The forms and the themes may be inseparable, but are they necessarily reactionary? There is just room for three typical examples.

First, Aragon's "Le conscrit des cent villages" (*DF* 54-8). The villages' names are usually grouped together for their alliterative quality and for their cumulative picturesque suggestiveness. Take these five stanzas:

L'Ame Sommaisne Flammerans
Sore Sormonne Sormery
Sommeilles La Maladrerie
Bussy-le-Repos Sommerance

Mon pays souffre mille maux
S'en souvenir monte à la tête
Ah démons démons que vous êtes
Versez-moi des mots et des mots

Il reste aux mots comme aux fougères
Qui tantôt encore brûlaient
Cette beauté de feu follet
Leurs architectures légères

Angoisse Adam-les-Passavant
Bors L'Aventure Avril-sur-Loire
La Balme-d'Epy Tréméloir
Passefontaine Treize-Vents

Adieu le lieu dit l'Ile-d'Elle
Adieu Lillebonne Ecublé
Ouvrez tout grands vos noms ailés
Envolez-vous mes hirondelles

Some of the elements in the first stanza, if taken as common nouns, have denotative value ("Ame", "Sommeil[les]", "Maladrerie", "Repos"). "Sommeilles" generates a connotation of *somme* in "Sommaisne" and "Sommerance". The *rance* element in "Sommerance" may be brought to the surface by "Maladrerie". Through its relentlessness, the alliteration on [s] and [m] combines with these semantic hints to suggest an overwhelming sickness of heart and body and a craving for rest. In similar ways, the fourth stanza hints at the life of a fugitive or a Resistance courier, hunted, afraid, elusive, constantly on the move. These elements accord with the themes of exile, journey and the wind, so important in the poem.

It is striking that these semantic sketches should be achieved through lists of names, without the help of any other parts of speech – particularly as a limited number of sounds is repeated with great frequency in a short space. The greater the phonetic density, the more obtrusive the verbal sound, and the greater the threat that meaning will evaporate and leave a residue of pure sound. The threat is very clear in the first two lines of the fifth stanza quoted. This tension between meaningfulness and meaninglessness is formally analogous to that between the order and coherence of a country and the disorder and incoherence of a random collection of villages (such as the routed army or the refugees of the *exode* passed through).[13] There is a manifest effort at organisation in the text. The analogy is reinforced by the fact that in the lines of "commentary", where the conscript expresses his feelings, there is often a similar phonetic density. For example, the second stanza takes up the insistent [m] of the first. This, the repetition of "démons" and the homonymy of "maux/mots/mots" again result in sense starting to give way to sound. The sounds are dizzying. Perhaps this is because of earlier references to the "odorante fleur du langage" (p.54), to drunkenly drinking the "vocables où flambe et tremble la patrie" (p.55), and now to intoxication and pouring out words like drink. At all events, the *signifiant* is analogous to the *signifié* in this stanza, and the stanza as a whole is an example of what is then referred to in the following one: even if meaning, like the burning countryside, seems to be vaporising, the acoustic "architecture" is left. In like manner, a new obtrusive alliteration, on [v], is set up in the last two lines of the fifth stanza, and the four rhymes permutate related sounds: [dɛl/ble/ɛle/dɛl]. There is almost as great a phonetic density in the second two lines as in the first two, and the rhymes draw the four together into a unit. Just as the heady alcohol of words was poured out in the second stanza, words are invited to fly away in this one. The common feature is volatility. And in this stanza as before, there is an analogy between the *signifiant* (the phonetic alcohol) and the *signifié* (the flight of birds). This volatility is an all-important part of the motif of wind. The poem ends:

> Musiques s'il n'est pas trop tard
> Parfumez le vent parfumé
> Sanglotez les cent noms aimés
> Que j'écoute au loin vos guitares (*DF* 58)

France is not the hundred separate villages, nor the soil, nor the burning countryside. It is a particular way of talking about them, a "musical" way, a set of words turned into an "ancienne antienne" (but of course it is quite new) and released into the air like alcohol to join isolated people together in shared intoxication.

The traditional form is part of the manifest effort to impose order, and therefore essential. In all verse, the shorter the line, the more obtrusive the rhyme, especially when the lines are end-stopped, as they usually are in this poem. The obtrusiveness is increased in the poem by the frequent rich rhymes. Given the almost ubiquitous alliteration and assonance, the whole poem resembles a wager: how far can one abuse the traditional octosyllabic quatrain by turning it into sheer sound, and still use it to make sense? In this connection, even the humdrum question of the mute e is important. It has to be sounded, for the lines to have eight syllables. As usual, its effect is to put extra stress on the preceding syllable. In this poem, because so many of the lines are lists of names, the mute e's role is often to cut the names off from each other. The first stanza quoted here is a good example. So, like rhyme and length of line, the mute e is exploited to increase the threat of disorder (a succession of disconnected names).

Tradition is traditionally a guarantee of order, witness Vichy's authoritarian traditionalism. Here, an ancient French prosodic tradition (the rhyming octosyllabic quatrain) is used both to generate disorder (sheer verbal sound) and to establish a fresh order, that of the manifestly willed analogy between *signifiant* and *signifié*. This paradox is itself a deeper instance of the analogy: behind the lists of names and their subtle distillation into heady music lies the struggle between the divisively traditionalist *patrie* of Vichy and the subversively, creatively traditionalist *patrie* of the Resistance, the voluntarist Revolutionary tradition of *fraternité*, returning to which will be so radical as to be another Revolution. The France of this poem is a *mythe* in Péret's sense; but Aragon's act of writing about it, in the particular way we have seen, has already turned it into a proverbial myth.

Péret talks about the alexandrine, of course, not the octosyllable. There is great variety in the use made of the alexandrine by the Resistance poets. Let us just take the case of another former surrealist, Robert Desnos. His sonnet "Le legs" (*DA* 223) is an attack on the Nazis and Vichy:

Et voici, Père Hugo, ton nom sur les murailles!
Tu peux te retourner au fond du Panthéon
Pour savoir qui a fait cela. Qui l'a fait? On!
On c'est Hitler, on c'est Gœbbels ... C'est la racaille,

Un Laval, un Pétain, un Bonnard, un Brinon,
Ceux qui savent trahir et ceux qui font ripaille,
Ceux qui sont destinés aux justes représailles
Et cela ne fait pas un grand nombre de noms.

Ces gens de peu d'esprit et de faible culture
Ont besoin d'alibis dans leur sale aventure.
Ils ont dit: «Le bonhomme est mort. Il est dompté.»

Oui, le bonhomme est mort. Mais par-devant notaire
Il a bien précisé quel legs il voulait faire:
Le notaire a nom: France, et le legs: Liberté. (© Editions Gallimard)

The reference in the first line is to an anti-Resistance poster which quoted Hugo's initial fear that the insurrection of June 1848 would result in a bloody "République de Marat". Hugo, of course, soon developed into the great Republican hero who wrote *Châtiments* when in exile from the Second Empire. After his return in 1870, his name was associated with resistance to the Prussian as well as to tyranny. It is important to note, however, that at the end of the poem Hugo's legacy is not a free France, but freedom itself: France is the legal witness and guarantor of freedom. This France is, like Aragon's, the supra-national *patrie* of Sieyès and Péguy, a custodian of universal values.

It is also, however, a France of *légèreté* and irrepressible wit. This is embodied in the contrast between the traditional dignity of the sonnet form and the familiar language – "Père Hugo", "racaille", "ripaille", the comically contrived rhyme in line 3. The almost parodic *grand siècle* grandiloquence of line 7 and the rhetorical repetition of "ceux qui" also contrast comically with "ripaille". The utter simplicity of line 8 is increased by its contrast with this comedy, and acquires an overtone of quiet determination and threat. There is another contrast, between the down-to-earth expression of distaste in line 10 and the more schoolteacherly knuckle-rapping in line 9. The straightforwardness of the rest of the poem is enhanced by the mobility of the internal rhymes ("esprit/alibis/dit/oui"). These coincide with a pause each time, and act as a kind of phonetic punctuation to introduce the key notion: "le bonhomme est mort". The sonnet form is in this poem very far from being a reactionary constraint. Desnos' nonchalant manipulation of tones, and his easy integration of sonnet and alexandrine, those traditional emblems of "culture" (line 9), with more popular culture is an affirmation, and an example, of the vitality and flexibility of a French tradition. The *signifiant* of this poem contrasts sarcastically and vividly with the atrophied, reactionary culture preached by Vichy, and wittily represented here by Bonnard, who was an academician and Pétain's minister of education![14] Desnos was to take the same process further in the hilarious vituperative sonnets of 1944, which combine the alexandrine and strict sonnet forms with an exclusive use of *argot* (*DA* 216-21).

An important variation on the alexandrine is the near miss. Seghers' poem "Dans la nuit" (*TM* 21-2) is a good example. Here is an extract:

Les chemins de notre pays sont sans cloches
Le bronze, une Pâque de sang nous l'a pris
Dans la nuit. J'écoute un chant que j'ai appris
jadis, est-ce lui qui naît et qui s'approche

Sonnailles des vieux béliers, est-ce vous qui
Ressoulevez la houle immense là-bas
Dans la nuit? L'espoir ou le silence bat-
Il à votre cou? N'êtes-vous pas conquis

Comme une terre, comme une chair esclave
Et pouvez-vous toujours chanter l'avenir
Dans la nuit? O mon pays qui sait tenir
Son drapeau qu'un temps de chiens un temps délave

Est-ce toi ce troupeau de nuit, la colère
Contenue, avec des airs d'airs défendus
Dans la nuit, est-ce toi grondant et tendu
Vers le jour et vers le ciel à nouveau clairs?

The poem as a whole is built on the image of transhumance and shearing. The flock alternately represents captivity and nomadic freedom. In every stanza, the phrase "dans la nuit" opens the third line, and is followed by some degree of pause. This repetition is an element of order and stability. So, of course, are the quatrains and the regular rhyme-scheme. The stability even threatens to become a straitjacket, inasmuch as three successive stanzas contain the rhyme [i]. This stability is, however, undermined by a number of factors: the [i] alternates between the outer and inner pairs of rhymes from stanza to stanza; it is consequently anticipated and echoed by the repeated "dans la nuit", and by other occurrences of the same sound in varying stressed positions within the line (for example, lines 1, 4, 11, 13 of this extract); and there are also other interior rhymes in stressed positions (notably "sang/chant", "immense/silence", "terre/chair", "drapeau/troupeau", "contenue/défendus"), together with clusters of alliteration or homonymy ("est-ce vous . . . ressoulevez la houle", "un temps . . . un temps", "des airs d'airs défendus"). Quite apart from their semantic functions, these phonetic features in themselves inject an anarchic fluidity into the formal stability; indeed, as in "Le conscrit des cent villages", sound sometimes threatens to overwhelm sense.

This phonetic fluidity is reinforced by a rhythmic one. Above all, each line has eleven syllables. This is what I mean by a "near miss". The "failed" alexandrine is formally analogous to the repressed but powerful urge to expression which is the central theme in the poem. It also contrasts with the formal rigidity noted above. There is a further contrast. The balanced classical hemistich is impossible in a line of eleven syllables, and this irregularity contrasts all the time with the presence inside the lines of regular groups, notably octosyllabic and hexasyllabic, often ending with a rhyme. The first stanza quoted is a good example: "Les chemins de notre pays" and "J'écoute un chant que j'ai appris" each have eight syllables, and echo the regular rhyme in [i] in this stanza.

There is, then, a constant and varied rhythmic and phonetic rise and fall, or ebb and flow ("la houle immense" is a key image in the poem), within the (irregular) prosodic constraints. This does not only highlight essential ideas; it is itself analogous to the heaving struggle between acceptance, resignation and silence (fixity) and refusal, resistance and protest (movement). The *patrie* in Seghers' poem ("notre pays", "mon pays") is this seething, pent-up song of hope, an "air défendu" (like the *Marseillaise* and the *Internationale*). The function of traditional form here is to convey a successful struggle with recalcitrant language, so that the poem symbolises the struggle with a recalcitrant past out of which the still-ideal *patrie* may emerge.

All the poems I have mentioned have one theme in common, namely that "la patrie se fait tous les jours".[15] The *mythe* – in Péret's sense – to which the poets give voice is that of a future France, enjoying freedom of speech once more and using it in the promotion of a universalist liberal humanism like that which originally, and all too briefly, inspired the French Revolution. That this France is a *mythe* is confirmed by the many references to hope, collective silence and the urge to speak, and by its presentation not as just the soil or just history, but as a function of language – as the way we utter or "name" events and the soil. The poems go further. They are linguistic acts, characterised by a manifest and conscious mastery of language. This contrasts greatly with the *submission to* language normal in a state founded on propaganda and terror. The poems are acts which deliberately contribute both to the making of history and to its transformation into proverbial myth.

IAN HIGGINS

St Andrews

NOTES

[1] Republished in B. Péret, *Le déshonneur des poètes* précédé de *La parole est à Péret* (Paris: Pauvert, 1965). Reference is to this edition. Péret's attack is on *L'Honneur des poètes*, an anthology published with an introduction by M. Simon (Rio de Janeiro: Atlantica editora, 1944). This is not to be confused with either of the anthologies bearing that title published clandestinely in Paris by the Editions de Minuit in 1943 and 1944. Péret does make this mistake (p.82), but this is explained by a misleading reference to the 1943 anthology in Simon's introduction (p.8). I define Resistance poetry as poetry written and/or distributed in France during the Occupation, and which the reader sees as implicitly or explicitly conveying hostility to Nazism and Collaboration.

[2] In fact, just over half the poems are in alexandrines, and not all of them rhyme. Most of the others are in rhyming octosyllables, decasyllables or heptasyllables. The use of fixed form certainly was a feature of much Resistance poetry, but it was less universal, and more varied, than Péret suggests.

[3] Repeated reference to poets' works will be by abbreviated title and page number, as follows. The place of publication is Paris, unless indicated otherwise. ARAGON: *DF*: *La Diane française* (Seghers, 1945); *EP*: *En étrange pays dans mon pays lui-même* (Seghers, 1947); *YE*: *Les Yeux d'Elsa* (Seghers, 1945). R. DESNOS: *DA*: *Destinée arbitraire* (Gallimard (coll. "Poésie"), 1975). P. ELUARD: *OC* I: *Œuvres complètes*, vol.I (Gallimard (Pléiade), 1968). P. EMMANUEL: *CD*: *Combats avec tes défenseurs* suivi de *La Liberté guide nos pas* (Seghers, 1969); *Can*: *Cantos* (Neuchâtel: Ides et Calendes, 1944). L. MASSON: *DM*: *Délivrez-nous du mal* (Seghers, 1945); *Lum*: *La Lumière naît le mercredi* (Seghers, 1945); *PDI*: *Poèmes d'ici* (Neuchâtel: Baconnière, 1943). P. SEGHERS: *TM*: *Le Temps des merveilles* (Seghers, 1978). J. TARDIEU: *JP*: *Jours pétrifiés* (Gallimard, 1948).

[4] A. Frénaud, *La Sainte face* (Paris: Gallimard, 1968), p.154.

[5] J. Marcenac, *Poésies 1932-1969* (Paris: Temps Actuels, 1983), p.69.

[6] *Contrebande* poetry, being legally published and therefore submitted to the censor, smuggled in under the surface a subversive message which was clear to the alert reader.

[7] Gabriel Péri, a former Communist *député*, was shot as a hostage in 1941. He quickly became a legendary martyr, and many poems were inspired by his death.

[8] P. Emmanuel, *Qui est cet homme?* (Paris: Egloff, 1947), p.318.

[9] Cf. Seghers' "Octobre 41" (*TM* 19). The theme of Tardieu's "Oradour" (*JP* 99-101) is this transformation of an event into a legend and then into a proverbial myth, and the poem is itself an example of such a transformation.

[10] Or that of Vichy. The significance of *patrie* changed automatically with Vichy's substitution of *Travail, famille, patrie* for the Republican *Liberté, égalité, fraternité*. The *Etat français* was authoritarian, hierarchic, xenophobic, anti-semitic and officially committed to collaborating in the creation of a Fascist "new order" in Europe. The *patrie* of its three-part motto becomes a usurpation of its counterpart, *fraternité*: perhaps, after all, the patriotism of Republicanism could be an extension of *fraternité*, instead of the imperialist chauvinism denounced by, among others, Aragon, Desnos, Eluard and Péret, notably in 1925 and 1929-30. (See e.g. J. Pierre, ed., *Tracts surréalistes et déclarations collectives, 1922-1939* (Paris: Le terrain vague, 1980), pp.50, 129-30, 152, 394-5, 432-3.)

[11] *Deux voix françaises. Péguy. Péri.* Avec une préface de Vercors et une introduction par le témoin des martyrs [i.e. Aragon] (Paris: Editions de Minuit, 1944).

[12] P.Seghers, "Poésie à hauteur d'homme", *Le Figaro*, 12-13 septembre, 1942, p.3.

[13] Cf. Claude Simon's use of place-names, analysed by A. C. Pugh below (pp.67-8): the disorder of battle (advance and retreat through a succession of villages) and the phonetic suggestiveness of place-names contrast with the idealised order imposed on the battle by history.

As in Aragon's poem, this shows that what is "represented" in history or fiction is a function of the language that represents it. Simon, however, writing after the war, uses the place-names "centrifugally", subverting an established positivist, narrative historical order, whereas Aragon, writing during the war, uses them "centripetally", to express the will to impose a moral order on events.

[14] "Bonnard" is also a familiar word meaning "dupe". It is interesting to compare this poem with "Le conscrit des cent villages" and Eluard's "Gabriel Péri". Desnos goes some way towards turning the names in line 5 into common nouns by introducing each with an indefinite article. The monotonous repetition of the article isolates each name, throwing it into relief, so that each receives the listener's full attention as the speaker spits it out. This in turn highlights the semantic suggestiveness of the names (*aval, ravaler, avaler, péter, putain, bonnard*). "Hitler" and "Gœbbels" are similarly highlighted by the repeated introductory "on c'est". The introduction of "France" in line 14 is a quite different matter: Desnos brings in the word "nom", instead of saying e.g. "Le notaire est la France" or "Le notaire, c'est France", which would have been prosodically impeccable. Presenting France as a *name* ensures that it is seen as a function of utterance, something ideal and mythical (both *mythe* and proverbial myth). The presence of Gœbbels (propaganda) and Bonnard (education) in the poem confirms the importance of this theme.

[15] The phrase is the title of an anthology of Resistance writings edited by J. Paulhan and D. Aury (Paris: Editions de Minuit, 1947). The *patrie* which emerges from Resistance poetry is the one found in *Domaine français* (Geneva: Trois collines, 1943). This is a special issue of *Messages*, too incendiary to be published in France. It comprises nearly 450 pages, and most of the contributions make it aggressively plain that the "domaine" in question is not a stretch of land, but something universal, moral and liberal. J. Cassou's article, "Corps mystique de la France" (pp.87-92), is typical of the volume, and draws together many of the threads of my discussion: "Une maxime blasphématoire a prétendu jadis que la nation était faite de la terre et des morts. . . . Mais cette limitation est particulièrement inadmissible pour une France idéale, moins une terre qu'un ciel, faite non pour des morts, mais pour des vivants. Des vivants qui, de génération en génération, appliquent le meilleur de leur destin à se vouloir cette patrie et à la vouloir pour les autres, à la rêver, à la penser, à déployer son azur au-dessus de toute la diversité des nations du vaste monde. . . . Car la France n'est pas seulement la France des Français, la France manifestée, mais cette marge d'aurore, ce point du jour. Si les vivants perdaient un tel sentiment d'espérance, ils ne pourraient plus vivre. . . . Il leur faut l'appel rajeuni du bonheur, ce bonheur que Saint-Just voyait apparaître comme une 'notion nouvelle en Europe', ce je ne sais quoi de délicat et d'immense, d'actif et de fraternel que suggèrent les choses, les personnes, les pensées et les actes de la France manifestée, et qui la dépassent, et dont celle-ci n'est qu'une figure" (pp.91-2).

DEFEAT, MAY 1940: CLAUDE SIMON, MARC BLOCH AND THE WRITING OF DISASTER

Le désastre ou l'invérifiable, l'impropre.
Maurice Blanchot

Claude Simon's *La route des Flandres*[1] stands out among novels set against the background of the military defeat of France as a work displaying a rare degree of intellectual and artistic integrity. It concentrates upon a few incidents during the retreat following the battles on the Namur-Dinant sector of what had been intended to be the front, defended by General Corap's Ninth Army, along the West bank of the river Meuse. The chaotic withdrawal of regrouped remnants of the 31st Regiment of Dragoons (sent, on horseback, to fight aircraft and armour) is not, however, described directly: the slow progress of the small band of survivors making their way back towards the (already non-existent) French lines, following in the paths of the Vth and the VIIth Panzer Divisions of General Hoth's XVth Armoured Corps (the latter commanded by the then unknown General Rommel) is depicted much of the time as taking place in an uncannily normal Spring countryside.[2] The war seems already to be over; it is only perceptible in terms of its effects: corpses of men and horses, burned-out wrecks of vehicles, and a lingering smell of decomposition and burning rubber. Only an intermittent artillery duel in the distance indicates that elsewhere the battle continues.

The reader of *La route des Flandres* is placed in a situation in some ways equivalent to that of the riders: there are no secure references in the text to either dates or any of the well-known names I have mentioned, and the novel is more a commentary upon war as such than a guide, in fictional form, to a specific event. Indeed, what makes *La route des Flandres* much more than an "authentic" war novel, based upon a writer's personal experiences, is the way it unerringly focuses upon questions which have come to be seen, in the light of the contemporary preoccupation with narrative forms and the functioning of figural language, as crucial to our understanding of the ways in which history is written, and historical knowledge achieved.

All representations, as modern theory shows, signal as much the codes upon which depend the impressions and effects they produce as those same impressions and effects. "Decoded", such effects do not disappear; instead, our appreciation of works of art is enhanced, for we not only learn how their meanings are constructed and transmitted, but we begin also to ask more searching questions about the values we assign to them. If *La route des Flandres* did not *return* its readers to questions concerning perception, recollection, and representational and figurative[3] writing, the bold formal and linguistic aspects of its narrative structure and its descriptive technique would reduce the text's meanings to an elaborate game played against more conventional fiction, or to a parody of realist assumptions. Certainly, the novel questions many such assumptions, but since they also underpin historical narratives, history is not so much banished from the scene, as brought back to centre-stage, in the form of a whole series of issues involving the ways in which we imagine the past and try to understand what has come before.

All these issues come to a head when it is a question of describing adequately the most violent form of historical change, and it is made clear, in a scene some twenty pages into the text, that the particular disaster in which the novel's protagonist-narrator was involved has caused him to rethink the view of history supplied to him, before his brief period as a combatant, by the cultural and educational tradition represented by his father, a teacher and writer.

In the scene in question, father and son argue about the nature of war. Georges, the son, rejects bookish knowledge, and any view of history as progress or process, as well as his father's disillusioned appeals to the psychology of human aggression and economic explanations of conflict (*RF* 33). All such speculation is dismissed impatiently by Georges as a useless stringing together of words (*RF* 34). The brief fragment of dialogue in which we catch a glimpse of Georges during the period prior to the commencement of hostilities occurs as a flashback. The outer frame of the narrative is situated after the war, and in the interim he has experienced directly the reality not only of modern warfare, but defeat and captivity. He has been lucky enough to survive, but the military fiasco in which he has been involved causes him to react angrily to the faith in an essentially literary culture to which his father still clings, for while the father laments the bombing of libraries (*RF* 210), Georges sees not just accumulated historical knowledge and philosophical wisdom as the casualty of war, but the possibility of meaningful knowledge of the past in general as a dream without foundation.

After rejoining his regiment, Georges has spent the first ten days of the war (the real one, as opposed to the "phony" one) more or less continuously in the saddle. His cavalry regiment has been sent forward to head off the German attack, but has been caught in a series of ambushes by the faster-moving motorised units of the enemy. Following the retreat from the Meuse, which has taken several days, Georges's regrouped squadron is virtually wiped out just as they thought they had reached the safety of the frontier fortifications (*RF* 145-152). Georges, having finally lost his horse, wanders through fields and woods trying to orient himself according to the position of his shadow on the tracks he follows, until he unexpectedly comes across the captain commanding his squadron, together with a lieutenant and an orderly, riding along a country road as if nothing had happened. Obliged to mount one of the spare horses, Georges, with the orderly, follows the two officers, who continue an urbane conversation about horse-racing (*RF* 286-294). As they go through a village, they are warned by some wounded men along the road-side that Panzer units have already been active in the area, and that there are snipers waiting for them if they continue in the same direction. The captain takes no notice of these warnings, and a few minutes later, together with the lieutenant, he is cut down by a burst of fire from behind a hedge. Georges and the orderly spend another two or three days trying to evade capture, but are eventually taken prisoner.

The final ambush marks both the beginning and the ending of the part of the novel dealing with the narrator's experiences of warfare. Indeed, the scene in which the captain raises his sabre in a last gesture of defiance – or resignation, for Georges is not certain how to interpret this action – recurs like an image in an obsessive dream (*RF* 12, 84, 216, 279, 295). It is more, however, than a *leitmotif* illustrating a tragic theme, even though it symbolises the anachronistic attitudes and beliefs of the tradition-bound military hierarchy, for Georges's attempts to make sense of the captain's apparent acceptance of his fate become the focus of wider issues, notably the possibility, and even the purpose, of any reconstruction of the past. Georges's desire to comprehend this event, in both its real and its symbolic dimensions, thus introduces, superimposed on the lacunary intrigue of the novel, problems as germane to strictly historical writing as to modernist fiction of the "self-reflexive" kind.

The raw material of historical narratives consists largely of eye-witness accounts of events, or parts of events, which are submitted to a cumulative process of selection and rewriting. It is therefore instructive to see how *La route des Flandres* stresses the difficulties involved in the subjective reporting of incidents in cases where the witness has no access to the accounts of other witnesses or information retrospectively acquired. Georges, having no such secondary sources at his disposal, is obliged, when telling his story to a sceptical companion in the prisoner of war camp, to rely largely upon his own memories. Since then, he has learned more about the overall situation, for example that not just his regiment but the whole army of which it was a part was, as it were, absorbed into the ground, and disappeared without trace (*RF* 282). He also knows that the general commanding his regiment, unable to accept the impossible situation in which he had been placed, committed suicide.[4] The general's act sums up, for Georges, the uselessness of retrospective knowledge, and as he tries to imagine the unfortunate officer's reactions to the evidence of catastrophe, it is made clear that the suicide symbolises not just a military defeat but a failure which is ironically repeated in the narrator's attempts to describe it.

Not only does Georges doubt the accuracy of what he remembers, realising that at the time his perceptual and cognitive responses were numbed by fatigue, but his desire for certain knowledge of what happened is contaminated by the indeterminacy of the overall situation: nobody, from the captain leading the group of survivors, to the general himself, had any idea of how to respond to a kind of war for which they were totally unprepared (*RF* 16). The narrator's difficulties are compounded, moreover, by his inability to separate his memories of the recent past from other memories involving family legends, his mother's gossip, and even a childhood fantasy centring on the portrait of an ancestor, which used to hang in the family home.

Doubts over the circumstances of the ancestor's death are amplified as a series of mythical prehistories are superimposed upon the history he is trying to reconstitute; the "knowledge" he desires – on the assumption that behind all these layers of narrative there is an original truth to be found – reveals itself as founded in a more basic form of curiosity, powerfully exemplified, by displacement, in the sexual quest which leads him to Corinne, the captain's widow (*RF* 243-246).

The protagonist-narrator's knowledge of the past is thus shown to depend very much upon the ways in which an uncertain history deriving from a multitude of unreliable sources is represented in the ongoing present. Each attempt to "go back" is rendered more difficult by the memories of previous attempts, and in the text, this layering process is seen to become an essential motor in the production of a fiction. The writing now begins to illustrate aspects of its own history and to assert itself according to its own laws, as the search for an origin for truth in the past is transformed into what is both a regression into myth as the symbolic articulation of impossible desires, and the progress of an artistic adventure in language.

History, as the possibility of certain knowledge of the past, thus appears more and more like a discursive form which papers over the problematic issues concerning its sources and the reliability of its explanations. However, Georges's awareness of these problems, following his engagement with "real" history, causes his previous objections to his father's reliance upon discourse ("enfiler des discours . . . " *RF* 34) to rebound, for all Georges can do, in his quest for the truth of what happened, is to re-tell his story and produce more and more strings of words. The pressure of this contradiction causes the character to "split", and the reader eventually realises that "Georges" is not so much the psychological vehicle for what the text represents, as the support for the text's own productivity. There is no centred "point of view", no reliable and constant "presence" providing the reader with an opening onto a pre-existent world, and thus no way of separating what is represented from the medium of representation, that is to say a fragmented narrative which shifts unpredictably from the first to the third person.[5]

It is noteworthy, in *La route des Flandres*, that the move into the third person is not exploited by the novelist in order to correct or complement the limited perspective of the first person narrator; instead, the system of alternation between the narrative "voices"[6] is used in such a way as to ensure that any one description, or attempt at narration, is liable to be disconfirmed by another. Without access to either objective criteria for the establishment of truth conditions, and in the absence of any way of verifying subjective impressions and recollections, the writing constantly brings the desire for "knowledge" back to its discursive origin and to the problem of "original" discourse, for representation, by definition, should be the replication, or the attempted repetition of a logically and chronologically prior entity. The concept of mimesis appears more sophisticated, but by introducing the element of *difference* it also emphasises the problem of iterability. When it is shown that literary mimesis must necessarily take diegetic form (a central plank in modern literary theory), it becomes clear that the "object" of a representation has always been lost. The orphic quest thus symbolises, in mythical form, the "temporal paradox" explored by both fiction and history.

Simon's novels regularly question the intelligibility of "history itself" by implicitly denouncing such a concept as nothing more than a figure of speech,[7] if not a figment of the collective imagination. However, if this might seem to amount to an artistic overstatement of the case against accepted views of history, it is worth recalling that *La route des Flandres* echoes a generalised uncertainty within the discipline of history which was already apparent during the inter-war years, and which the disaster may well have caused to come to a head, thus contributing directly to what has become, in the post-war period, an ongoing revolution in the field of historiography.

Some of the evidence for such an assertion is to be found in two works by a noted historian expressing views parallel to those implied (as opposed to being overstated) in Simon's novel. They are *L'Etrange défaite*[8] and *Apologie pour l'histoire ou métier d'historien*[9] by Marc Bloch, who was the co-founder, with Lucien Febvre, of the review initially entitled *Annales d'histoire économique et sociale*. Since 1945, the so-called "Annales School" has become synonymous with critiques of narrativism and its traditional preoccupation with "events". Shortly before the foundation of the journal, Raymond Aron, in 1938, summed up many of the objections to both narrativist and positivist conceptions of history in a book which had considerable influence, and which also reflects the then current "existentialist" attitude towards "objective" historical knowledge. In it can be found many statements which illuminate any comparison between the limitations inherent in both historical and fictional representations of the past, among them the following: "Les constructions irréelles doivent rester partie intégrante de la science, même si elles ne dépassent pas une vraisemblance équivoque, car elles offrent le seul moyen d'échapper à l'illusion rétrospective de fatalité."[10]

As a reservist captain serving on the General Staff, Marc Bloch had an inside view of the rapid collapse of communications which prevented the French Army from responding to the accelerated pace of a battle which did not correspond to their expectations. Having observed the sometimes pathetic effects of the disintegration of a tradition-bound "order" (*ED* 89), Bloch analysed the long-term causes of the defeat in a way which many fellow historians find to remain exemplary, given the fact that he wrote the book without access to either verifiable information or the kind of archive material available to those who followed him. Obliged to rely on his own memory and the anecdotes of other witnesses, in which rumours had frequently substituted themselves for facts, Bloch had to be very much on his guard against the accusation that he was merely writing his memoirs or telling another soldier's story (*ED* 22). Wary of narrative history, and equally suspicious of claims for causal hypothesis made by means of appeals to scientific models such as those employed by positivist theorists, Bloch felt it necessary to play down the narrative elements in his account. Without access to "objective" evidence, however, he had to present his credentials, and ground his account in his authority as an internationally celebrated historian, a soldier decorated for bravery during the First World War, and above all, a staunch patriot. Indeed, these factors guarantee *L'Etrange défaite* the kind of authenticity underwritten by the "contract" binding the author and the reader of an autobiographical work.[11] The historical value of the book is enhanced by its sustained sense of moral outrage at the laxity of those entrusted with crucial decisions, and whose procrastination created what one military historian called "the war of lost opportunities".[12] Bloch's acute analysis of the complex historical factors which culminated in the defeat has not been seriously challenged.

Since *La route des Flandres* does not present itself as anything other than a novel there is no need for any contractual element which might ground its narrative in an agreed definition of historical truth. The question of the text's "realism" or otherwise is thus an impertinent one, unless, of course, it is accepted that literary realism is part of a larger ideological apparatus involving shared beliefs in the persuasiveness of specific discursive forms, such as "novels" and "histories", which can be shown to depend upon a system of relays (in the sense of both connections and mutually supportive techniques) grounded in the same representational code.[13]

Whereas the cognitive dilemma of the narrator of *La route des Flandres* can encourage the reader, at one level, to accept the view (powerfully orchestrated by the Formalist tendency in modern critical theory),[14] that the world presented by the novel is closed off from reality – and thus from real history too – it is also demonstrable that the fiction leaves open enough "routes to reference"[15] to enable that same reader to relate the text to other descriptions of the same overall "event", many of which pose exactly the same questions regarding the *vraisemblance* of historical narrative.[16]

The Formalist argument is thus revealed to be based upon one of the oppositions it most fiercely denounces, namely a polarisation between "reality" and referential or projective illusions; *La route des Flandres* illustrates how all writing mediates between the real and visible world of experience and appearances, and the rhetorical and discursive forms we traditionally classify as pertaining to more or less real worlds, according to whether we are discussing historical, fictional or other kinds of representations.

As a consequence of the virtual taboo placed upon both "reality" and "history" by the principal spokesmen of the "New Novel" movement, with which Simon, for better or for worse, has been associated since the late 1950s, the question of the referential status of *La route des Flandres* has either been dismissed as naïve or reduced to a purely anecdotal level. In a companion piece to this article,[17] I shall set out some of the reasons for challenging this view, but before providing the historical evidence, it is necessary to establish that such "evidence" does not so much consist of "hard facts" as of an intertextual framework of other narratives. It is by illustrating the relays (as defined above) between a diversity of texts that the value of the novel, as a "supplement" to more conventional history, can be demonstrated.

Marc Bloch's "Apology" for history usefully supports some of the elements of such an argument, for the historian makes it clear, in this posthumously published work, that many of the claims hitherto made on behalf of his discipline as a form of "scientific" inquiry have been overstated. A reconsideration of the foundations of historical method must start with the same question asked naïvely by Bloch's son: "Papa, explique-moi donc à quoi sert l'histoire" (*AMH* ix). The question is one of major importance: "Notre civilisation occidentale entière y est intéressée" (ibid). Had Bloch survived the war (he joined the Resistance after the defeat and was shot by the Nazis in 1944) he might have seen his views reflected by the subsequent move towards the Human Sciences, and the acceptance (in some, but by no means all schools of historical thought) of all the problems involved in establishing a "scientific" basis for all the allied disciplines seeking to explain human behaviour in historical, economic and cultural terms. As developments in recent years have shown, especially in continental philosophy, this is by no means easy, if concepts of historical knowledge are themselves reflections of ideological structures.

Catastrophic events, like the defeat of 1940, reveal the fissures in such concepts, and Bloch's awareness of this is very evident when it is seen that the son's innocent question is in fact the one asked by men betrayed both by some of their fellows, and by "history itself": "Dans le jardin normand où notre Etat-Major, privé de troupes, traînait son oisiveté, nous remâchions les causes du désastre: 'Faut-il croire que l'histoire nous ait trompés?', murmura l'un de nous" (*AMH* x). Bloch had written many times about battles, but first as an historian detached from his subject, and then as a former soldier whose country had eventually been victorious. After 1940, there was nothing to alleviate the "atroce nausée" (*AMH* 14) of defeat, and Bloch stresses how his view of history as writing has been changed by such a bitter experience by questioning the value of the kind of knowledge proposed by histories which neglect subjective accounts in the interests of objectivity. The "témoignage" is the base matter of history (*AMH* 23-4, 85) and the historian deals not with facts but with the "traces" (*AMH* 34) of human actions, whose effects are essentially psychological (*AMH* 101). The "récit" of a witness is of course not reliable evidence in itself, and in certain periods, especially periods of instability or violent change, such narratives can be untrustworthy (*AMH* 51), but their comparison excites the historian's "sens critique" (*AMH* 52), and Bloch concludes, on this point, with a remark which seems to apply particularly well to *La route des Flandres*, not only because of the retrospective framing of the narrative, but because the novel itself was not written until nearly twenty years after the events it describes: "Au contraire, on croit fortement le narrateur qui, à longs intervalles, apporte par des chemins difficiles les rumeurs lointaines" (*AMH* 52). Bloch's metaphor usefully underlines the argument I am advancing here, namely that Simon's novel is not a purely self-contained fiction, but a highly poetic exploration of "routes to reference" more complex and problematic than those all too often abused by both crudely realist fiction and a great deal of popular historical narratives.

When Bloch describes his professional activity as "une science dans l'enfance" still at the stage of its "premiers tâtonnements" (*AMH* xiv), which he has downgraded to the level of a "trade" or "craft" (*AMH* xvii), the parallels between the metaphors he uses, and those frequently employed by Claude Simon when describing his activity as a novelist,[18] are particularly striking, as is the historian's recourse to a cinematic metaphor similar to ones which occur many times in Simon's novels, for Bloch speaks of the historian as someone obliged to look back at the past as if it were a film in which only the last reel is intact: "Pour reconstituer les traits brisés des autres, force a été de dérouler, d'abord, la bobine en sens inversé des prises de vues" (*AMH* 15). The historian, no more than the novelist, can claim to represent the past as in a mirror, nor as a continuous sequence of logically related images. The past resurfaces as fragments,[19] and cannot be delineated by means of neat contours without falsifying the "traits brisés", or the cracks which reach back into the prehistory of the edifice of historical knowledge.

The matter of history, as represented in *La route des Flandres*, is essentially fragmentary. War as such cannot be represented, only its material and psychological consequences, or what could be called its after-effects and "after-affects". In his most pessimistic mood, Georges (or perhaps Blum, his companion in the prisoner of war camp) defines the past as waste matter and history as the "disinfected" version of events: the aftermath of war, the filthy residue of disaster, epitomises the "dustbin" view of history, as expressed in the conclusion of an extraordinary diatribe: "ce formidable amoncellement d'ordures, cette décharge publique où figurent en bonne place, au même titre que les képis à feuilles de chêne et les menottes des policiers, les robes de chambre, les pipes et les pantoufles de nos penseurs" (*RF* 176).

Such a passage does not sum up a "message" of a merely negative kind, for the images employed have a critical function: they illustrate how the institutionalisation of thought leads us all to don "uniforms" of one kind or another, all of which, together with the works of thinkers and writers who continue to rely upon unquestioned value-systems (such as the code of verisimilitude supporting realist fiction and uncritical narrative history), will end up on the same rubbish heap. The metaphor is a frequent one in Simon's work, and if we stated earlier that *La route des Flandres* brings history to the centre of the stage, the text obliges us to correct the implication that this stage is peopled with living presences, for even the actors seem to have departed (*RF* 291), having shed their costumes. A whole series of interconnected metaphors, too numerous to be examined here, indicate that history, to become "authentic", has to accept the gaps and the uncertainties in the conceptual and cognitive ground supposedly supporting it.[20]

La route des Flandres thus shows us some of the reasons why such issues are left to be discussed in the theoretical margins of historiography or raised by self-reflexive fictions. It has even been suggested, by a noted specialist in hermeneutics and narrative theory, that history deals not only with imaginary entities (which have of course been real at some time in the past), but that its discursive and explicative structures are equivalent to "transitional objects", that is to say symbolic substitutes for absence whose function is to allay anxiety and uncertainty: by *playing* with the past we come to terms with the reality of the contingent present and an unpredictable future.[21] By organising the past according to logical, theological, theoretical or even purely tropological models,[22] or "mapping" time and space in such a way as to give it design and formal coherence, a similar purpose would appear to be served. But how many historians draw attention to the creative freedom they could enjoy, if they so wished, in the organisation of their material?

The imaginary dimension of historical mapping of time and space is clearly signalled in *La route des Flandres*, where the few references to real locations and dates are suspended, and subjected to fictional elaboration. In military histories of the battles of 1940, references are taken for granted: they denote real events, places and persons. Seldom, however, is the "cartographic" perspective of historical narratives shown up to be an idealisation so clearly as it is in Simon's novel:[23]

> cherchant à nous imaginer nous quatre et nos ombres se déplaçant à la surface de la terre, minuscules, parcourant en sens inverse un trajet à peu près parallèle à celui que nous avions emprunté dix jours plus tôt en nous portant à la rencontre de l'ennemi l'axe de la bataille s'étant entre-temps légèrement déplacé l'ensemble du dispositif ayant subi de ce fait une translation du sud vers le nord d'environ quinze à vingt kilomètres de sorte que le trajet suivi par chaque unité aurait pu être schématiquement réprésenté par une de ces lignes fléchées ou vecteur figurant les évolutions des divers corps de troupes (cavalerie, infanterie, voltigeurs) engagés dans les batailles sur la carte desquelles figurent en grosses lettres parce que passées à la postérité les noms d'un simple village ou même hameau ou même une ferme un moulin ou une butte ou un pré, lieux-dits
>
> les Quatre Vents
> L'Epine
> L'Ecrevisse
> Trou des Loups (*RF* 280)

Maps, as this extract shows, have their own poetry, and place-names do more than organise a topographical space. Indeed, the signs which normally represent security not only produce historical echoes (which Simon develops in the more recent novel *Les Géorgiques*),[24] but become emblems of disorientation, as the text distorts and plays with them in such a way as to suggest the psychological effect produced upon the weary horsemen by their repeated evocations of other times and other places, or some exit from the contingent situation. Their ironic solicitations emphasise the anachronistic slowness of the riders' progress, caught in the middle of the rapid advance of a highly mechanised enemy.

The link between the uselessness of purely referential knowledge and the symbolic satisfactions of writing (whether fictional or historical) is established in *La route des Flandres* in a passage where the novelist clearly pays tribute to his master, Marcel Proust:

> le bruit du canon s'éloignant lui aussi, sur la droite à présent, vers l'ouest, on pouvait voir un haut clocher gris à bulbes au-dessus de la campagne mais savoir s'ils avaient pris le patelin comment savoir comment savoir nous pouvions voir leurs noms énigmatiques sur les plaques indicatrices les bornes, coloriés eux aussi et moyenâgeux Liessies comme liesse kermesse Hénin nennin Hirson hérisson hirsute Fourmies tout entier vermillon-briques théorie d'insectes noirs glissant le long des murs
>
> (*RF* 291)

Wherever we turn, in the novel, the question of the language of representation looms large, constantly demonstrating how the depiction of the past is coloured by the play of sound and sense in what we might otherwise assume to be non-problematic "references". *La route des Flandres* is a brutally down-to-earth novel not only because it represents principally the waste matter of war seen (literally) at ground level (and not from the ideal aerial perspective of military or other histories) but because it reveals that once set to work in a text all references refer to absences: we are forced to admit that it is not so much historical knowledge that is groundless, but writing which assumes that there is a "proper" way to write history, for what poetic writing reveals is that there are no proper meanings beneath the surface of a text, only references to other meanings in other texts and other contexts.

Marc Bloch expressed the hope, in *Apologie pour l'histoire*, that the new generation of historians would adopt the habit of reflecting upon what he called the "hésitations" and the perpetual "repentirs" of his craft (*AMH* xvii). He also recommended that they take care not to deprive it of its "part de poésie", adding that it would be "une étonnante sottise de croire que, pour exercer sur la sensibilité un si puissant appel, elle doive être moins capable de satisfaire aussi notre intelligence" (*AMH* xi).

Returning the compliment, we might add, as a rider to Bloch's remark, that the powerful appeal of *La route des Flandres* illustrates the necessity of seeing poetic writing not just in formal and linguistic terms, but within the context of the history it evokes and the reality it reflects, albeit in brilliant fragments which can never be reassembled so as to replicate the past, but which can be so skilfully composed as to keep open the question of how and why we seek to represent and explain it.

ANTHONY CHEAL PUGH

Durham

NOTES

[1] Henceforth, *RF*. Page references are to the paperback edition (Paris: Editions de Minuit ("Collection Double"), 1982). Originally published by Ed. de Minuit in 1960.

[2] See below, pp.121-130, for a bibliography of historical treatments of the defeat of 1940, and a short chronicle of Claude Simon's experiences generously provided by him, together with some extracts from the correspondence with the writer generated by my research into the historical background to his novel.

[3] What has been called "The Figurative Thesis" involves the view that "Whatever can be represented can also be described, and moreover, can be described in concrete terms" (Richard Wollheim, "On Representation: The Philosophical Contribution to Psychology", *Critical Inquiry*, vol.3, no.4, Summer 1977, p.710). Wollheim's critique of this and other representational theses is a useful introduction to a topic more exhaustively dealt with by J-F. Lyotard in *Discours, figure* (Paris: Editions Klincksieck, 1978).

[4] General Barbe, the officer in command of the 31st Regiment of Dragoons in which Claude Simon served, shot himself after the defeat. It seems likely that a postcard mentioned by Paul Reynaud, in *La France a sauvé L'Europe*, vol.II (Paris: Ernest Flammarion, 1947), p.102, was sent him by this same officer: "Hélas, le 25 mai, je reçois une carte postale adressée à mon nom, trouvée, en gare du Mans, sur le corps d'un officier de l'armée Corap, qui venait de se suicider. Il me disait: 'Je me tue pour vous faire savoir, Monsieur le Président, que tous mes hommes étaient des braves, mais on n'envoie pas des gens se battre avec des fusils contre des chars d'assaut.'"

[5] For a bibliography of articles on the novel written before 1975, see *Claude Simon, Colloque de Cerisy* (Paris: Union Générale d'Editions (Coll. 10/18), 1975) p.441. For an account of some of the ways in which the novel confronts the problem of representation see "La crise de la représentation", by Alastair Duncan, in the special number of *Critique* devoted to Claude Simon (novembre 1981, pp.1181-1200).

[6] See "Voices, absence and presence in the novels of Claude Simon", by Celia Britton, *French Studies*, Oct. 1982, pp.445-453, and my commentary on the opening pages of *Histoire* (1967) in *Simon: Histoire* (London: Grant & Cutler Ltd., 1982) pp.34-43.

[7] See my article "Facing the Matter of History: *Les Géorgiques*", forthcoming in *Claude Simon: New Directions*, ed. A. Duncan (Edinburgh: Scottish Academic Press), in which some of the ways in which history is described in Simon's latest novel are examined (notably as a *figure*, in the sense of trope, character and face).

[8] Paris: Albin Michel, 1957 (first published, 1946). Henceforth, *ED*.

[9] Paris: Armand Colin, 1949. Henceforth, *AMH*.

[10] Raymond Aron, *Introduction à la philosophie de l'histoire: essai sur les limites de l'objectivité historique* (Paris: Gallimard (Coll. "Idées"), 1957), p.120.

[11] See Philippe Lejeune, *Le pacte autobiographique* (Paris: Editions du Seuil, 1975).

[12] This was the first title of *The Battle of France*, by Colonel A. Goutard (London: Frederick Muller Ltd., 1958). See Ch.3, "The Battle of the Meuse".

[13] For an informed discussion of Jacques Derrida's use of the concept of the *relai*, see Marian Hobson, "Deconstruction, Empiricism and the Postal Services", *French Studies* July 1982, pp.290-314.

[14] In particular in the works of Jean Ricardou, whose hold over much of the critical discussion during the *colloques* on the New Novel held at Cerisy-la-Salle is very much in evidence in the published proceedings. See *Nouveau roman; hier, aujourd'hui*, vols.I & II (Paris: Union Générale d'Editions, 1972), and the volume devoted to Claude Simon (see note 5).

[15] See the chapter entitled "Sense and reference" in *Frege, Philosophy of Language* by Michael Dummet (London: Duckworth, 1981), esp. pp.93-4.

[16] See Gérard Genette's seminal article, "Vraisemblance et motivation", in *Communications* 11, 1968, pp.5-21.

[17] See below, pp.121-130.

[18] Notably in Simon's introduction to *Orion aveugle* (Geneva: Skira, 1970).

[19] The provisional title for *La route des Flandres* was "Description fragmentaire d'un désastre". See the extract from an interview (*Le Monde*, 8 October 1960) which appeared in the "Collection 10/18" edition of the novel. Also the many comments on fragmentary writing in Maurice Blanchot's *L'Ecriture du désastre* (Paris: Gallimard, 1980) from which the epigraph to this article is taken (p.15).

[20] For a discussion of the "unreal", or imaginary nature of causal hypothesis in the philosophy of

history see the chapter entitled "L'intentionnalité historique" in Paul Ricœur, *Temps et récit*, Tome I (Paris: Editions du Seuil, 1983). For a sophisticated defence of narrative see Hayden White, "The Value of Narrativity in the Representation of Reality", *Critical Inquiry*, Autumn 1980, pp.5-27, and the same writer's article "The Question of Narrative in Contemporary Historical Theory", *History and Theory*, Vol.23, no.1, 1984, pp.1-33.

[21] Ricœur, p.270. The remark is made almost as an aside, and is not developed. I have drawn out some of the implications of Winnicott's concept, as expounded in *Playing and Reality* (London: Tavistock Publications, 1971, and Pelican Books 1974).

[22] See Hayden White, *Metahistory* (Baltimore: Johns Hopkins Univ. Press, 1973) and *Tropics of Discourse* (ibid., 1978).

[23] "Un rêve secret de cartographe ou de diamantaire meut l'entreprise historique." Ricœur, p.248.

[24] Paris: Editions de Minuit, 1981.

ATTACKS ON THE GAULLIST "MYTH" IN FRENCH LITERATURE SINCE 1969

"Il faut qu'il y ait un idéal. Il faut qu'il y ait une espérance. Il faut que, quelque part, brille et brûle la flamme de la résistance française."[1] When de Gaulle uttered these words on 24 June 1940, a few days after his famous *appel*, he was reiterating the main theme of all his early speeches – having adopted the role of "soldat et chef français",[2] working in the best interests of *la patrie* and maintaining the nation's honour, he incarnated French hope for the future. In short, he was the true representative of "la France". The problem with his embodying an ideal in this way, however, was that an idealised view of events tended to be put forward, especially as far as the extent of his following and influence was concerned.[3] Of course, the need to boost French morale, the attempt to impress the Allies and the very recourse to rhetoric encouraged exaggeration, as is only to be expected in wartime. What is more surprising, perhaps, is the fact that a distorted view of occupied France seems to have been widely expressed and accepted long after the war had ended.

In other words, it can be seen that a myth grew up around the Resistance and principally around de Gaulle.[4] Indeed, so strongly was its impact felt over three decades that at the end of the 1960s extensive reaction to it began to emerge in the form of the *mode rétro*. It is this recent trend towards demythification which will be the ultimate focus of the present study, but if the phenomenon is to be fully understood it will initially be necessary to see how the myth developed down through the years.

The liberation of Paris and the walk down the Champs-Elysées marked the climax of de Gaulle's four years of resistance – the nation was finally able to express its recognition of the man who had embodied "la France éternelle". This was significant because "la légitimation populaire . . . consacrait la légitimité originelle – celle de 1940 – et transformait de fond en comble ses fonctions de chef du Gouvernement provisoire".[5] With this acceptance came the legitimisation of the views expounded by the General. He had always claimed that virtually the whole of the country was behind him in his struggle; he could now add, with scant regard for the role of the Allies, that the French had liberated themselves.[6] National redemption thus ensued: "le gaullisme de gouvernement . . . emporte l'adhésion confuse et souvent ambiguë d'un pays victorieux sans avoir beaucoup combattu, et dont de Gaulle est la bonne conscience."[7] On the basis of this consensus, the General could pursue the interests of the nation by stressing that France remained great, using her now massive participation in the war to ensure that she took her place alongside the other formidable world powers – the United States of America, the Soviet Union and Great Britain. It is not without cause that Jean Touchard says of de Gaulle's speeches from 1944 to 1946: "le thème fondamental est celui du rang, le rang de la France dans le monde."[8]

The press of the period reveals just how strongly the myth was establishing itself at this time. For example, Raymond Aron criticises the General's power, but nevertheless recognises his charisma:

> A la fin du mois d'août 1944, le général de Gaulle prit le pouvoir avec l'assentiment unanime de la nation. De l'extrême-gauche à l'extrême-droite, tous les partis, toutes les familles spirituelles acclamaient le premier Résistant de France, l'homme qui symbolisait l'honneur de nos armes, qui avait maintenu la patrie dans la guerre et dans la victoire.[9]

A setback came, however, when the temporary government fell in 1946, a victim of its inability to unite the nation – the post-Liberation excesses and the shameless exploitation of the Resistance had left their mark.[10] De Gaulle tried to make the best of a bad situation and continued to propagate his version of events, taking care to distinguish between passive and active *résistants*. This is illustrated by his speech of 16 June 1946:

> [Le salut] vint, d'abord, d'une élite, spontanément jaillie des profondeurs de la nation et qui, bien au-dessus de toute préoccupation de parti ou de classe, se dévoua au combat pour la libération, la grandeur et la rénovation de la France . . . de cette élite partie de rien et qui, malgré de lourdes pertes, devait entraîner derrière elle tout l'Empire et toute la France.
>
> Elle n'y eût point, cependant, réussi sans l'assentiment de l'immense masse française. Celle-ci, en effet, dans sa volonté instinctive de survivre et de triompher, n'avait jamais vu dans le désastre de 1940 qu'une péripétie de la guerre mondiale où la France servait d'avant-garde. Si beaucoup se plièrent, par force, aux circonstances, le nombre de ceux qui les acceptèrent dans leur esprit et dans leur cœur fut littéralement infime.[11]

To increase the impact of such speeches, de Gaulle refused to form a political party. He could thus portray himself as being outside the party system and so maintain the purity of his image, attributing all the blame for leading the Resistance astray to the Communists.[12] Supporters were quick to follow the lead of the "chef dont toute la politique, depuis qu'il s'est éloigné du pouvoir, tient dans la conscience qu'il a d'incarner cet esprit auquel tant de Français sont devenus infidèles et que la surenchère des partis a disqualifié".[13]

This defensive action appears to have been reasonably successful, and as the 1940s drew to a close de Gaulle's prestige seems to have suffered less than might have been expected. Indeed, the continued expression of certain, if not all aspects of his view of the Occupation can be seen by reference to a piece by Sartre, first published in 1945 and reprinted in *Situations III* (Gallimard, 1949). Sartre could in no way be accused of adherence to the Gaullist cause, and yet he agreed that "la Résistance active devait, par nécessité, se limiter à une minorité. Et puis, il me semble que cette minorité qui s'est offerte au martyre, délibérément et sans espoir, suffit amplement à racheter nos faiblesses" (p.42). However, although the myth was still widely accepted, the element of hagiography involved had not gone unnoticed: "Depuis la Libération, les livres sur les Français libres n'ont pas manqué. Mais se réclamant en général de l'orthodoxie gaulliste ces écrits taisent ou déforment ce qui ne cadre pas avec la légende."[14]

The 1950s arrived and the acrimonious debate within the ranks of the Resistance persisted.[15] Some of the mud thrown was bound to stick, of course, despite de Gaulle's attempts to remain pure. This is apparently what happened – Claude Mauriac, the General's secretary, noted in his diary on 18 March 1952 that "le mythe de Gaulle est très atteint".[16] It is significant that this is the time when the former leader of the temporary government slowly began to move out of the political arena. He was evidently concentrating on other matters because 1954 saw the publication of the first volume of his *Mémoires de guerre*.[17]

In this work, powerful new expression was given to the myth, the basis of which remained the same: France was still seen as a nation of *résistants* committed to the General, their sole representative:

> La France avait choisi d'elle-même. Les renseignements qui en arrivaient chaque jour démontraient, en effet, que la résistance ne cessait pas d'y grandir, qu'autant vaut dire tous ceux qui y prenaient part avaient moralement rallié le général de Gaulle et que tout gouvernement bâti en dehors de lui serait rejeté par la masse dès l'instant de la libération.
> (II, p.36)

Portraying himself as a prophet, a chosen man of destiny, and employing literary skills to play on the patriotic emotions of his reader, de Gaulle once more imposes a certain interpretation of events.[18] In fact, the whole work is summarised in the very first line: "Toute ma vie, je me suis fait une certaine idée de la France" (I, p.1).

A secondary effect of the publication of the *Mémoires* was that reviewers were also given the opportunity to propagate the legend. André Rousseaux, for example, wrote:

> Le portrait le plus grandiose des *Mémoires*, nulle part dessiné mais partout visible, est celui de ce sauveur de la France qui s'est senti appelé et que le destin a élu. Des malveillants ne manqueront pas de dire que l'auteur de ce livre y sculpte sa propre statue. Et c'est vrai qu'il y a une statue. Mais un homme vivant s'en est senti devenir le glorieux captif.[19]

In this way, the *Mémoires* regalvanised the press. They also offered lots of information and documentation which historians and biographers could use. In brief, they became recommended reading for anyone with an interest in the war years.

More than in the literary sphere, it was on the political front that de Gaulle's popularity made tremendous progress in the late 1950s. The Algerian war was going badly, France was in a state of crisis and the government fell. Many believed it was 1940 all over again – once more a saviour was needed for the nation. Ever ready, de Gaulle stepped into the breach. The Resistance epic consequently received its second legitimisation; de Gaulle's presidency from 1959 to 1969 was to lead to its institutionalisation.

This success had not been achieved easily, however. The myth-makers who stressed France's heroism and allegiance to the General had continually had to fight a rearguard action against those who expressed unorthodox views, frequently novelists. A good example of such a novelist is Jean-Louis Curtis, whose *Les Forêts de la nuit* (Julliard, 1947) illustrates the disillusionment common at the time by criticising the *épuration* and exposing the Gaullist notion of redemption by the few (p.367).

Although many literary critics, including the Goncourt judges, appreciated the work, other commentators were less pleased. For instance, André Rousseaux complained: "A la Résistance trahie, bafouée, il manquait encore de recevoir ce que le fabuliste représente par le coup de pied de l'âne. Maintenant c'est fait."[20]

As the years went by, the reviewers remained vigilant, always quick to decry not only unheroic depictions of the Resistance, but also the second threat to the myth – the attempt to rehabilitate the Collaboration. Roger Peyrefitte's *La Fin des ambassades* (Flammarion, 1953) is a defence of the *épurés* and seeks to rehabilitate Pétain by repeating the thesis that the Maréchal was the *bouclier*, de Gaulle the *épée* (p.351); it is significant that François Nourissier had to confess: "On se prend à regretter que les commentaires qui l'attendent n'aient rien à voir – Grands Dieux! – avec l'histoire des idées, ni – cela va sans dire – avec la littérature."[21]

Jacques Laurent also fell victim to this climate when he published *Le Petit Canard* (Grasset, 1954), "petit drame infini où la critique trouva de la politique parce que le jeune héros s'y engageait à la LVF alors que je voulais montrer seulement le hasard d'une vie et le peu de part qu'y prend un choix délibéré".[22] It was obviously not acceptable to suggest that someone could join the *Légion des volontaires français contre le bolchevisme* quite by chance and with no sense of commitment.

The omnipresent François Nourissier draws the conclusions from the above analysis when he says of the period from 1945 to 1955:

> Les moyens d'expression, ces années-là, furent mis au service d'une mythologie et d'une consolation. Quoi de plus explicable? Bien que la France n'ait jamais été experte à chanter ses grandes heures nationales, sa geste collective . . . tout se passa comme si la tentation nous était venue, insidieusement, de nous offrir alors une grande fable collective.[23]

As already noted, this situation did not improve in the late 1950s. Indeed, when de Gaulle returned to office in 1959, the myth was not only legitimised once again, its defences became even more secure. As long as the General remained at the head of the nation, any attack on the Resistance and on his involvement in it would be unpatriotic, and might be punished.[24]

The orthodox view of the Occupation was thus dominant until de Gaulle fell in 1969, as is illustrated by Claude Jamet's *Le Rendez-vous manqué de 1944* (France Empire, 1964), the record of a meeting he arranged between collaborators and *résistants*. Jamet's aim was to reconcile the two sides but his venture ended in failure (the famous Rémy refused even to sit at the same table as his former opponents). The book is an attempt to salvage something from the wreckage: "Ce livre, enfin, est pour qu'on cesse d'enseigner la haine à nos enfants. Qu'on désarme les manuels. Qu'on fasse taire les menteurs. Que l'on déchire enfin ces images d'Epinal, idiotes et féroces, sur lesquelles nous vivons – et dont beaucoup sont morts – depuis vingt ans" (p.28). When one considers what was at stake here, the failure is significant: "bien que je n'aime guère ce mot, dont on abuse, il s'agit bel et bien d'une entreprise de *démystification*" (p.305). It was not until the late 1960s that such enterprises would start to be more successful.

Examination of the twenty-five-year period from the Liberation to 1969 would now seem to have indicated that a myth grew up around the Resistance and that this myth comprised four basic propositions for the Gaullists. First, the number of real collaborators was minute; second, the vast majority of French people were basically patriotic, even if some were misled; third, the true cause of France was actively expressed by an elite of heroic *résistants*; and finally, the Resistance was incarnated by Charles de Gaulle.[25] While it is true that attempts to reassess the Resistance and the Collaboration had been made, their impact had been minimal. National redemption had been achieved and France's greatness asserted.

By the start of the 1970s the tide had turned. Demythification was becoming more popular and it soon developed into a definite fashion, *la mode rétro*. Two probable causes of this change of atmosphere can be discerned. Perhaps the more noticeable one is the demise of de Gaulle. Georges Pompidou, the man who replaced him as president in 1969, was "volontiers agacé par la geste de la Résistance et de surcroît soucieux de réconcilier pour des affaires plus sérieuses les honnêtes gens".[26] The General's death a year later confirmed this new approach: "il semble que ce soit la mort du général de Gaulle qui ait abattu le grand obstacle, dressé par lui, entre la nation et le juste reflet qu'elle voudrait mériter d'elle-même."[27]

The second reason is that the late 1960s and early 1970s was the time when the young generation, those who had no direct adult experience of the war, had come to maturity. Members of this generation felt deprived of a heritage because they knew little about the Occupation, the period in which they had their roots. Part of the problem was that their parents had not provided the necessary information on the *années noires*.[28] Possibly more important was their own awareness that most of the facts which were available elsewhere could not be trusted. As André Harris says:

> Cette espèce de mythologie un peu tricolore, un peu paranoïaque sur l'occupation m'agaçait depuis très longtemps. . . . Ce qui m'agaçait ce n'était . . . pas la Résistance mais le résistancialisme qui ne représentait pas la réalité de l'Histoire et dont on a encombré la littérature, le cinéma, les conversations de bistrot et les manuels d'histoire.[29]

The solution to the problem was to go in search of the true heritage which lay behind the myth, to take up the points made by the earlier demythifiers. In Harris's case, he joined Alain de Sédouy and director Marcel Ophüls to make

Le Chagrin et la Pitié (1969). This four-and-a-half-hour film, which is generally accepted as the start of the trend towards demythification, demonstrates in the most striking fashion that "les résistants actifs, sous l'Occupation, constituaient une infime minorité des Français".[30] Originally intended for television, the documentary was banned by the ORTF. The director-general explained why: "Ce film détruit des mythes dont les Français ont encore besoin".[31] It was only when the Socialists came to power in 1981 that *Le Chagrin et la Pitié* got its first television showing, even though it had played to packed houses in a Latin Quarter cinema during the ban.

After this initial assault by the film-makers, the challenge was taken up in the novel. Young writers reinforced the attack, and once they had started to gain ground they were joined by members of the older generation, those with direct adult experience of the war to call upon. The consequences for the myth were catastrophic, as is illustrated by the three novels former *résistant* Alphonse Boudard has written on the *années noires*.[32] In his *style parlé*, reminiscent of Céline's, and with a sense of humour which belies the powerful demythification taking place, Boudard concentrates on the crimes and *bavures* of the Resistance. *Le Corbillard de Jules* provides a good example of the way he recalls the injustice of the Liberation: "Ceux qui n'ont pas vécu ces événements, même à travers les livres les plus sérieux, n'y reconnaîtront jamais les leurs. Etaient déclarés collabos, bien souvent, des gens dont on voulait prendre la place, l'appartement, le buffet Henri II, le cosy-corner convoité" (p.36). In other words, the *résistants* could be compared to the *gestapistes*: "On se comportait pas mieux qu'eux, je dois bien reconnaître, avouer. Nous étions, nous aussi, des salauds" (p.183).[33] Added to these admissions is criticism of the way in which the Resistance was cynically exploited. The author's main regret is that he did not use his war record to make a career in politics and business.[34]

The Resistance depicted by Boudard is evidently not the one embodied by de Gaulle, for the heroism and the idealism essential to the latter's version of events are missing in the former's. The novelist leaves his reader in no doubt that mythification explains the discrepancy: "Tout l'art du général de Gaulle fut de monter le blanc en neige, de nous faire croire qu'on était des lions alors que nous étions de pauvres clebs calamiteux."[35]

Boudard's destruction of the myth can be compared to Brigitte Friang's. Her novel, *Comme un verger avant l'hiver* (Julliard, 1978) recounts how Gérard, a *salaud* who betrayed his network during the war, is nevertheless able to exploit his past commitment. He rises in the post-war hierarchy of the Resistance thanks to his money, his contacts and his heartless manœuvring of all about him. In a bitterly ironic ending, he achieves his aim of becoming a *commandeur de la Légion d'honneur* and the top personalities present at the celebrations are treated to a summary of "la vie exemplaire de ce grand résistant . . . " (p.344).[36]

Exactly the same points are taken up by Pierre Daninos in *La Composition d'histoire* (Julliard, 1979). The work is a demythification of many historical periods, but the Occupation is the one where the facts are judged to have been distorted most. Daninos is astounded by the picture of occupied France which is being passed on to French schoolchildren: "Voilà. Voilà la France héroïque de l'Occupation; la France tout entière dressée comme un seul homme (une seule femme) contre l'ennemi; la France passant par bateaux entiers en Angleterre tandis qu'une poignée de traîtres à la solde des nazis collabore avec le gouvernement de Vichy" (p.73). Like Boudard and Friang,[37] he has no doubts as to the source of this disinformation – the "grand maître du lifting, esthéticien hors classe, habile comme pas un à raffermir les chairs meurtries de Marianne et à remodeler son visage selon 'certaine image' qu'il s'est toujours faite d'elle, incomparable magicien parvenant à faire admettre de nouveau la nation vaincue dans le Jockey Club des grands: Charles de Gaulle" (p.77).

Faced with this situation, Daninos reacts by taking five key statements from the textbooks and adding his own comments. The result is a witty, and therefore appealing, yet extremely powerful demythification, as the four points which relate directly to the Occupation demonstrate:

> 2 – "*Tandis que le maréchal Pétain signe l'armistice, le général de Gaulle lance son appel. La résistance s'organise.*" Pas question, là encore, de dire que l'armistice a été accueilli avec soulagement par 85% des Français et que l'appel du général de Gaulle n'a guère été entendu. Le jour où il a été lancé, on était occupés, ou occupés à autre chose.
>
> 3 – "*La France subit les tortures de l'Occupation.*" Pas question de parler de la proportion – infime par rapport à l'ensemble de la population – des héros de la Résistance (48 000 médaillés, soit 1 pour 1 000 habitants); ou du fait que la France est le seul pays occupé (avec le Danemark) à avoir conservé un gouvernement légal sur son territoire.
>
> 4 – "*Les Anglo-Américains débarquent en Normandie.*" Pas question des Canadiens, Australiens ou Néo-Zélandais qui, sans doute parce qu'ils sont morts pour du beurre, sont enterrés en Normandie. Des photos de De Gaulle, de De Lattre, de Leclerc, de FFI, de résistants – pas d'Eisenhower. (Plus tard, on passera sous silence le Plan Marshall.)
>
> 5 – "*C'est le signal de l'insurrection nationale. Paris se soulève.*" C'est le bouquet, si l'on ose écrire. Que ceux qui ont été témoins d'un tel événement lèvent la main: on pourrait les compter, comme il est facile de compter les Français qui ont pris part à cette insurrection dite nationale. Sur 42 millions de citoyens 41 800 000 se sont terrés chez eux, ont vaqué à leurs occupations, ou courageusement craché à la figure de quelques soldats allemands faits prisonniers par les FFI. (pp.75-76)

Two basic points are being made here. First, by stressing the tremendous debt owed to the Allies, without whose aid nothing could have been achieved, Daninos effectively negates the contention that France's liberation was secured by the Resistance.[38] Second, with statistics to help, he shows that there were extremely few active *résistants* (the number of holders of the *carte de combattant au titre de la Résistance* is revealed to be 148,173 (p.76n.)). As a further illustration of his case, he tells of an archivist he knows who has photos of the Paris crowds acclaiming Pétain in May 1944 and de Gaulle three months later in August; with enlargements, at least four different people can apparently be seen to figure in both pictures.[39] The implications concerning the commitment of the *Français moyen* to the Resistance are clear.

Analysis of the representative works of Boudard, Friang and Daninos has now shown that many different, but related attacks were brought to bear on the Gaullist myth in the 1970s. Most important was the insistence on the limited nature of active resistance, but recognition of the debt to the Allies, charges of exploitation and criticism of crimes and *bavures* all served the cause of demythification too.

However, this cause was not served merely by refuting the notion of an heroic *France résistante*; there was also a second manœuvre, one which led to the rehabilitation of the Collaboration. An important contribution was made here by the now mature sons and daughters of collaborators. Pascal Jardin, son of Laval's *directeur de cabinet*, was by far the most productive of these writers and his approach to the Occupation is representative of that of the whole group.[40] Very much aware of the stigma attached to his name, Jardin attempts an exorcism in the four works he has produced on his Vichy childhood.[41] He does this by creating a more acceptable heritage for himself, undermining the orthodox view of the period which classifies him as the son of one of the rare French traitors.

Part of this procedure involves removing the Resistance from its pedestal – he recalls the *bavures* and names de Gaulle as a mythifier.[42] But most of his efforts go into re-evaluation of Vichy, as is evident in his reference to Pétain's residence, l'Hôtel du Parc, in *La Guerre à neuf ans*:

> Si la collaboration qui se faisait là était indispensable à la survie économique de la France, elle se révéla pourtant, après coup, intolérable au regard de l'histoire. Pourtant, dans un pays occupé, noyauté par la fantastique infrastructure militaire et policière du Troisième Reich, collaborer, c'était la raison. Résister, c'était l'espérance. De toute manière, Vichy a perdu. En politique, "c'est plus qu'un crime, c'est une faute". (p.87)

With this reassessment of Vichy goes the rehabilitation of the father, who is seen in a favourable light. He is oppressive, authoritarian and domineering, it is true, but he has none of the evil characteristics frequently bestowed upon collaborators by the myth; in short, he is viewed through the eyes of his loving son. Many commentators were well aware that the result of this was in effect "la *rentrée en grâce* de tout le passé qui s'insinue d'un air de rien".[43]

Re-examination of the Collaboration was also provoked by other writers who stressed the ambiguity of the Occupation. They depicted unmotivated characters who could not be classified or judged according to the myth because chance had decided their commitment for them. Patrick Modiano's *La Ronde de nuit* (Gallimard, 1969) is a particularly good example to consider. The narrator is indifferent and indecisive; quite fortuitously, he joins the Gestapo. His new masters do not tarry in asking him to infiltrate a Resistance network; he accedes to the request, only to be asked by the *résistants* to infiltrate the Gestapo. In this way he becomes both a *résistant* and a *gestapiste* and so demonstrates that there was often little difference between members of both sides. As he says:

> Ne me sentant aucune vocation particulière, j'attendais de mes aînés qu'ils me choisissent un emploi. . . . Le plus curieux avec les garçons de mon espèce: ils peuvent aussi bien finir au Panthéon qu'au cimetière de Thiais, carré des fusillés. On en fait des héros. Ou des salauds. On ignorera qu'ils ont été entraînés dans une sale histoire à leurs corps défendant. (pp.101-102)[44]

It is worth recording at this point that Modiano also worked on Louis Malle's *Lacombe Lucien* (1974), the film which portrays the archetype of the problematic character, the best-known illustration of how people can commit themselves to a cause without ever making a conscious choice to do so. In Lucien's case, a freak puncture results in his being taken to the local Gestapo building where he is plied with drink and encouraged to betray the Resistance leader, which he does. He thus becomes a *gestapiste*, but he could just as easily have joined the *résistants* (they had refused him earlier).

The orthodox interpretation of the Occupation cannot accommodate this kind of collaboration, as Malle recognises: "Pour beaucoup, un garçon qui rentre dans la Gestapo en 1944 est un salaud. Il faudrait même, pour la mythologie, qu'il ait un pied bot, qu'il louche, que ce soit, en fait, un monstre que l'on extermine sans avoir à essayer de comprendre pourquoi de telles choses ont pu se produire."[45] This is why the myth is challenged – Lacombe Lucien and his novelistic counterparts demonstrate, as did Jardin's presentation of his father, that not all collaborators were the exceptional creatures they are made out to be.

Rehabilitation of the so-called traitors did not merely rely on reference to ambiguity or on a loving son's re-enactment of a happy childhood – the *mode rétro* also saw the reappearance of the committed collaborationist hero who unrepentantly argued his case. Paul Werrie's *La Souille* (Mercure de France, 1970) and the sequel *Les Chiens aveugles* (Mercure de France, 1972) are two good examples.[46] The second of these novels shows that the narrator still takes pride in his past actions, despite his present isolation: "On est les rebuts, nous, les rebuts de l'humanité, des détritus, les rescapés du grand naufrage, ceux qu'on appelle les salauds, ceux qui ont cru, ceux qui n'ont pas su se retourner à temps, qui auraient eu honte de faire machine arrière, de retourner leur veste, comme il y en a eu tant" (p.19). He argues that the plight of the *collabos* can be put down solely to misfortune – for him, there is no absolute Good or Bad, no Right or Wrong, there is only the justification of the acts of the victors and condemnation of the acts of the vanquished: "si nous avions gagné . . . serais un héros. Et maintenant qu'on a perdu, tu vois . . . ne suis plus bon qu'à jeter aux chiens" (p.224).

Perhaps more significant than the reappearance of fictional collaborationist heroes was the return of the real collaborators, who could now publish memoirs in a less hostile atmosphere. Lucien Rebatet's *Les Mémoires d'un fasciste* . . .

(Pauvert, 1976) are worthy of mention in this respect.[47] The two volumes comprise a restatement of the Fascist point of view and Rebatet, like Werrie, claims that he could so easily have won complete recognition if the war had gone differently: "Paris dans sa majorité attendait pour choisir son opinion de voir de quel côté pencherait la balance de la guerre. Si nous nous trouvions à l'épilogue sur le bon plateau, sans aucun doute une belle foule de partisans nous rejoindrait avec empressement" (II, p.64).

It is clear from these statements that the *réprouvés* did not feel as detached from the masses during the Occupation as the myth would seem to imply. Rehabilitation once more ensues.

Three reasons to explain why the *mode rétro* saw the Collaboration in a favourable light can thus be discerned. First, the sons and daughters of actual *collabos* were able to show that their parents were lovable people, not monsters; second, many *gestapistes* and the like were depicted as ordinary human beings, mere victims of Fate who could have joined the Resistance if fortune had smiled on them; finally, the Collaboration was allowed to put its own case at length, either in memoirs or through the mouthpiece of a fictional character. Such *banalisation du mal* offered as great a threat to the myth of a *France résistante* as the direct criticisms of the Resistance had done.[48]

It would be wrong, however, to assume that a truer picture of the Occupation is now being given. As examination of certain representative works has revealed, *la mode rétro* encourages the belief that there were no heroic *résistants* and no totally despicable collaborators. This version is just as misleading as the one it seeks to replace, as the critic Mona Ozouf noted:

> Ainsi s'achève le conte bleu où, grâce à de Gaulle, les Français s'entendaient dire qu'ils avaient été collectivement héroïques. Il s'est mué en son contraire exact, également trompeur car il dispense tout autant de l'interrogation personnelle: si la France occupée ne peut sécréter que des débrouillards et des bourreaux, plus quelques résistants grotesques du dernier quart d'heure, ce destin collectif, bien que peu reluisant, absout l'individu aussi sûrement que l'épopée.
>
> Ce n'est donc pas encore le temps de l'objectivité.[49]

In short, myth is being replaced by counter-myth.

Such is the situation to date. Over forty years, the same points have been raised to reassess the status of Resistance and Collaboration alike and counter-mythification has usually been the consequence.[50] The only change since 1969 has concerned the frequency of this re-evaluation, the fact that a new orthodoxy has asserted itself. So, what has the result of this long process been? It is still too early to say with any great certainty, for *la mode rétro* is not yet over. One can merely suggest possible outcomes. It is quite conceivable, for example, that the present counter-mythification will eventually lead to the reassertion of the original myth (elements of this reaction are already evident in Henri Spade's *Et pourquoi pas la patrie?*). Just as plausible is the opposite occurrence, an upsurge in Fascism, mainly because the collaborators are rehabilitated, but perhaps also because a string of indecisive, indifferent characters will create the need for a leader-figure (Le Pen's National Front party has been doing well lately).

Although both these scenarios can be envisaged, the most probable development would seem to be that a more realistic view of events will ensue from the conflict of the two contradictory myths. In fact, François Nourissier suggests that this may already be the case: "Bien entendu le risque est grand . . . de montrer une nation lâche et veule dans sa majorité après avoir abusé des clichés d'une France blessée, digne et courageuse. Entre l'excès d'honneur et l'indignité perce pourtant la vérité."[51] Even if Nourissier's judgment is correct, only time will really tell if the national self-analysis has proved therapeutic, only time will confirm that France is finally coming to terms with her past. Nobody yet knows how the next generation will view the *années noires*. Perhaps a new *mode rétro* is about to emerge. For the sake of the French, let us hope not.

ALAN MORRIS

Strathclyde

NOTES

* I gratefully record my indebtedness to David Gascoigne and Ian Higgins, whose encouragement and suggestions have been invaluable.

[1]Charles de Gaulle, *Discours et Messages*, 5 vols (Plon, 1970), I, p.8.
Hereafter, wherever practicable, publication details and page references will be incorporated into the text. All works are published in Paris unless otherwise stated.

[2]*Discours et Messages*, I, p.4 (19 juin 1940).

[3]See, for example, his speech of 15 November 1941: "pour quarante millions de Français, l'idée même de la victoire se confond avec celle de la victoire des Français Libres" (op.cit., I, p.134). Contrast the depiction of occupied France given by the historian Robert Aron in *Histoire de l'Epuration*, 3 vols (Fayard, 1967-1975), I, pp.281-82.

[4]Reference to myth creates certain difficulties, for there is no general agreement as to what myths actually are, even if there is consensus that they can be of many different types. My use of the term here can be compared to one of the classical interpretations summarised by Christopher Nash: "myths are regarded as attempts at *history*, in the course of which the confused memory and imagination of early peoples have transfigured human leaders into 'gods' and the record of their acts into theology" ("Myth and Modern Literature", in *The Context of English Literature 1900-30*, edited by Michael Bell (London: Methuen, 1980), pp.160-85 (p.161)). Although de Gaulle will be the human leader in question in the present study, it should not be forgotten that the Communists also played a part in glorifying the Resistance, but without "deifying" the General. Their role will accordingly be referred to in notes, where relevant, in order that comparisons and contrasts can be made.

[5]Jean-Pierre Azéma, *De Munich à la Libération* (Seuil, 1979), p.351. The "légitimité originelle" refers to the fact that on 5 June 1940, in Reynaud's last cabinet reshuffle before Pétain took over, de Gaulle was made *sous-secrétaire d'Etat à la Défense nationale et à la Guerre*.

[6]See, for example, the Hôtel de Ville speech of 25 August 1944, op.cit., I, pp.439-40. This is where de Gaulle refers to "la France éternelle".

[7]Jean Touchard, *Le Gaullisme 1940-1969* (Seuil, 1978), p.353.

[8]Ibid., p.86.

[9]"Les Désillusions de la liberté", *Les Temps Modernes*, 1 (1er octobre 1945), pp.76-105 (p.77).

[10] The national disillusionment is revealed by contrasting two of François Mauriac's articles: "La Vocation de la Résistance", *Le Figaro*, 3-4 décembre 1944, p.1, and "L'Esprit de la Résistance", *Le Figaro*, 18 mai 1946, p.1.

[11] *Discours et Messages*, II, p.6.

[12] See, for example, *Discours et Messages*, II, pp.317-18.

[13] François Mauriac, "L'Esprit de la Résistance". Cf. André Frossard, *Histoire paradoxale de la IVe République* (Grasset, 1954), p.147.

[14] Louis de Villefosse, "Témoignage: Les Petites îles de la liberté", *Les Temps Modernes*, 49 (novembre 1949), pp.868-95 (p.869). Cf. Alfred Fabre-Luce, *Au nom des silencieux* (L'Auteur, 1945), p.11.

[15] See Jean Paulhan, *Lettre aux directeurs de la Résistance* (Minuit, 1952).

[16] *Un autre de Gaulle. Journal 1944-1954* (Hachette, 1970), p.368.

[17] Charles de Gaulle, *Mémoires de guerre*, 3 vols (Plon, 1954-59).

[18] Cf. Jean Touchard: "les *Mémoires de Guerre* . . . ont parfois le caractère d'une recomposition a posteriori" (op.cit., p.53).

[19] "Les *Mémoires* du Général de Gaulle", *Le Figaro Littéraire*, 30 octobre 1954, p.2.

Cf. Marcel Arland, "Sur les mémoires du Général de Gaulle", *La Nouvelle NRF*, 24 (1er décembre 1954), pp.1073-79. Not all the reviews were favourable, however. The Communists in particular were not impressed. See, for example, Pierre Daix, "Du culte de la personnalité", *Lettres Françaises*, 12-18 novembre 1959, pp.1, 10.

[20] "*Les Forêts de la nuit*", *Le Figaro Littéraire*, 13 décembre 1947, p.2.

Cf. the Communist reaction, as expounded in Louis Parrot, "Prix Littéraires", *Les Lettres Françaises*, 18 décembre 1947, p.5.

[21] "Roger Peyrefitte: *La Fin des ambassades*", *Nouvelle NRF*, 10 (octobre 1953), pp.720-21 (p.721).

[22] Jacques Laurent, *Histoire Egoïste* (Table Ronde, 1976), p.285; cf. also p.271.

[23] "Les Français, étaient-ils des veaux en 40?", *Réalités*, juillet 1974, pp.18-25 (p.20).

[24] See, for example, Laurent, *Histoire Egoïste*, pp.300-311. Laurent describes how *La Bataille de France*, a film he made with Jean Aurel, was criticised by François Mauriac for not having the happy ending of 18 June 1940. This led him to conclude that "omettre de se référer à de Gaulle était coupable en soi" (p.300). The controversy continued when Mauriac published a very favourable biography – *De Gaulle* (Grasset, 1964) – to which he felt obliged to reply with *Mauriac sous de Gaulle* (Table Ronde, 1964). After a trial, Laurent was fined and about twenty pages of his work were cut.

[25] The Communists, while accepting the heroic view expounded by the first two propositions, rejected the second two. For them, the Resistance was the rising of the masses; it was not the work of an elite. As such, it was best represented by the Parti Communiste Français. See "Premier maurrassien de France", *Les Lettres Françaises*, 16 octobre 1947, pp.1-2. This analysis of the two versions of the myth is confirmed by Jean-Pierre Azéma in *De Munich à la Libération* (p.356).

[26] Jean-Pierre Azéma, *La Collaboration 1940-1944* (P.U.F., 1975), p.11.

[27] François Nourissier, "Le cadavre dans le placard", *Le Point*, 11 mars 1974, pp.86-87 (p.87).

[28] The parents themselves admit to this neglect. See Henri Spade, *Et pourquoi pas la patrie?* (Julliard, 1974), p.12. Cf. Roger Ikor, *Pour une fois, écoute mon enfant* ... (Albin Michel, 1975), p.10.

[29] Pierre Loubière and Gilbert Salachas, "Libre cours: André Harris", *Télé-Ciné*, 171-72 (juillet-septembre 1971), pp.34-41 (p.38).

[30] Marcel Ophüls, "Regardez donc dans vos greniers", *Avant-Scène-Cinéma*, 127-28 (juillet-septembre 1972), pp.9-10 (p.10).

[31] Danièle Heymann, "Français vous saurez", *L'Express*, 4 septembre 1981, pp.18-19 (p.19).

[32] *Bleubite* (Table Ronde, 1975; first published by Plon in 1966, under the title *Les Matadors*); *Les Combattants du petit bonheur* (Table Ronde, 1977); *Le Corbillard de Jules* (Table Ronde, 1979).

[33] For similar views of the Liberation, see José Giovanni, *Mon ami le traître* (Gallimard, 1977) and Laurent, *Histoire Egoïste*, p.242ff.

[34] See e.g. *Les Combattants du petit bonheur*, pp.150-51 and 208, and *Le Corbillard de Jules* pp.239-40. See also Erik Orsenna, *La Vie comme à Lausanne* (Seuil, 1977), p.193.

[35] *Les Combattants du petit bonheur*, p.257. Cf. *Bleubite*: "On a l'autre pour sauver la face, notre Charles qui plastronne en V, qui bouffe du micro, qui se sent la France à lui tout seul. Très chétive revanche ... piètre cinoche! Autant tout de même en profiter" (p.20).

[36] Such ironic treatment of Gérard can be compared to the exposure of Darricade's rise to fame in *Les Forêts de la nuit*. It can also be noted here that Boudard's demythification of the Resistance frequently repeats criticism already made in Marcel Aymé's *Uranus* (Gallimard, 1948) and that

Patrick Modiano's *La Ronde de nuit*, to which reference will be made on pp.78-9, bears striking resemblances to Roger Nimier's *Les Epées* (Gallimard, 1948). These comparisons serve to illustrate that the writers of the *mode rétro* are accepting their literary heritage, re-stating exactly the same points which had been raised to little effect until 1969. For further analysis of this aspect of the trend, see my St Andrews Ph.D. thesis, *The German Occupation in Modern French Fiction: An Analysis of the Literary "mode rétro"*.

[37] Friang, op.cit., p.269.

[38] Cf. Giovanni, op.cit., p.136. See also Frédérique Moret, *Journal d'une mauvaise Française* (Table Ronde, 1972), p.237.

[39] The two visits are also mentioned as significant in the following works: Giovanni, op.cit., pp.189-90; Boudard, *Les Combattants*, p.149; Michel Robida, *Le Déjeuner de Trieste* (Julliard, 1974), p.235. For perhaps a more objective assessment, see Azéma, *De Munich à la Libération*: "rien ne prouve – comme on l'affirme généralement – que ce furent bien les mêmes qui se déplacèrent pour acclamer à Paris Philippe Pétain en avril et Charles de Gaulle en août: il subsistait un public vichyssois" (p.323).

[40] See also Marie Chaix, *Les Lauriers du lac de Constance* (Seuil, 1974); Jacques Bonny, *Mon père, l'inspecteur Bonny* (Laffont, 1975); Jean-Luc Maxence, *L'Ombre d'un père* (Editions Libres-Hallier, 1978).

[41] *La Guerre à neuf ans* (Grasset, 1971); *Guerre après guerre* (Grasset, 1973); *Le Nain jaune* (Julliard, 1978); *La Bête à bon dieu* (Flammarion, 1980).

[42] See *Guerre après guerre* (pp.197-98) and *Le Nain jaune* (pp.170-71) respectively.

[43] Luce Giard, "La Honte", *Esprit*, 25, no.1 (janvier 1979), pp.71-78 (p.74). Cf. Spade, *Et pourquoi pas la patrie?*, p.14.

[44] Cf. Boudard, *Le Corbillard de Jules*, p.243, p.251, *Les Combattants du petit bonheur*, p.93. See also Laurent, *Histoire Egoïste* (pp.216-17) and Denis Lalanne, *Le Devoir de Français* (Table Ronde, 1974), pp.128-29.

[45] Jean-Jacques Olivier, "L'engagement de Louis Malle", *Le Figaro*, 26 janvier 1974, p.15.

[46] See also Pierre Serval, *Une boule de neige en enfer* (Albin Michel, 1980).

[47] See also Christian de la Mazière, *Le Rêveur casqué* (Laffont, 1972) and Robert Poulet, *La Conjecture* (Table Ronde, 1980).

[48] For a lucid summary of the demythifiers' aims, see J.-P. Azéma, *La Collaboration 1940-1944*, pp.11-12.

[49] "Sans chagrin et sans pitié", *Le Nouvel Observateur*, 25-31 mars 1974, pp.54-56 (p.55).

[50] As early as 1947, Maurice Bardèche was being criticised for producing a counter-myth: "Il démolit d'une manière très réjouissante une certaine mythologie de la résistance; mais s'il est bon de la dénoncer, il ne faut pas que ce soit au profit d'une autre. C'est pourtant ce qui se passe" (Jean Pouillon, "Notes: *Lettre à François Mauriac*", *Les Temps Modernes*, 26 (novembre 1947), pp.949-55 (p.951)).

[51] "Le cadavre dans le placard", p.86.

STAGING THE WAR IN GERMAN

German *Theaterwissenschaft* has an enviable reputation for academic thoroughness, yet on the whole it has been more at ease with foreign subjects like the sources of *commedia dell'arte*, than with delicate matters nearer home like the presentation of the German army on the stage. The book by Roswitha Flatz, which appeared in 1976, on "war in peace-time", was therefore something of an exception in dealing directly with the military play in the days of the old Reich.[1]

What came after is not so well documented. It is difficult, for example, to say when the anti-war movement on the stage started, despite the strong tradition of German pacifist literature.[2] What is clear, is that powerful anti-war plays were written right up to the end of the First World War and beyond.[3] Undoubtedly the most original of them all was Karl Kraus' *Die letzten Tage der Menschheit*, written in a time of most stringent censorship and using the censored war-time press itself as its sources of ridicule. Following the war there was no break in the literary discussion of the problem of "War and Literature", neither was there any gap between the end of the war and the appearance of war literature. It was some time, however, before Remarque's novel *Im Westen nichts Neues* (1929) appeared, which not only set new standards (and new records for numbers of copies sold), but which also set in motion a counter-reaction resulting in a hunt for works proclaiming the positive aspects of war. From the end of the twenties onwards the World War began to be acclaimed from the stage as well as from the narrative page as the one great historic event which had made possible the birth of a nation. While the dramas which could be mentioned in this connection can in no way compare with a truly international phenomenon like Remarque's novel, nevertheless they do indicate that there was a strong current running the other way, saying "yes" to war.[4]

The most successful of all such war plays in the Weimar Republic was *Die endlose Straße* (1929) by Sigmund Graff and Carl Ernst Hinze. Described in its subtitle as a "front-line play", it was acclaimed by theatre critics of all complexions. This was a play whose apparently objective picture of the soldier at war rightly invited comparison with the world of Remarque's novel, yet the objectivity was only apparent. In fact the general tenor of the play pointed rather towards a glorification of the togetherness and the sacrifices of the front-line soldier (a favourite Nazi theme). The increasing popularity of the play in the dying years of the Weimar Republic obviously derived from powerful elements in the play, which encouraged former front-line fighters, now languishing in the homeland, to relive the experience of the soldiers in the play. So it is reported for example, that for one performance, all the walk-on parts were performed by real members of Stahlhelm (the militaristic returned-soldiers league), who actually brought on their own real guns, and wore their own real army equipment.

Die endlose Straße showed the endless martyrdom of the front-line soldiers engaged in trench warfare. Other such plays followed. Paul Joseph Cremers' "Deutsche Tragödie" *Die Marneschlacht* (1933) moved from the trenches to command headquarters. The plot, such as it was, had echoes of Kleist's *Prinz Friedrich von Homburg*, which was not surprising, for in just the same way that Hölderlin was appropriated by the Nazis as the elevated poet of national sentiment, so too Kleist was taken over into the militaristic camp. In this play, as in *Prinz Friedrich von Homburg*, a general fails to follow the battle-plan to the letter and as a result victory is not as complete as it should have been. In another similar play by Friedrich Bethge called *Reims* (1937), a character appears, who has obviously been modelled on Jünger. Jünger himself never concealed his contempt for the Nazis, despite his worship of war. Bethge was rather different. Starting as a volunteer for military service, he had fought through every year of the war from 1914 till 1918, being wounded *each* year. After the war he took part in every form of counter-revolutionary activity and eventually joined the Nazi party in 1932. In 1937, as an SS Sturmführer, he received the National Book Prize for his earlier soldier play *Marsch der Veteranen* (1935).

It must not be thought that the army engaged all the attention of the pro-war school: the navy too received its share. Indeed, nationalist dramatists no doubt felt compelled to demonstrate on the stage the navy's genuine devotion to the true cause, because the navy had in fact mutinied, and the navy munity had been powerfully dramatised by Marxist playwrights like Friedrich Wolf. That the navy, despite this, was ready to make the ultimate sacrifice for the national cause was demonstrated by Karl Lerbs in his play *U-Boot 116* (1931). Finally, though not a war play as such, Hanns Johst's *Schlageter* (1933) must be mentioned, because its Freikorps characters (among them the eponymous hero Schlageter) refuse to believe that the war has ended in 1918, and instead wage their own war against Germany's enemies. This play marked the end of Weimar Culture and projected Schlageter, the Freikorps leader and terrorist bomber as "the First Soldier of the Third Reich".[5]

It has often been claimed that there was no Nazi literature.[6] A modification of this theory is the claim that Nazi literature did exist, but that most of it was written before 1933 and that the seizure of power and the creation of the Reichsschrifttumskammer, controlling *all* literary production, meant the death of creative literature as such. What the preceding brief examination of the treatment of war has shown is that there was a powerful, nationalistic, militaristic tradition on which the National Socialists could build, and that the transition from the war dramas of the Weimar Republic to the ideology of National Socialism was an easy one. Given the essentially warlike nature of the Nazi ideology it is tempting to assume that after 1933 a spate of war plays would flow from the pens of Nazi dramatists, swamping the repertoires of the nation's theatres and drowning out all other themes. As has been seen, war plays were written, though generally on themes from the First World War. In fact, however, the theatres were not drowned in war plays and other themes did survive. There were various reasons for this. For a start there was Goebbels' famous doctrine of "steely romanticism" for the new literature.[7] This did (it was true) advocate the heroic view of life, but at the same time, as the mention of "romanticism" indicates, Goebbels did not want realism and he certainly did not want all Nazi literature to be reduced to direct and aggressive propaganda. He knew how counter-productive that would be. As a result National Socialist drama eschewed realism (particularly in the treatment of war) and while encouraging the heroic *Weltanschauung*, tended rather towards treatment of the past rather than the present, and that too in highly literary, neo-classical, traditional terms.

As far as the theatre was concerned, the National Socialist victory meant a chance to clear out the notorious "decadence" of the Weimar Republic, and this was done ruthlessly. In line with the nationalistic longings for a new theatrical form consistent with the demands of the Conservative Revolution, the concept of the so-called Thing-play gradually crystallised. Thing-theatre meant open-air spectacles, and this appealed immediately to the Nazi leaders, whose minds were already attuned to monumentality of this order from their experience of choreographed party rallies. However, the Thing-plays written represented dramatic experiments from an early phase of the movement and, no matter how aggressive, they were unlikely to be successful, once a real war was in the offing.[8] In the end party support for the Thing-play was withdrawn. Instead the new party line, instigated in an essay about "Nordic Culture" by Reichsdramaturg Schlösser, pressed the case for a "new" tragedy. Most leading dramatists like Möller, Curt Langenbeck and Gerhard Schumann pursued this policy vigorously but the result in terms of actual plays written was remote, classicistic drama of a kind which was rarely successful. Similarly, in spite of a great deal of government support, Blood and Soil dramas about heroic, Aryan peasants and legendary historical fighters became boring after a very short time. In terms of the theatre the war, when it came, was fought more successfully on the cinema screens than on the stage. The cinema was after all the modern art form really favoured by Goebbels and Hitler and one capable of showing, in however idealised a fashion, the modern war in the air, in which at least at the start the blitzkrieg tactics and the use of Stukas were remarkably successful.

As has been seen, the glorification of war in dramatic form was well under way long before 1933. On the pro-Nazi side *Schlageter* had reminded audiences of the continuing role of the Freikorps in the fight for a new Germany, and on the other side Horváth's *Sladek, der Schwarze Reichswehrmann* (1928) had recorded the growth of para-military organisations bent on avoiding the limitations on army size imposed by the Treaty of Versailles. Despite Hitler's constant claims that he was a man of peace and despite his initial diplomatic successes, which made it possible for him to achieve his ends without having recourse to war, it was generally recognised that a Nazi victory at the polls would inevitably lead to armed conflict with other countries. Not surprisingly, oppositional dramatists wrote plays which stressed this theme in an attempt to hammer home the message that employment of the kind a Hitler regime would have to offer, could only be in the form of concealed preparations for war, and that neither individual nor national unemployment problems could be solved in this way. With this general situation in mind, Paul Zech, one of the first to go into exile in South America, added a scene to his play *Windjacke* (1932) showing workers arguing the pros and cons of whether war would bring back full employment. Erich Weinert moved to France, where he wrote a sketch called *Gegen die Brandstifter* (1933-35), which adopted the *Sprechchor* form, commonly used by the Communist Party in the Weimar Republic, in order to make the same kind of point. Not two individuals, but two choruses, put the opposing points of view, leading to "a group of new recruits, eager for war, being dissuaded by the arguments of anti-war groups, comprising workers, crippled war victims and mothers".[9] Such fairly primitive propagandistic works had little effect and, as expected, Germany did move towards war, though not at first openly, but rather through fairly covert involvement in the Spanish struggle. Anti-Nazis in exile quickly realised the significance of the Nazi rehearsal for war in the Spanish arena and Brecht, for example, included various references to the Spanish situation in his cycle of scenes called *Furcht und Elend des dritten Reiches* (1935-38). To him and to other anti-Nazis at the time it was clear that the war in Spain with German involvement would soon spread and develop into the Second World War.

This was indeed to be the case, and dramatists who had been forced to leave Germany recorded the impact of German expansionist policies as they affected one country after another. Friedrich Wolf escaped from Germany to Austria and from there to Switzerland and France. As a Communist Party member since 1928 he then made his way to Soviet Russia. His play *Das Schiff auf der Donau* (1938) is based on newspaper reports of a floating concentration camp on the Danube, following the Anschluß with Germany. *Der Rattenfänger bei den Schildbürgern* (1938) was written by the less well-known dramatist Albin Stuebs, who was to spend fourteen years in exile, partly in Australia, partly in Oxford and London, where he worked for the B.B.C.[10] Like so many of his contemporaries, he first made for Czechoslovakia, and there he wrote this play in the fairy-tale mode of the Pied Piper of Hamelin, to show the Czechs and the Germans of the Sudetenland the dangers of the Fascist Henlein, who was inciting them to wage war on the "rats". The moral of the epilogue: "Der Krieg bringt uns kein Brot ins Haus", seems rather tame and despairing in the face of the German threat, and Czechoslovakia was lost soon after. The volume of the exile journal *Das Wort* which contained part of Stuebs' play also included a short dramatic satire called *Die Räuberbande*. Although the playlet, like its author, is now almost completely forgotten, it is a useful reminder that there was in Engels a German-speaking Volga Republic. This was where its author Hans Rosenberg was working as a producer. While this work takes up, from a

Russian perspective, the progress of the German advance into Europe, Brecht, from exile in Scandinavia, also took up the theme of German aggression against Austria, Czechoslovakia and Poland in the one-act plays *Dansen* and *Was kostet das Eisen?* (1939). Jennifer Ann Taylor sums up the changing scene as follows:

> Until the outbreak of the Spanish Civil War the argument centred round attempts to demonstrate the economic disadvantages war would bring to the working classes, while after that the dramatists turned to a castigation of German aggression, offering a detailed chronicle of the subjugation of Eastern Europe before the official declaration of war.[11]

So far only the period between the Nazi assumption of power in 1933 and the declaration of war in 1939 has been dealt with. When the war came it had no immediately noticeable effect on the output of émigré dramatists. One country after another was occupied by German forces, and one possibility after another for the performance of plays in German disappeared, leaving only Switzerland outside the National Socialist sphere with real theatres prepared to accept such material. Despite this, the productivity of the dramatists in exile did not diminish, though there were obviously difficulties in the path of those attempting to deal directly with the military events of the time. Exile meant that authors were limited to the restricted sources made available by censored bulletins and ministries of "information". Audiences abroad were not always familiar with the places in the news or with the peoples involved. For these and other reasons dramatists in exile turned as often to classical and historical themes as dramatists inside Germany itself did. If therefore, in what follows, the stress is on war plays, it has to be remembered that this by no means exhausts the range of theatrical material produced in these years; indeed the example of Brecht shows that the parabolic approach was far more effective in putting the anti-war message across than crudely realistic plays might have been.

Even as far as outright war dramas are concerned it has to be admitted that war in terms of actual fighting plays a less important part than discussions of the implications of the war. One of the results of the blitzkrieg tactics of the German army was that "action" was over almost as soon as it started. Dramatists dealing with this situation in various countries tended to focus on the problems of occupation, rather than on those of fighting, shifting the attention from the soldier to the civilian population. Of necessity this meant dealing with the differences which the Nazi ideology brought about, when it came into conflict with established ideas of military honour and proper soldierly behaviour. One of the best examples of a play of this kind is *Geiseln* (1941), written by Rudolf Leonhard, while the author was imprisoned in the notorious French camp at Le Vernet. *Geiseln* takes up a story from the press about ten French hostages condemned to death as a reprisal for attacks on German soldiers. Leonhard's play was "the first German drama on the French Resistance", and as such deserves to be remembered.[12] Unfortunately its over-long speeches make it too prosily pro-communist, and too lacking in theatrical life. By contrast Peter Martin Lampel's *Überall schreit ein Vaterland* (1941), based on reports of a British raid on the island of Lofoten in occupied Norway has somewhat more dramatic action. Lampel had enjoyed an even more sensational and successful career than Leonhard. Like him a volunteer in the First World War, he not only did *not* become a pacifist, he ended up a bomber pilot and after the war fought on with the Freikorps in the Baltic and Upper Silesia, and was still with the "Black" Army until 1923. From these years he gathered extensive knowledge of the earlier stages of the NSDAP, which he was later to put to very good use in his literary works. He became most famous in the Weimar Republic for problem plays like *Revolte im Erziehungshaus* (1928) and for *Giftgas über Berlin* (1928), the play which blew the whistle on the build-up of the secret army by General von Seeckt. After 1933 Lampel thought it would still be possible for him to stay on in Germany, but he had underestimated the extent of Nazi hatred for former sympathisers like himself. In exile he wrote many plays, most of which have remained unpublished. Very much like Lampel's play about the Lofoten raid is *Denn seine Zeit ist kurz* (1943) by Ferdinand Bruckner, another successful dramatist from the Weimar Republic.[13] The title, a quotation from the Bible, indicates not only the theological background to the play, but the optimistic message that the reign of evil on earth, in this case National Socialism, will be short. This play, which has all the hallmarks of the accomplished dramatist, finishes with a burst of action, in which Werfen, the representative of Nazi youth bent on destroying the church and imposing the new German pagan ideology, is himself shot following an armed uprising by the local fishermen, led by a young Lutheran clergyman. What the play hopes to reveal is that in such extreme cases of the incursion of an evil belief into the modern world, the use of violence is not only justifiable, but consistent with Christian theology. However, dramatic discussion of the problem of violence was by no means limited to Christian dramatists. Friedrich Wolf was a convinced Communist, yet his play *Patrioten* (1942) deals with a very similar problem, though his setting is occupied France.

In the war plays considered so far, discussion of moral issues arising from conflicts between occupying army and occupied civilians generally formed the basis for such interest as they were able to arouse. The war on the Eastern Front gave rise to entirely different problems. For a start the blitzkrieg phase was comparatively quickly over, and once the advance was stopped, the inevitability of German defeat instead of total victory became more readily apparent. In addition, as far as dramatic treatment of the war on the Eastern Front was concerned, such plays were generally written by politically committed dramatists who had not only a long history of opposition to National Socialism behind them from the days of the Weimar Republic, but who had also found refuge in the Soviet Union. This meant that they not only had the psychological security of a political faith to support them through the traumas of exile, they also had the physical support of a government which offered not only shelter but also publishing, and to some extent, production facilities. Doubtless there were disadvantages; only certain themes and certain styles were acceptable, practically all forms of modernism were taboo, and the ideological stance of the attacks on Fascism had to be clear at all times. Nevertheless, the authors now to be discussed seem to have accepted these restrictions. Generally speaking, the dramatic works written were small-scale pieces for instant propaganda effect and for immediate performance; however, one major play, J. R. Becher's *Schlacht um Moskau*, did emerge.[14]

Before looking at Becher's vast play in some detail it is perhaps advisable to remember the kind of propaganda work, written in Russia by Becher's fellow Germans in exile, against which it has to be measured. Dramatists were sent directly to the front to take part in such work, indeed Erich Weinert and Friedrich Wolf were members of the group led by Walter Ulbricht, which directed its efforts against the German army at Stalingrad. Weinert's propaganda material was mostly of a non-dramatic nature, but Wolf composed some fifty dramatic scenes, set in both home-front and battle-front situations. Their aim was generally to encourage defection or desertion from the German army to the Russian side. Similar dramatic scenes by Berta Lask, another veteran anti-Fascist, also centre on the issue of defection and the tainted German cause. Given the nature of the new German army and the atrocities in which it had become embroiled in Poland and Russia, it is not surprising that this whole question of loyalty and military honour, complicated by the oath of allegiance to the Führer, should become such a crucial one. However, in the sphere of the theatre, the appalling dilemma of the German fighting man, forced to long for a German defeat rather than a German victory, was most forcefully presented on the stage, in a play with a home-front setting. This, the most famous of all German plays written in exile, was Carl Zuckmayer's *Des Teufels General*, a play written in the United States between 1942 and 1944, by yet another dramatist with a successful career in the Weimar Republic behind him. Zuckmayer chose a situation far from the front to show the dilemma of a high-ranking officer in the German Air Force, called upon to deal with a case of sabotage at the highest level. When he unmasks the saboteur who is crippling the aircraft industry and asks him why he is damaging his own side instead of the enemy, he receives the answer:

> Wenn Deutschland in diesem Krieg siegt – dann ist Deutschland verloren . . . Es gibt keine Unterjochung, die nicht Befreiung wäre – für unser Volk . . . Wir dursten nach Untergang. Wir müssen dazu helfen – mit eigener Hand. Nur dann können wir gereinigt aufstehen.[15]

One line of criticism levelled against Zuckmayer's enormously successful play was that it focused most attention on the dashing and heroic general in the glamorous uniform and hardly any attention on those hidden heroes actually engaged in resistance to National Socialism. This fault, if it was one, was remedied by other dramatists, who attempted more explicit plays about resistance, but their efforts enjoyed little success, perhaps because of the problematic nature of their material. The collapse of the National Socialist regime, when it came, was brought about not by any resistance groups undermining the brave efforts of the front-line soldiers: it came to pass thanks to the victories of the Allied armies and the Allied air-forces. Some dramatists did attempt to capture the final stages of the war in dramatic form, showing for a change not the German Army as an army of occupation, but the Allied armies as occupying forces in a crumbling Reich. Such plays by exile dramatists failed and remained unpublished and unperformed. In this respect Lampel has suffered more than most. A play like his *Eine Ortschaft bei Aachen* (1945) set in a small town before the final surrender, remains completely unknown to this day, as does most of the exile work of this once famous dramatist.[16]

The Weimar Republic had been extremely successful in encouraging the work of exciting, new dramatists, though the Nationalists did not approve of their efforts and denounced what they saw as "decadence" on the stage. One might have expected that the great war play would be written in exile by one of them, by Friedrich Wolf or Ferdinand Bruckner, by Peter Martin Lampel or Carl Zuckmayer. All of these famous dramatists continued to write plays in exile; Zuckmayer even managed the unique feat of a come-back after the war, with *Des Teufels General*. However, it has to be admitted that the weightiest of all the war plays came from a most unexpected quarter, namely from the pen of Johannes R. Becher. After the war he tended to be looked down upon in the West as a party hack, who had rejected his wild, Bohemian, expressionistic beginnings and prostituted his talents with poems in praise of Stalin. The fact that he had survived his long period of exile in Soviet Russia so well, while so many of his contemporaries had perished there, and the additional fact that he had been rewarded by such high office in the new German socialist republic diverted attention from his undoubted literary achievements. The result was that he was for long reviled in the West and lauded to the skies in the East. Of unique significance in the present context, however, is the play he wrote while the war in Russia was at a critical stage. He called it *Schlacht um Moskau*.[17] At first sight it has to be admitted that the text does not look very promising. Becher's play, in this version, is some two hundred pages long and a mixture of prose and elevated verse, leavened with several long monologues. It is a "play for reading" in the German tradition of that genre, and hence one doomed to seem lacking in dramatic life. It *was* performed at the time; however, the play really only came to life when Becher revised the work, shortened it and tightened up the structure. The play then attracted far more attention and resulted in several successful productions, including one by Brecht with the Berliner Ensemble to music by Hanns Eisler. Further productions followed and there was also a radio version, a TV version and an operatic version, which in turn was televised. Some of this theatrical activity around an otherwise apparently unpromising script might perhaps be attributable to the official respect due to the German Democratic Republic's leading literary statesman and to the state's desire to "come to terms" with the Fascist past; however, it does also suggest that there is more to the play than Western critics have been prepared to admit.

The first fascinating feature of Becher's play is that it was written in a few weeks while the Battle for Moscow was still going on. On 14 October 1941, when the advancing German troops were practically at the gates of the city, Becher and other literary figures were evacuated. When, in February 1942, he returned to a Moscow which, contrary to all expectations, had *not* fallen, the play was finished. It was first published in Moscow in the émigré journal *Internationale Literatur* and, remarkably, this version moved German émigrés in far-away Mexico to stage a production of it. Egon Erwin Kisch, the famous "Raging Reporter" commented as follows:

> Bechers großes Dokument, wenn auch in gekürzter Form, darstellerisch zu gestalten, hat als erste auf dem amerikanischen Kontinent die Kulturorganisation der deutschsprachigen Emigranten in Mexiko, der Heinrich-Heine-Klub, zu unternehmen gewagt. Diesem Mut und dazu einer mühseligen Sorgfalt in der Vorbereitung und einer kollektiven Begeisterung der Darsteller ist es zu danken, daß Mexiko einen deutschen Theaterabend erlebte, wie kaum je zuvor.[18]

This is a salutary reminder of the fate of plays written in exile; that a German play composed and published in Russia should be first performed on another continent altogether was typical of the problems dramatic works had to face. With enormous efforts Brecht could find clubs or groups and sometimes even real theatres to put on his plays in Paris, Zurich and New York. Other less well-known writers encountered greater difficulties, never saw their plays performed and after the war were dismissed as "dated" and committed to oblivion. Becher was fortunate in being such a prominent figure after 1945 that his war play could not be ignored in this way.

Becher's *Schlacht um Moskau* then, was one of the first dramatic works to deal with a major military defeat of the German Army in the Second World War. The first version was subtitled "dramatische Dichtung" although as has been noted it was far from dramatic. The second, shortened version had the new title *Winterschlacht* and (like Paul Joseph Cremers' *Marneschlacht*) now had the subtitle "Eine deutsche Tragödie". Between 1933, the date of Cremers' play, and the Battle for Moscow, the whole nature of the "German tragedy" had changed. The tragedy resides not in the possibility of a German defeat as in the First World War, but in the victory of Fascism over the German army and the German people. Defeat for the German army outside Moscow is now no tragedy, but the means of purifying the German soul.

In his introduction to the revised version of the play in 1953 Becher draws attention to the fact that his aim now was not only to remind the German people of the significance of this turning point in history, when the Nazi invasion of Soviet Russia was repulsed, but also to point to the relevance of the play for the post-war period, when revanchist elements in West Germany and elsewhere seemed to be threatening the Soviet Union once again. This also explains the motto, at the head of the revised text of the play: "Merkt euch: für Feinde führt kein Weg nach Moskau! Den Freunden aber öffnen wir das Herz!" Above this is a quotation from Hölderlin. An examination of the text of the play itself quickly reveals that it is replete with such literary allusions, not only to Hölderlin, but also to Goethe and Schiller. Becher's play, in other words, is still extremely bookish. However, the Hölderlin quotation is perhaps particularly significant, because as has been noted, the great German poet of peace had been appropriated by the Nazis and turned into a Germanic prophet of war. He therefore had to be rescued from the contaminating National Socialist grasp, and this Becher sets out to do. In addition, Becher, the Minister for Culture, strongly supported the party line, which stressed the importance for the new state of establishing its roots in Germany's cultural heritage. Hölderlin and the classical literary canon are lovingly invoked in this play as a demonstration that a passion for things German does not have to be the hate-filled "German passion" which the Nazis had evoked.

In the introduction to his play Becher also mentions his intention of creating a Hamlet figure as his protagonist. Here again Becher was drawing on a long German literary tradition. Just as Goethe's Faust was often interpreted as expressing the divided nature of the German soul, so too Shakespeare's Hamlet was traditionally taken to be the key to another split in the German psyche. Viewed thus, Hamlet's indecisiveness derived from the Germanic conflict between sickly thought and strong-willed action. Becher has deliberately built into his Hamlet figure, Hörder,

> die schwankende Haltung deutscher Intellektueller . . . , die durch ihre humanistisch geprägte Vaterlandsliebe in immer stärkeren Widerspruch zur faschistischen Wirklichkeit gerieten und von hier aus den Zugang zu einer antifaschistischen Haltung finden konnten.[19]

In the play Hörder is a student and a poet, confronted in the army with the atrocities committed by it and forced to recognise what allegiance to Hitler means. Yet characteristically he never reaches the point of outright opposition, he never acts against the army or the regime. The climax for him is reached only in the *refusal* to act, when he will not obey an order to murder Russian partisans. Such indecisiveness does not make for exciting drama. Instead of action, Becher offers the gradual revelation of ethical and philosophical positions through soliloquies, sequences in elevated verse and deliberately contrasting scenes. The result is long-windedness, improbability of plot and a great lack of convincing realism. Becher is not a born dramatist and his lengthy play has great weaknesses, yet despite this the central situation is well chosen. Two soldiers, Johannes Hörder and Gerhard Nohl, are seen on a hill-top one hundred kilometres from Moscow. This is a "historic moment", when the heart of Russia lies exposed and there seems to be nothing to stop the invincible German army. The two soldiers occupy this height and nail up the board pointing the way. For this symbolic act Hörder is awarded the Knight's Cross by the Führer personally, but what should be his greatest moment turns into the opposite, for his comrade who has helped sow the seeds of doubt goes over to the Russians, the winter comes, the advance is halted, and the play ends with the hill being re-taken by the Russian Commander, who in a final, elevated speech heralds the defeat of the Nazis. This Winter Battle has freed the Russians from the Germans, but the hope is that this victory at a place 100 kilometres from Moscow will also mean the ultimate liberation of all peoples of the world, including the Germans themselves.

Becher's Shakespearean play cannot by any stretch of the imagination be described as modern; indeed it seems rather to represent a deliberate shift away from modernism back to traditional forms. Cäcilia Friedrich has even suggested that Becher has gone back to a "classical" model like Schiller's *Wallenstein*. Following this model, no historical panorama is unfolded, and instead the action is concentrated on one particular place at one particular time, and on a strictly limited number of central characters, though the structure is opened up slightly by means of the contrasting scenes from the home front. Little or no background information is given, for example about the roots of National Socialism, and great reliance is placed on "types", particularly as a means of exposing the brutal Nazis. In the same way as the Nazis are presented in caricature, the anti-Nazis tend to be equally predictable. Hörder's comrade who defects has a proletarian background and an anti-Nazi father, while Hörder's father is a middle-class, fanatical hanging judge. Improbably, Hörder's mother turns against her Nazi husband and shoots him. None of these figures are particularly convincing and only the Schweykian cook Oberkofler shows any real life. If there are good qualities in this play they have to be sought elsewhere, and not in the plot or in the characterisation. Most important is the fact that the play does raise effectively all the major problems of the period. Although the action at the front takes place in Russia, this is essentially a play about Germany and the German tragedy and clearly too a play imbued with a love of Germany. Hörder is a seeker after that other, better Germany, which only defeat can help to bring about. Like Zuckmayer's *Des Teufels General* this is a plea for a German defeat to save Germany.

As has been noted, Brecht knew Becher's play and took it into production for the Berliner Ensemble. The part of Johannes Hörder presented special difficulties for the actor, as Brecht's notes indicate.[20] Acting him as an indecisive Hamlet-figure could make him appear negative, on the other hand he was also far from being the "positive hero" normally looked for in the German Democratic Republic. As far as realism in general was concerned, there were further problems, because Becher's elevated language constantly moved away from the normal to the higher plane. However, Brecht himself was not noted for simple socialist realism and, when presenting war on the stage in his own plays, preferred to go back to historical or legendary settings as he did in his

Mutter Courage (1939). *Schweyk im Zweiten Weltkrieg* (1943) is the only one of his major plays in which he moved into the twentieth century and let his play end, like Becher's, in the snowy wastes of the Russian battleground. Indeed there are also great similarities between his crafty Czech Schweyk and Becher's cook Oberkofler, and it is not surprising that Brecht, who tended to base his plays on the Marxist concept of "contradiction", should see Becher's play as a series of fruitful contradictions, with the greatest of them all in Oberkofler himself.

> Die Tragödie ist eine bürgerliche Tragödie. Der Kampf (Hörder gegen Nohl) findet in der Bourgeoisarmee Hitlers statt. Die Oberkoflergruppe überredet Nohl zum Überlaufen. Hier tauchen die echten Widersacher auf, hier erscheint die echte Lösung des Hauptwiderspruchs.
>
> Oberkofler zuerst ein "Original", Einzelgänger, Narr. In Wirklichkeit der Vertreter der breitesten Massen und der Vernunft.[21]

Brecht's final words on the nature of the music which Eisler composed for Becher's play also sum up the contradictory nature of this German tragedy, for Eisler composed music for the retreat of the German army in *Winterschlacht*, which expressed triumph and mourning at one and the same time, "Triumph über die Besiegung Hitlers durch die Sowjetarmee und Trauer über die Leiden der deutschen Soldaten und die Schmach ihres Einfalls in die Sowjetunion."[22]

J. M. RITCHIE

Sheffield

NOTES

[1] Roswitha Flatz, *Krieg im Frieden. Das aktuelle Militärstück auf dem Theater des deutschen Kaiserreichs*, Frankfurt am Main, 1976.

[2] J. M. Ritchie, "Germany – a peace-loving Nation? A Pacifist Tradition in German Literature", *Oxford German Studies*, 11, 1980, 76-102.

[3] German Expressionist war plays are discussed in chapter 4 of J. M. Ritchie, *German Expressionist Drama*, TWAS 421, Boston, 1976.

[4] Pre-Nazi war plays are discussed in detail in Bruno Fischli, *Die Deutschen-Dämmerung. Zur Genealogie des völkisch-faschistischen Dramas und Theaters*, Bonn, 1976.

[5] J. M. Ritchie, "Johst's *Schlageter* and the end of the Weimar Republic", in Alan Bance (ed.), *Weimar Germany*, Edinburgh, 1982, 153-167.

[6] J. M. Ritchie, *German Literature under National Socialism*, Beckenham, Kent, 1983.

[7] J. M. Ritchie, op.cit., p.92.

[8] J. M. Ritchie, op.cit., p.105. The rise and fall of the Thing-play concept is discussed here in this book.

[9] I here rely very heavily on Jennifer Ann Taylor, *The Third Reich in German Drama 1933-1956*, Ph.D. dissertation, University of London, 1978, which I also used extensively for my book *German Literature under National Socialism*. She is the only scholar who has gone to the sources and knows about published and unpublished plays by all writers in exile. All of the following section draws on her work. I have not overloaded the footnotes by referring to her thesis as often as justice would demand. References to rare works by Zech, Lampel, Weinert, Wolf et al. come from her.

[10] Now readily available in *Stücke aus dem Exil*, Henschelverlag Berlin, 1984.

[11] Jennifer Ann Taylor, op.cit., p.129.

[12] Jennifer Ann Taylor, op.cit., p.134-5.

[13] Now readily available in *Stücke aus dem Exil.*

[14] Jennifer Ann Taylor discusses Zuckmayer and Becher in "The Dilemma of Patriotism in German Plays of the Second World War", *New German Studies*, vol.ix, No.3, Autumn 1981, 181-192. More details on Becher in Hans Dieter Schäfer, "Johannes R. Becher im Exil", in *Das gespaltene Bewußtsein. Deutsche Kultur und Lebenswirklichkeit 1933-1945.* Munich, 1981, 96-106. For Becher as dramatist, see also Horst Haase, *J. R. Becher. Leben und Werk*, West Berlin, 1981, 190-208.

[15] Quoted from Jennifer Ann Taylor, dissertation, p.180.

[16] Lampel is discussed by Jennifer Ann Taylor, but more information about his exile plays is also contained in Mennemeier and Trapp, *Deutsche Exildramatik 1933 bis 1950*, Munich, 1980, who in addition to Becher and Brecht, also discuss Bruckner, Hasenclever, Hay, Hochwälder, Horváth, Leonhard, Mostar, Gustav von Wangenheim, Wolf, Wüsten and others.

[17] I have drawn most extensively on the discussion of Becher's play by Cäcilia Friedrich, "Bechers Hamlet-Tragödie: *Winterschlacht*", in Hartung, Höhle and Werner, eds., *Erworbene Tradition*, Berlin, 1970, 119-147.

[18] Quoted from Becher's "Vorbemerkung", Johannes R. Becher, *Gesammelte Werke*, vol.8, Berlin und Weimar, 1971, 597.

[19] Cäcilia Friedrich, op.cit., p.125.

[20] Bertolt Brecht, *Gesammelte Werke 16, Schriften zum Theater 2*, werkausgabe edition suhrkamp, Frankfurt am Main, 1963. "Brief an den Darsteller des jungen Hörder in der *Winterschlacht*", 891-4. "Einige Irrtümer über die Spielweise des Berliner Ensembles", 901-919.

[21] Bertolt Brecht, *Gesammelte Werke 17, Schriften zum Theater 3*, werkausgabe edition suhrkamp, Frankfurt am Main, 1963, p.1291.

[22] Bertolt Brecht, op. cit., p.1292. It is interesting to note that in May 1943, on the occasion of the tenth anniversary of the Burning of the Books in Berlin, a programme under the title "Fires in May" was put on at the Scala Theatre, London. The second half of the programme was a very abridged version of Becher's "Battle for Moscow". Approximately eleven hundred people saw this performance.

THE BRUTALIZATION OF WARFARE ON THE EASTERN FRONT: HISTORY AND FICTION

After 1945, one of the tasks that fell to German writers dealing with the Second World War was the attempt to salvage something positive from the national catastrophe. Neutral topics which seemed to offer the chance of some redemption included, for example, wartime love relationships, and the medical profession. (In the popular novels, like Heinz Konsalik's *Der Arzt von Stalingrad*, 1956, they are often combined.) Both themes embody a human interest that transcends politics or the moral tangles of war. A third area resorted to in this way was, curiously enough, the Army itself, commonly seen as the repository of uprightness and pre–National Socialist values within an evil system.

The Army had at least maintained an air of independence from the National Socialist state in the pre-war years, and in fact, despite humiliations and inroads into its autonomy, its claim to be a last bastion outside the general *Gleichschaltung* had a substantial basis of truth. The military clearly managed to protect its relative political intactness, epitomised by Gottfried Benn's phrase "the army is the aristocratic form of emigration".[1] (Benn joined the medical corps as early as 1935, in order, by his own account, to escape from other importunate commitments within Nazi society that would have been difficult to avoid had he remained a civilian.)

It is obviously comforting for German writers to concentrate on what is left of the reassuringly independent tradition of the Army. Identification with this tradition can, in extreme cases, offer almost complete detachment from implication in the black side of Germany's war, which is safely left to Hitler and his SS henchmen. Ernst Jünger, in the first part of his war diary, *Gärten und Straßen* (1942), takes refuge from the pain the regime obviously caused him by drawing upon his pride of lineage as a member of the Prussian officer caste, whose military achievements run in an unbroken line from 1814 through to 1870, 1914 and 1940. Generally speaking, where war crimes are mentioned, like the execution of partisans in the East, they are attributed to Nazi units, rather than to the Army.

Not that all war novels are completely uncritical of the Army. On the contrary, the critical dissection of the mentality of the Prussian officer caste becomes practically a *topos*, most memorably in Theodor Plievier's *Stalingrad* (1945: this first volume of his trilogy was written during his wartime Moscow exile, and is all the more trenchant for it) or the less incisive *Moskau* (1952),[2] in Heinrich Gerlach's *Die verratene Armee* (1957), or in Alexander Kluge's Stalingrad novel *Schlachtbeschreibung* (1964). But the target of these authors' criticism is a comfortably familiar one. In the context of 1939–45, the concepts of Prussian militarism and the backwardness of the Junker type whose heritage it is to incorporate it, conjure up a degree of integrity – however archaic – which enhances rather than accurately analyses the German Army as seen in operation in the Second World War. Particularly in respect of the Eastern Front, the *topos* seems to have little to do with the reality perceived by recent historians of Operation Barbarossa.

Even as late as 1974, in his novel *Winterspelt*, Alfred Andersch can present without much negative ballast the suggestion that "die Ehrbegriffe von preußischen Offizieren und amerikanischen Südstaatlern [i.e. 'Southern gentlemen'] sich ziemlich ähnlich sind" (Zurich, 1974, p.437). Sadly, however, since the late 1960s historians have been hard at work destroying this myth of a "gentlemanly" German Army. War fiction reflects, as much as it contributes to, a German delusion of the post-war years that the Army was exempt from guilt for the crimes committed in the name of Germany. There may have been theatres or branches of war where "decent" standards applied (the war in the air, for example, or to some extent the war at sea), but for most Germans – because of the enormous concentration of effort in Operation Barbarossa – the Second World War meant primarily the land war in the Russian campaign, and it has now been demonstrated to the hilt that, apart from the SS and SD *Einsatzgruppen* ("task forces" specially assembled and detailed to carry out political liquidations in Eastern Europe), the German Army was involved in the atrocities of the Eastern Front, and that by the later stages of the war in the East the Army and Heydrich's "security police" units together with the SS played more or less indistinguishable roles in executing the policy of annihilation.

There is a striking relationship here between fiction and history which I want to comment on before proceeding. If history as written before the 1970s was incomplete (to say it was fiction would be too extreme), fiction could be accepted as authentic history, in the absence of historical correctives. It was only in 1978 that historiography achieved a real breakthrough to public awareness. Although not the first important historical contribution relevant to this subject, Christian Streit's *Keine Kameraden* established among other things a direct relationship between the treatment of Russian prisoners of war and the systematic mass execution of the Jews: in the process, the Army's complicity in crimes against humanity was for the first time demonstrated beyond a doubt. If the history had been written and assimilated earlier, the fiction could not possibly have taken the form it did. I am not inclined to believe that most writers are simply evasive and immoral when it comes to recording the facts of their national past. And yet it is incontrovertibly true, on all the evidence, that many thousands of German troops had either witnessed or taken part in atrocities, especially during the advance of 1941, when, in a prelude to the terrible "Final Solution", Eastern European Jews were being "combed out" by actions such as the massacre at Babi Yar. It is unlikely that writers could have failed to know or hear of these events. They simply wrote about other aspects of the war. (Even Heinrich Böll, who sets most of his war fiction on the Eastern Front, and in *Wo warst du, Adam?* deals with events in a concentration camp, centres his interest in the debilitating effects of the nihilistic vacuum created for his unwilling soldiers by their army existence, rather than exposing the full moral catastrophe that the war in the East represented.) This suppression of knowledge by writers, or usurping of "memorial rights", as the anthropologist might say, was a part of the general West German displacement of complicity through collective amnesia, which prevailed, in the absence of an objective writing of history, to "create" a national memory.

It is, of course, a circular argument to propose that all would have been different in the world of literature if the history had been written – since the reasons why the history was not written are effectively the same as those which caused the writers' amnesia. Professor Volker Berghahn recently dealt in a lecture with the hagiography – and the demonology – of the changing historical record.[3] He suggests that the early post-war phase was dominated by opinions formed in response to the strong moral condemnation of the German armed forces and the consequent hostile Allied policy towards Germany. The work of historians such as Meinecke, Ritter and Herzfeld emphasised the demonic nature of National Socialist rule and the revolutionary aspect of the Third Reich, the product of the "Socialist" part of the National Socialist programme. It was an approach which diverted attention from critical questions about the role of the German élites in bringing the National Socialist regime into being. Early studies suggested that Germany's military leaders were too naïve and ill-prepared by their background to grasp the dangers of Nazism: that, however, the military eventually did their best to rectify their mistakes by undertaking the belated act of resistance of 20 July 1944, a symbolic rescue of Germany's honour.

Some of the work being done abroad in the early post-war period indicted the fellow-traveller, anti-democratic tendencies of the military, but the hint was not taken by West German historians of the 1950s. Part of the reason lies in the Cold War climate of Korean War days and the new Allied perception of the usefulness of a rearmed Germany. "The outcome of such work [i.e. post-war German history-writing] was the powerful picture of the 'unpolitical' soldier, free from any real taint of Nazism, defending the fatherland – against communism above all."[4] The vehement public reaction to Christian Streit's revelations was evidence enough of how deeply the image of the unpolitical soldier had engraved itself upon the collective public memory, shared, and in part no doubt formed, by those who wrote fiction about the war. This failure of the West German writer – on the whole – to perform his proper function and go against the grain (which is what a free democratic society is supposed to pay writers to do) only indicates, perhaps, that you cannot have instant democracy. Yet, since war novelists otherwise faithfully respected the circumstantial detail of authentic reporting, realistic time-scale and historical accuracy, their omission or evasion of certain aspects of the Second World War amounted to an even more successful hidden persuasion practised upon a willing public.

What I want to do in the following pages is, firstly, to provide an outline of the process by which the military gradually became caught up in the brutalisation of warfare on the Eastern front; and secondly, to look at some of the characteristic ways in which German war literature (including war-diaries and memoirs) dealing with that front responds to what it perceives to be its material; in particular, the ways in which the fiction evades or neutralises the question of the barbarisation of warfare. The results will show, if nothing else, that the much-cited "Bewältigung der Vergangenheit", or coming to terms with the past, in West German literature has certainly not taken place in respect of experience on the Eastern Front.

This is a good point at which to make a progress report on developments in the history of the subject. Christian Streit's book was preceded, a decade earlier, by a pioneering study called *Das Heer und Hitler* (1969), by Klaus-Jürgen Müller, on the undermining of the Army's conscience and the limiting of its moral room to manœuvre between 1933 and 1940 by the subjugation of the upper echelons of the military to National Socialist authority (symptomatic of which is the obligation to swear the traditional oath of loyalty to Hitler personally). Manfred Messerschmidt's *Die Wehrmacht im NS-Staat* (1969) detailed the efforts of the OKW and OKH (Supreme Command of the Armed Forces and Army High Command) to indoctrinate the Army in the Nazi *Weltanschauung*. Following Streit, there appeared another monumental work of investigation, *Die Truppe des Weltanschauungskrieges* (1981), by Helmut Krausnick and Hans-Heinrich Wilhelm. It takes us through from the annexation of Austria to the fulfilment of the "Final Solution", and studies the interinvolvement of the *Einsatzgruppen*, sent into Russia to exterminate "Jewish Bolshevism", and the regular armed forces. The achievement of all these revisionist historians has been crowned quite recently by the long-awaited publication of what almost amounts to the official West German history of the Second World War, *Das Deutsche Reich und der zweite Weltkrieg*, published by the Militärgeschichtliches Forschungsamt in Freiburg. Volume Four (1983) is the one dealing with the Eastern campaign, *Der Angriff auf die Sovjetunion*. Other works are in progress,[5] and there is plenty of scope for further research. I merely want to give a broad outline of some of the stages in the process revealed by all this new "history from below", and I do not intend to take the story back any further than the Polish campaign which opened the war.

In fact, what happened in Poland between the Army and the executive arms of the National Socialist state, SS and "security" forces, effectively settled for the duration of the war the Army's abject role in relation to the extermination policy in the East. Alongside the Army there operated in Poland a parallel, politically trusty civilian authority, and SD *Einsatzgruppen* were already being deployed. Following close behind the combat troops, they were nominally subject to Army authority, but in practice answerable only to the *Reichsführer* SS. This division of command was fatal from the beginning. Much as it may have disliked the "unmilitary" (and murderous) activities of the "security forces", the Army found its authority and integrity suffering the death of a thousand cuts. Army officers did their best to control the behaviour of the German forces towards the civilian population, but in an attempt to "keep its hands clean", the Army allowed the civilian command in the occupied territory to do the dirty work. The effect was, however, drastically to curtail the Army's impact when it came to further protests about the SS.[6] The military progressively forfeited the right to intervene. There was eventually intense friction between the SS and "policing" forces and the Army, but the latter was apparently helpless, and its complaints were in any case often couched in *realpolitisch* terms, and not humane ones (op. cit., pp. 438, 448).

When the Russian campaign opened in the summer of 1941, the pattern had already been set. Having "sold the pass" over Poland, the Army found that any protests about SS and SD brutality in Russia were mere formalities. There were, in any case, several new factors in the Soviet operation which led to extreme brutalization of the mode of warfare there. One was the attitude of the German generals. They tended to view the USSR as an "Asiatic" state, and to regard Germany as a defender of European culture and a bulwark of the white races stemming the Asian tide. From the start, some of the conditions which made warfare more or less humane in other theatres of the Second World War were missing in Russia. You were more likely to encounter *jus in bello* when the battle was between antagonists of similar race, culture and ethical persuasion, not inflamed by negative preconceptions or a propaganda of hatred, led by officers trained in a classic European manner, and fighting in more or less recognised traditional ways. Notions of chivalry and humanity survived up to a point in land operations on the Western Front in both World Wars.[7] However, the German Army was prepared before Operation Barbarossa to accept that war in Russia could not be conducted according to normal military and legal conventions of warfare. They also expected a successful and rapidly-concluded *Blitzkreig*, justifying a short-term suspension of legality. National Socialist ideology held that the war in the East was to be a *Vernichtungskampf*, an extermination campaign against "Jewish Bolshevism" (which the officer caste had been conditioned by propaganda ever since 1918 to hold responsible for the destruction of the *Kaiserreich* at the end of the First World War). The message was reinforced by Hitler personally in his address to the leading military of 30 March 1941, warning the Army that, in the coming operations, "the leaders must require of themselves the sacrifice of overcoming their scruples".[8] The Army and SS had arrived at what appeared to be a reasonable division of labour for the forthcoming campaign. In March 1941 SD chief Reinhard Heydrich and Generalquartiermeister Generalmajor Wagner had hammered out an agreement by which the only power the Army retained over the *Einsatzgruppen* was that of keeping them out of the immediate front line combat area. The Army agreed to leave the "political" questions to the "security" arm, and to bury the disputes that had arisen over the governing of occupied Poland. The military were left in no doubt about the fate of the Jews in occupied Soviet territory. The *Einsatzgruppen* leaders orally received orders from Heydrich, on the command of Hitler, to execute all Communists, Jews and other "radical" elements (op. cit., p.426). The only lingering disagreement between Army and SS/SD was over the question of *Militärgerichtsbarkeit* – to what extent martial law should prevail. What it amounted to was whether the Army should retain the right to go through the formality of a court martial when soldiers took unilateral action against "Träger des jüdisch-bolschevistischen Systems". The verdict would always be one of not guilty, anyway, since the universal plea of "Erbitterung" of German personnel against the Bolsheviks was regarded as complete exoneration of any "crime" against civilians. As usual, the Army's main concern was with maintaining the discipline of the troops. The only concession from the SS/SD side was that the Army command could order courts martial, but only (even in cases of offences against military regulations) if there was a threat of the *complete* breakdown of Army discipline, "Verwilderung der Truppe" (op. cit., p.431). This was incorporated in the notorious *Führererlaß* of 13 May 1941, which also offended against the international laws of warfare by requiring that *Freischärler* (*francs-tireurs* or irregular troops) should be shot out of hand by the Army. "Collective measures" (that is, mass reprisals) must be taken by the troops against villages or settlements used as a base for "covert and malicious" attacks upon army personnel. With Operation Barbarossa, the Army had in every sense gone far beyond Poland. It was now hopelessly implicated in National Socialist crimes.

The *Kommissarbefehl* which followed on 6 June 1941 commanded army officers to shoot any captured Soviet Army commissars (political indoctrination officers, but with the status of military personnel in uniform). These were by definition guilty of the usual "Jewish-Bolshevist" crimes: against whom, or when, need not be specified – presumably because, by ideological agreement between the Army and the National-Socialist apparatus, these crimes were "self-evident". The *Kommissarbefehl*, though Führer-inspired, does not seem to have been an order from Hitler, but, significantly, to have originated within the Army command itself (op. cit., pp.436-438).[9] Controversy about war crimes committed by the Army in Russia has centred much more on the *Kommissarbefehl* than on the Führer's order limiting military judicial power. The latter was to have more sinister and far-reaching consequences, but the attention given to the shooting of commissars was due to the fact that the illegality was more obvious: men were shot for what they were, and not for what they (allegedly) did. All ex-combatants since the war have (whether in war crime trials or in their memoirs) denied shooting commissars. Although the facts are hard to come by, the consensus is that it would be a mistake to assume that only a few cases occurred, or that most troops found ways to avoid carrying out the order.[10] The story is a mixed one, with some officers showing clemency, but mainly there is a display of zeal on the part of the Army.[11] The *Kommissarbefehl* was eventually rescinded because it was counter-productive for the war-effort: it led to a desperate resistance on the part of political cadres, and terrorist measures by them in retaliation against the Germans. It is noticeable that the first protests against the *Kommissarbefehl* by the Army only occurred in autumn 1941, when the initial German advance had lost its momentum and the Red Army's resistance had become stiffer. But it was not until the spring of 1942 that the directive was cancelled.

The partisan war was a particularly vicious aspect of the campaign in the East (if any aspect deserves singling out for this "honour"). Since the Franco-Prussian war of 1870, the German military with their traditional professional ethos had always had a particularly intense dislike of irregulars, guerillas, *francs-tireurs*, the Maquis.[12] If caught, they were summarily shot.

The massacre of Jews in the wake of the advancing troops was the biggest stain on the honour of the German Army, not least because such actions were not connected even by the merest thread to the conduct of war or the security of the armed forces (though the latter was often cited as a flimsy pretext), and because – at least according to Krausnick and Wilhelm – the only chance to prevent the liquidation programme of the *Einsatzgruppen*, which merged into the "Final Solution", lay with the relatively autonomous and potentially still powerful German Army. At all the points where the Army could have intervened, it missed the opportunity. That it did not do so was largely due, it is now clear, to a degree of conformity and affinity between the views of the highest-ranking officers and the National Socialist ideology. Indicative of the Army's enthusiasm for harsh measures against Jews is the zeal shown by General Karl-Heinrich von Stülpnagel in going far beyond the call of duty, and any agreement with Heydrich, by personally suggesting reprisals against Jewish members of Comsomols (Krausnick/Wilhelm, op. cit., p.219). (Von Stülpnagel was later to play a prominent part in the 20 July 1944 conspiracy to assassinate Hitler: his case shows the possibility of being anti-Hitler but *also* anti-Bolshevik and anti-semitic.) German troops were subject to constant indoctrination. "Men and officers alike spoke in terms borrowed from Hitler's, Goebbels' and Rosenberg's rhetoric."[13] (This linguistic pollution is certainly not apparent in the war fiction.) Orders went out to the troops, from the highest to the lowest levels of command, couched in terms that could have emanated unaltered from the SS. Many of the young officers, far from being members of the old Prussian officer caste (not that *that* proved much of a check!), were products of National Socialist schooling. The many excesses by Army personnel themselves must have been connected with the ideological incitement to which they were subject. Even the Nazi commander of the 6th Army, Generalfeldmarschall von Reichenau, whose communiqués to the troops had done so much to urge them to crimes against the "Jewish Bolsheviks", was obliged to prohibit soldiers from volunteering in their off-duty hours to help the SD to carry out executions, from attending as witnesses of such measures and taking photographs of them.[14] The fact that the General's own language was so rabidly provocative probably had something to do with his failure (to judge by the frequency with which such orders had to be repeated) to curb the troops' antisemitic zeal. Official support was equally forthcoming from the Army to the *Einsatzgruppen*. A pioneer unit was placed at the service of *Sonderkommando* 4a to blow up the sides of the ravine at Babi Yar (Kiev), to bury the dead – and the evidence. In Zhitomir the Army lent transport for the execution of 3,145 Jews. The German Army as a whole could not conceivably have been unaware of operations on such a scale.[15] Indeed, there are on record many instances of participation by the Army in the extermination plan (Krausnick/Wilhelm, op. cit., p.237). As the partisan threat became ever more real, so the Army relied increasingly on the SD/SS forces, with their good intelligence network, to deal with the problem (op. cit., p.243), and this too increased the integration of the two branches. There *was* revulsion at the extermination policy, and this is on record, too: but the frequency of its occurrence and its intensity can easily be exaggerated (op. cit., p.256). There was no consensus in the officer corps to produce a condemnation of brutalisation, and, since Poland, no likelihood of support from the highest echelons if there *had* been purposeful resistance.

I have not yet mentioned the appalling treatment of Russian prisoners of war, more than half of whom died in German captivity (one in ten was shot by the *Einsatzgruppen*). The root cause of the disaster lay in a preconceived plan on the part of the Berlin *Ostministerium* – popularly known at the time as the "Chaostministerium" – to strip the USSR of food in order to supplement the diet of Germans in the Reich; a plan adhered to even after it became clear that there was not enough food in Russia to feed the Army, let alone the home population in Germany – not to speak, of course, of the Russian people or, still less again, the Russian prisoners of war. Here the Army once more played its part. Thousands of prisoners were shot while on the move between camps, because they were physically incapable of continuing the march. (This particular atrocity *is* mentioned in Plievier's volume *Stalingrad*; see p.106 below.)

In the end, not even a formal distinction between Army units and *Einsatzgruppen* meant anything at all. Does it matter now? Should we simply consign these atrocities to the dustbin of history as an inevitable product of total war? I would suggest that it does matter in Germany that the true history of the Eastern campaign should be known and acknowledged. In the words of Ralph Giordano's novel *Die Bertinis* (1982), the denial is almost worse than the deed: "fast noch schlimmer als die Tat ist ihre Leugnung." The failure of denazification, and the presence of moral "unfinished business", has played its part in forming some of the less attractive aspects of the *Bundesrepublik*. That the bulk of the German population for decades after the war managed to maintain an astonishing blindness to the true state of affairs is well attested by opinion polls in West Germany and demonstrated by the impact of the TV series *Holocaust* at the end of the seventies.

In fiction as in reality, the tendency in the *Bundesrepublik* has been to separate the fighting aspect of the Second World War from its political context. One of the most far-reaching results of the revisionist history that has sought to investigate the political role of the fighting forces is the establishing of a link between the military and the Final Solution. The Army's weakness in resisting political interference led to its gradual incrimination in the evolution of the Holocaust.[16] The annihilation policy was not born complete;[17] it was developed piecemeal, by a process of trial and error, in which the Army played a crucial role. For its concrete realisation

> required several intermediary stages, including extending the activities of the *Einsatzgruppen*, trying out mass annihilation on the Soviet prisoners of war [gas lorries were first introduced for this purpose] and a deadening of moral reaction on the part of the Army to the basic elements of Hitler's "Ostraum" policy, as a token of ideological agreement.[18]

There is a direct link (shown by Christian Streit) between the question of prisoners of war and the systematic mass liquidation of the Jews.

If we now turn to the *fiction* of the Eastern Front, we find first of all that "the catastrophe in the East" is widely understood, not as the fate of Jews or Russians, but as the catastrophe of the German defeat at Stalingrad and the long, bitter retreat across Eastern Europe to Germany. The events of the early, fast-moving parts of the campaign – the would-be *Blitzkrieg* of 1941 – tend not to be treated by the novelists. Apart from sketchy references, most of the aspects of the eastern campaign mentioned in the preceding pages are omitted: the persecution of the Jews, the horrors of the German occupation policy in the USSR, the complicity of the German generals in war crimes, and the all-pervading indoctrination of the troops by National Socialist ideology.[19] Such a silence cannot be considered as neutral, of course: the absence of adequate questioning or condemnation of German policy in the East is itself a political position.[20] There are exceptions that prove the rule, but they are very incomplete ones, such as Jochen Klepper's war-diary, *Überwindung* (1958), in which he notes the effectiveness of anti-semitic propaganda among the troops, but scarcely mentions German atrocities, while constantly referring to Rumanian pogroms against the Jews. For the most part, National Socialist influence is very little in evidence in day-to-day life as lived in the war novels or diaries: Nazis, where they appear at all, tend to be stereotyped, caricatured, or clearly exceptional pathological cases, emphasising by contrast the essential sanity of ordinary, decent soldiers. German guilt is indeed a frequent subject for discussion, but usually guilt in the abstract, as in Wolfgang Borchert's story "Die lange lange Straße lang", where the white-coated marionette figure of the inventor of a sinister powder (suggestive of Zyklon B) is owned and manipulated by a barrel-organist. The first-person narrator destroys the puppet, but the real enemy, the manipulating barrel-organist, is out of reach, faceless and inaccessible: "Nein, ich schlag ihn nicht, denn ich kann sein Gesicht das fürchterliche Gesicht nicht finden" (*Draußen vor der Tür und ausgewählte*

Erzählungen, Hamburg, 1956, p.90). It is a metaphor that captures the generalized and undirected rage of early post-war writing. In other writers, less trenchant and original than Borchert, guilt is dissipated, attaching itself to the human race in general. The popular writer Johannes Mario Simmel provides a good example of this approach. His influence, to judge by sheer sales figures (almost all of his novels had reached an edition of 500,000 by 1975), must be enormous.[21] However, we find in his writing nothing approaching a social-historical account of war or National Socialism, though he passes for a leftish writer "with his heart in the right place" and without political jargon. As Herbert Zand puts it in his novel *Letzte Ausfahrt* (1953): "who was guilty, who was innocent? There were only points on a sliding scale." This kind of confession of "guilt" is, in fact, as with Simmel, a subtle method of exculpation.

Even where German crimes in Russia are listed, as they are by a writer who is also by no means on the right politically, Theodor Plievier in *Moskau* (Munich, 1975, p.261), they do not include the liquidation of the Jews. Weighing up what has occurred since the invasion of the USSR to nullify any suggestion that the Germans are liberators (!) or crusaders against Stalinist terror, the hero Vilshofen throws into the scales against the Reich a discarded non-aggression pact, the *Kommissarerlaß* (*sic*), SD (be it noted) destruction of villages, and the failure to dissolve the collective farms. In the (chronologically) second volume of the same author's trilogy, *Stalingrad* (Munich, 1975), he once again foregrounds German atrocities, but this time conveys a little of the true scale of events. The young soldier, Matthias Gimpf, has become obsessed and deranged by his memory of the massacre of thirteen thousand Russian men, women and children on the march between prison-camps. (Vast though it seems – Vilshofen's reaction implies that it is an unheard-of figure – the number is dwarfed, nonetheless, by the figures for Jews shot in a "normal" month's work by the *Einsatzgruppen*.) The horror of German guilt is somewhat mitigated by the fact that Gimpf was sent to a punishment battalion for refusing to participate in the massacres (carried out by regular troops). What is more, he never recovers from his delirium, and his death suggests at least a representative expiation of German guilt. Once again, crimes against Jews are not mentioned (pp.391-392).

There are a number of ways in which the central questions of the Eastern campaign are deflected in war literature. Common to most war books (but particularly useful when dealing with the war in the East) is the limitation of perspective to that of the small man, a "corporal's point of view" which permits a very limited grasp of the war as a whole, concentrates on the individual, and rules out extensive discussion of German policy or war aims. Heinrich Gerlach formulates the point for us: "Wenige nur sahen über den engen Rahmen ihrer eigenen Division hinaus" (*Die verratene Armee*, 1957: Munich, 1978, p.173). The responsibilities of the typical hero are too narrow to permit him to incur much personal guilt, and his minor role very easily allows him to appear in his own eyes a passive victim of circumstance. By concentrating mainly on the period of defeat and retreat that begins with Stalingrad, many authors justify a strong sense of self-pity on the part of the German soldier, like the one in Plievier's *Moskau* who complains bitterly at having to surrender hard-won territorial gains back to the enemy. His protest is innocent of political overtones, but must have an ironical ring for anyone who knows the history of the German Army in Russia: "Mein Gott, was haben wir verbrochen, daß uns das angetan werden muß?" (p.373). It is common for the good and conscientious soldier to claim ignorance, or to assign all guilt for brutal acts to the Nazis, as the paragon Oberst Luschke does towards the end of the second volume of Hans Helmut Kirst's best-selling trilogy *08/15*, a volume quaintly entitled *Die seltsamen Kriegserlebnisse des Gefreiten Asch* (Munich, 1954/55, p.411). (Here Nazi atrocities are mentioned – though previously not hinted at in the book, and certainly never *shown*, apart from one token shooting of partisans by military police in the second volume, p.171.) Kirst epitomizes a not untypical displacement of focus from the fateful events in which the Army is embroiled, to the little man's struggle with the Army hierarchy (rather than with his conscience). This theme is an international one, and probably accounts – together with his picaresque form and light-hearted style – for Kirst's great success in translation.

The kind of life lived by the ordinary soldier on active service is a good alibi (in terms of faithfulness to reality, mimesis) for the writer's own limitation of his perspective, for, as Ernest Hemingway once said, learning to suspend his imagination and live completely in the very second of the present moment with no before and no after is the greatest gift a soldier can acquire. In the case of writers reporting on the Eastern campaign, it is something of a gift for them too; but Hemingway also said that it is the opposite of all those gifts a writer should have.

The theme of betrayal of German troops (by their leaders, by the regime) is almost ubiquitously present, sometimes even in the titles of novels, such as Gerlach's *Die verratene Armee*, or Michael Horbach's *Die verratenen Söhne* (1957). "'Mensch, Mensch', stöhnt er, [the speaker, in *Die verratene Armee*, is a professional soldier with the rank of Captain] 'ich bin doch Soldat! Zwanzig Jahre bin ich Soldat... oder bin ich ein Räuberhauptman? – Himmel, wie haben sie uns zur Sau gemacht –'" (p.279). Gerd Gaiser's gallant little band of fighter-pilots (who remain gallant in the narrator's eyes even though on his own showing they bear the shame of complicity in the brutality of the Eastern campaign) in *Die sterbende Jagd* "waren getäuscht worden", but continue fighting desperately to the last, for "sie wollten selber nicht wieder täuschen" (1953: Frankfurt a.M, 1957, p.167).[22] So deep does this notion of the misuse of the German soldier's idealism run, even today, that a powerful dissident like *Bundeswehr* General Gert Bastian, associated very prominently with the radical Green Party in West Germany, gives a standard account of the unfortunate and exploited role of the *Wehrmacht* under Hitler. His words gain an unconscious irony from the context in which they appear, the foreword to a book by Heinz Artzt dealing precisely with the connexion between the army leadership and crimes in the East.[23] There cannot be a sense of betrayal, however, without an initial assumption that there is something to be gained in the first place, something of which it is possible to be cheated.[24] The "something", as offered by Hitler and accepted, was surely more than simply the chance to defend Germany against her enemies (as Gert Bastian believes the troops to have understood their role at the beginning of the war). At the very least there was no mistaking Hitler's policy of aggressive expansion to the East.

Wish-fulfilment dictates that brutality in the East is laid at the door of non-*Wehrmacht* organizations, as for example in Peter Bamm's *Die unsichtbare Flagge* (1952), where the Nazis, referred to as "die Anderen", infect and ruin the "clean" military ("die anderen haben uns hineingelegt", Munich, 1963, p.154), or in Plievier's *Moskau*, where Vilshofen, apparently close to death, is still reflecting on the way that the SS and SD have ruined the occupation policy in Russia, and suggests that fighting and shooting have been known to break out between SS and *Wehrmacht*, precisely over the issue of brutal methods: "die erschütternde SD- und SS- und Generalgouverneurspraxis liegt offen vor aller Augen. In Schlägereien, in Schießereien zwischen SS und Wehrmacht fand das Dilemma einen Ausdruck, aber keine Lösung" (p.396). I have come across no references to such conflicts in historical writing; which is not to say that something of the sort may not have taken place somewhere. The wish--fulfilment process is naturally complemented by a favourable, or at least tolerant, treatment of the generals and the Prussian officer caste to which they belong. They generally retain an aura of dignity, even of "the great man", despite defeat. Heinrich Böll is unusual in cutting his representative general – old, thin, scrawny, hopeless and Schnapps-sodden – down to size (*Wo warst du, Adam?*, 1951: Munich, 1976, p.7). Hans Helmut Kirst's generals are genial anti-Nazis, rejoicing in such popular nicknames as "Knollengesicht". In *Moskau*, Plievier suggests that it is only the generals who stand between Hitler and the horrific realisation of his plans for the Russian cities (p.310). On another occasion, in *Stalingrad*, the generals are allowed to plead a painful dilemma, caught between their ethics and their duty (p.307).[25] Alexander Kluge in his Stalingrad novel *Schlachtbeschreibung* asserts that the majority of the officer corps did not accept the Russian war as *their* war, but undertook it as a compromise which it was necessary to make in order to preserve intact their beloved Army tradition (1964: Munich, 1979, p.169). Much is made in a number of novels of the traditional and continuing power of the time-honoured oath of allegiance sworn by the military to the head of state, an elevated version of the defence plea of "superior orders" argued so often at Nuremberg. The classic statement is that of a general in *Die verratene Armee*, driven to a frenzy of unaccustomed soul-searching over the question of his allegiance to a law-breaker who also happens to be his head of state: "Dieser Eid galt. Daß er einem Verbrecher geschworen war, war schlimm. Aber es änderte nichts. Der Soldat durfte nicht fragen, er hatte zu gehorchen" (p.262). The general's attempts to convince himself of the truth of his own assertion fail, for "hier in Stalingrad verlor die Wehrmacht Hitlers die Maske, die ihr Gesicht verhüllt hatte. Was dahinter sichtbar wurde, war grauenhaft" (p.263). It is remarkable that in Gerlach's book – as in others – it takes Stalingrad to reveal the oath for what it is (the password to a criminal conspiracy). The initial crimes of the Russian campaign were apparently not sufficient. Sometimes Stalingrad is not sufficient, either. In Curt Hohoff's *Woina, Woina* (1951), the suggestion of a young officer cadet, made at the time of the last phase of Stalingrad, that he and his officer comrades should empty their pistols at Hitler, who is due to address them, is greeted by a reflex reaction: "War das erlaubt? War das Mord? Wo blieb unser Eid?... Daß über diese Dinge Unklarheit herrschte, war unsere Schwäche, war die Krise" (Düsseldorf/Köln, 1951, p.255).

Many more examples could be given of this particular line of defence or exoneration of the officer corps. For present purposes, the salient point is that the topic of Prussian obedience (itself a venerable *topos* in German literature) provides one of the clearest contrasts between the fiction and what the historians of the Eastern Front have to tell us. Compare, for example, Krausnick's and Wilhelm's *Die Truppe des Weltanschauungskrieges*, where we are informed that the eventual breakdown (where atrocities were concerned) of the formal distinction between Army units and *Einsatzgruppen* resulted

> teils aus Schwäche und Willfährigkeit der obersten Führung des Heeres, teils aus wachsender Übereinstimmung einer wachsenden Zahl von Offizieren und Soldaten mit Ideologie und außenpolitischer Zielsetzung der nationalsozialistischen Machthaber, teils wohl auch aus (berechtigter) Furcht vor den Folgen eines offenen Aufbegehrens, *doch sicherlich am wenigsten aus einem verabsolutierten soldatischen Gehorsam heraus...* (p.278, my italics).

A related discrepancy lies in Plievier's conviction, shared by other writers, that until Christmas 1941 (when the old guard of "traditional" generals, such as Guderian, Hoepner, von Brauchitsch, von Leeb, Hoth etc., was replaced, it is suggested, by young, loyal National Socialist commanders) the generals provided some bulwark against Hitler's worst intentions:

> ...Kommandeure, die ihre militärische Einsicht über den Parteibefehl stellten, die nicht in einer befohlenen Weltanschauung, sondern im eigenen Gewissen die höchste entscheidende Instanz erblickten, die internationale Abmachungen respektiert haben wollten und auch aus diesem Kriege mit "weißer Weste" herauszukommen trachteten. (*Moskau*, p.392)

Such a large-scale shakeout of commanders did indeed occur, but it did not mark the end of the "weiße Weste". The Army's hands had long ceased to be clean, and Plievier's picture is a hopelessly idealized one. It is hopelessly idealized *even without* the new evidence provided by the historians, for complicity between the Army and the National Socialist state was already present by virtue of the very fact of waging aggressive war on behalf of that state and throwing open conquered territories to the mercies of the Nazis.

Complicity cannot, therefore, be overlooked, even if we cared to believe assertions like those of a character in *Die verratene Armee*, who first of all claims that "we don't shoot prisoners", and then recalling as an afterthought the *Kommissarerlaß* of 1941, shrugs it off with "das ist schon lange her, und er wurde ja auch kaum befolgt" (p.105). Where the fiction attempts to find neutral territory by concentrating purely on combat, and especially on individual feats of arms (as in Gaiser's *Die sterbende Jagd*), it still indicts its heroes, for under an illegal regime to be a good soldier is to be a good accomplice to crime. Yet "good" (brave, loyal, tough, selfless, unassuming) soldiers abound in the fiction – in an apparent moral and political vacuum. The point is made very explicitly in Plievier's *Stalingrad*, the volume which was written (as already noted) during his Moscow exile, and contains a much sharper critique of the Army's position in the East than the later volumes, written back in Cold War Germany. The narrator lists GFP (Geheime Feldpolizei) and SD crimes against the civilian population, then tells us that his "good" soldier, Hauptmann Tomas, "wußte nicht einmal Genaues von 'GFP'- und 'SD'-Aktionen und wollte nichts davon wissen". He struggles against getting to know about these things, but to no avail, for the narrator goes on: "als ob die Front und die Etappenorganisationen, als ob das Niederschlagen des Opfers und das Ausweiden nicht Erscheinungen desselben Verfahrens wären!" (p.181). (Even *Stalingrad*, however, as we see from this quotation, does not on the whole implicate the Army *directly* in war crimes, but only in this secondary – though still serious – way.)

If it serves the purpose of German writers to enhance the integrity and status of the old Prussian officer corps or the Army, or the good soldier, another temptation for the apologist for German behaviour is to stress the atrocities committed by the other combatant nations. Particularly in the Eastern theatre, the argument is often advanced that warfare in that vast and unfathomable landmass was bound to revert to savagery, almost as a result of some law of nature which affects both "Deutsche und Russen als Opfer und Objekte der geheimnisvollen Natur dieses rätselhaften Landes" – to quote a typical "restorationist" commentator of the 1950s, writing in the military journal *Wehrkunde*. Both sides were equally guilty of cruelty, the author declares: "Das bestimmende Erlebnis war der Krieg im Osten, der sich nicht zuletzt aus der animalischen Angst der Gegner voreinander an Härte und Brutalität ständig steigerte."[26] Implicit in much war writing (even if only unconsciously) is the attempt to excuse the Germans' own crimes in terms of those committed against them and against third parties. The Russians maltreated German prisoners of war (though on the whole they treated them better than the Germans treated their Russian captives), and the NKVD conducted mass shootings of political prisoners. But, as the historian of *Das Deutsche Reich und der zweite Weltkrieg* remarks: "Ein Grund zur Rechtfertigung und Aufrechnung liegt darin nicht" (p. 1084). It will not do to explain German crimes as a mere reaction to Soviet atrocities. It was the invading and occupying power which determined the low price of human life. In doing so, it played into Stalin's hands, and an escalation of brutality thereafter became inevitable.

Early post-war historians and writers of fiction tended to agree on another exculpatory interpretation of events: the "Hitler-centric" view, which unconsciously perpetuates National Socialist mythology about the omnipotence of the Führer. As much as possible was blamed on the baleful demagogue. To attribute so much to any one figure is to elevate him to superhuman and demonic proportions. Such demonizations occur in the fiction, and tend to remove events beyond the grasp or the responsibility of ordinary humans. In the last, apocalyptic days in the *Führerbunker*, the character representing Albert Speer in Plievier's *Berlin* encounters even now the "Faszination der stumpfen, graublauen Augen, die Wirtschaftsführer zu Hasardeuren, ärztliche Helfer zu Mördern, Wissenschaftler zu Afterwissenschaftlern, einen Generalstab zu einem Konsortium von Affen, ein ganzes Volk in eine verschworene Gemeinschaft von Amokläufern verwandelt hatte" (p. 163). The theme is related to the very common one of the war as a natural catastrophe, like, for example, the disaster of Pompeii, a parallel drawn by both Plievier ("das pompejanische Schicksal des Begrabenwerdens", *Berlin*, p. 156) and Hans Erich Nossack (in the story "Dorothea", on the destruction of Hamburg, included in the volume *Interview mit dem Tode*, 1948).

"Objectively guilty" (as the Marxists say) of an evasion of the facts is the war novel that is a product of educated, lofty philosophical reflection, sometimes existentialist in nature, like Herbert Zand's *Letzte Ausfahrt* (1953), where the "Kessel", the pocket in which the hero finds himself trapped, is adopted as an existential metaphor. Jünger's war-diaries, products of rarefied contemplation, ignore the guilt and complicity around him, and in effect involuntarily lend support to the latter by doing so. Horst Lange's story of the Eastern Front, *Die Leuchtkugeln*, written in 1943, bears the mark of a certain kind of controlled, classical writing developed before the war under the National Socialist regime, and conveys little of the reality of the squalid war in the East. Peter Bamm's *Die unsichtbare Flagge* is pretentiously shot through with classical references, as is Gaiser's *Die sterbende Jagd*, Herbert Zand's *Letzte Ausfahrt*, or Hugo Hartung's novel on the fall of Breslau, *Der Himmel war unten* (1951), which begins with the apostrophe "Singe mir, Muse", and compares his subject (even if ironically) with the fall of Troy. The very style of most of these books precludes dealing with the degrading subject-matter of the German-Soviet war.

At the other extreme is the trivial war novel, which in its lowest manifestation is close to the popular *Landserhefte* publications, cheap magazines that carry formulaic war stories and in many ways clearly perpetuate certain war-time assumptions. The enemy is a stereotype – primitive Asiatic Russian, furtive Maquis. The typical commanding officer is a hard but caring father-figure to his troops. *Härte* is a highly-esteemed quality, but is more frequently invoked than shown. Trivial literature is even less likely to mention the sinister aspects of the German venture into Russia than are the serious books. Popular war novels which exist at a slightly higher level, such as Kirst's trilogy, often include a token anti-militarist message or indictment of Germany's "war-guilt", but in a way that makes the would-be serious message very obviously tacked on and misrelated to the fiction, so that the effect is a cheapening one (see p.288 of the third volume of Kirst's trilogy).

Finally, the historical perspective is a common device for shifting attention away from the particulars of the Eastern Front "here and now": it is especially prevalent in the more panoramic treatments of the war, such as Kluge's and Plievier's. The stress is on the recurrent patterns of history – Napoleon's invasion of Russia being an obvious point of reference – and on the impossibility of tracing the first causes of war (and therefore, for that matter, of war crimes), lost as they are in the mists of time. A clear example of this "historical deflection" is found in Hohoff's *Woina Woina*, a particularly useful illustration to end on because the device includes a rare acknowledgment of the liquidation of the Jews as the Army advanced, but is wrapped in a package of exonerating motifs exemplifying the evasions I have been touching upon in this chapter. The atrocities of the pogrom against the Jews in the Galician border-town of Brody are known to the troops, but *not their full extent*; they recall the long *history* of the persecution of eastern European Jews, it being therefore no novelty; such brutal actions are stupid, because *damaging to the German war-effort* (the latter being the one common form of protest by the Army recorded in historical sources); and finally, *Wehrmacht* soldiers had *nothing to do with them* (p.228 ff).[27]

German novels about the Second World War are very rarely militaristic in nature; indeed, whatever the political colour of their authors, to a man they warn against the horrors of war and a renewal of war. Yet the effectiveness of the message must be in doubt when we consider how the emphasis of the warning is shifted from the sufferings, partly at *Wehrmacht* hands, of the victims of German aggression – above all the Jews, but also the more frequently mentioned partisans and the ordinary Russian population – to the miseries of the defeated Germans, thus feeding the Germans' post-war conception of themselves as the betrayed and exploited victims of a conspiracy imposed upon them by a demonic tyrant. History written by a new generation of German historians is now saying otherwise.[28]

A. F. BANCE

Southampton

NOTES

[1]Gottfried Benn, *Doppelleben, Gesammelte Werke in vier Bänden*, Band 4, hrsg. Dieter Wellershof, Wiesbaden, 1961, p.94.

[2]This volume (*Moskau*) is the one that covers the period in which the *Einsatzgruppen*, in increasing co-operation with the Army, were pursuing their liquidation policy. If Plievier had written *this* part of his trilogy first, while still in Soviet exile, it is hard to imagine that he would not have been more explicit about the Army's part in war crimes, as was the case with the leading German writer in Soviet exile, J. R. Becher (see Professor Ritchie's comments on *Winterschlacht*, p.94 above, and Becher's *Schlacht um Moskau, Gesammelte Werke*, Band 8, Berlin & Weimar, 1971, pp.469 and 470). East German writers, many of them returned exiles, have taken a different approach to the moral problems of the Hitler period, sometimes going very far in the direction required by the official Soviet line (an approach that does not encourage treatment of the fate of the Jews, and occasionally results in a hopeless sanitizing of the Soviet record). There is no space to develop the subject here, but see my chapter "Germany" in *The Second World War in Fiction*, ed. H. Klein with J. Flower and E. Homberger, London, 1984.

[3]The lecture (delivered at the 1983 Regional Conference of the German History Society, which took the theme of "The Historiography of the Third Reich") does not exist in published form, but Professor Berghahn's arguments are summarised by John Hiden in *German History: The Journal of the German History Society*, No. 1, Autumn 1984, p.60-62.

[4]John Hiden, op. cit., p.61.

[5]Professor Volker Berghahn (private correspondence) informs me that another volume, on the political context of Operation Barbarossa, is being produced at the Militärgeschichtliches Forschungsamt, and a book on the Eastern Front by the German Historical Institute in London. Mr Omer Bartov of St Antony's College, Oxford has corresponded with me about his study of the record of some combat divisions, which seeks to achieve a clearer understanding of the various influences and pressures brought to bear upon the individual soldier during the Soviet campaign. There is scope especially for research into the role and attitudes of subaltern officers and lower ranks.

[6]See Klaus-Jürgen Müller, *Das Heer und Hitler: Armee und nationalsozialistisches Regime 1933-1940*, Stuttgart, 1969, p.426, n.19, and p.429.

[7]See Geoffrey Best, *Humanity in Warfare*, Ch.IV, "The Trials of Total War", London, 1980, pp.217-218.

[8]*Das Deutsche Reich und der zweite Weltkrieg*, Band 4, *Der Angriff auf die Sowjetunion*, hrsg. vom Militärgeschichtlichen Forschungsamt, Stuttgart, 1983, p.427.

[9]Heinz Artzt, however, suggests by omission that it *was* a so-called *Führererlaß* (and it was treated as such in fictional contexts: see Note 25 below). See *Mörder in Uniform*, Munich, 1979, p.144.

[10]Heinz Artzt, op. cit., p.146, asserts "daß der Befehl – bis auf wenige Ausnahmen – an der Ostfront mit letzter Konsequenz befolgt wurde". Charles W. Sydhor Jnr. estimates that between June 22 and December 31 1941, 16th Army units killed 57 commissars and 2,639 partisans, and destroyed 13 villages. See *Soldiers of Destruction: The SS Death's Head Division 1933-45*, Princeton N.J., 1977, p.201, n. 78. See also *Der Angriff auf die Sowjetunion*, p.1062.

[11]*Der Angriff auf die Sowjetunion*, pp.1067-1068.

[12]Geoffrey Best, *Humanity in Warfare*, pp.237 and 239.

[13]Quoted from an unpublished paper by Omer Bartov, "The Barbarisation of Warfare – German Officers and Men on the Eastern Front, 1941-1945", the text of which the author was kind enough to provide me with.

[14]Helmut Krausnick and Hans-Heinrich Wilhelm, *Die Truppe des Weltanschauungskrieges: Die Einsatzgruppen der Sicherheitspolizei und des SD 1938-1942*, Stuttgart, 1981, p.230.

[15]"And the German Army, in common with most German citizens, knew that this was going on": Albert Seaton, *The German Army 1933-45*, London, 1982, p.169. On this question of how much the Army knew, see Krausnick/Wilhelm, *Die Truppe des Weltanschauungskrieges*, "Die Kenntnis des Heeres von der Tätigkeit der Einsatzgruppen", pp.223 ff.

[16]The extent to which the Army has been assumed, even by experts in the field, to be free of such involvement, is demonstrated by Geoffrey Best's comment on the "Final Solution": "It was not something in which the German military were generally directly implicated, and was tried under a separate head at the 'war crimes' trials after the war" (*Humanity in Warfare*, p.219).

[17]It was not until the notorious Wannsee Conference of 1942 that a number of separate "special actions" were co-ordinated. Even if it is true that the conference decided on a single, centrally organized extermination campaign (and this has been disputed), the campaign moved forward

cautiously, step by step under a veil of secrecy which required the Army's increasing complicity. See a very recent contribution to this topic, Gerald Fleming's *Hitler and the Final Solution*, London, 1985.

[18] Hans Mommsen, review of Christian Streit, *Keine Kameraden: Die Wehrmacht und die sowjetischen Kriegsgefangenen 1941-1945* (Studien zur Zeitgeschichte Bd. 13), Stuttgart, 1978; in *Bulletin of the German Historical Institute London*, Spring 1979, Issue 1, p.21.

[19] See Jochen Pfeifer, *Der deutsche Kriegsroman 1945-1960*, Königstein/Ts., 1981, p.196.

[20] Cf. Hans Wagener, "Soldaten zwischen Gehorsam und Gewissen. Kriegsromane und Tagebücher", *Gegenwartsliteratur und Drittes Reich*, hrsg. Hans Wagener, Stuttgart, 1977, pp.241-264, especially p.257.

[21] See Heinz Brüggemann, "Johannes Mario Simmel – Deutsche Ideologie als Roman", *Deutsche Bestseller – Deutsche Ideologie*, hrsg. Heinz Ludwig Arnold, Stuttgart, 1975, pp.62-89.

[22] In *Die sterbende Jagd* there is a classic example of a reference to brutality in the East which both acknowledges the complicity – *at some level* – of all the German forces in atrocities (in this case the hanging of Russians) and yet subtly extricates "proper" soldiers from the net of guilt: "Das ist doch nicht die Truppe, Herr Hauptmann . . ." protests Leutnant de Bruyn, to which Hauptmann Vehlgast replies "Glauben Sie, man wird da einst einen so feinen Unterschied machen?" (p.174).

[23] Heinz Artzt, *Mörder in Uniform*, "Vorwort" by Gert Bastian, p.9. Cf. the words of Vehlgast in *Die sterbende Jagd*, "Verdammt sollen die sein, die uns so weit gebracht haben" (p.175).

[24] Cf. Jochen Pfeifer, *Der deutsche Kriegsroman 1945-1960*, p.118.

[25] This passage is significant for its suggestion that there *was* strong opposition and resistance by the generals to the "Kommissarerlaß" and other atrocities, invariably imposed from above: "daß wir immer, wenn die da oben ganz und gar verrückt wurden, ganz erhebliche Schwierigkeiten gemacht haben!" (p.307).

[26] Dr Franz J. Rappensberger, "Zur belletristischen Literatur des zweiten Weltkrieges", *Wehrkunde* ("Organ der Gesellschaft für Wehrkunde"), 6, 1957, pp.664 and 666.

[27] See J. Pfeifer, *Der deutsche Kriegsroman 1945-1960*, p.169.

[28] Cp. Walter Kempowski, *Haben Sie davon gewußt?*, Hamburg, 1979.

APPENDIX I

TAMBIMUTTU'S *POETRY IN WARTIME*: AUTHOR INDEX AND INDEX OF FIRST LINES

Author Index

Index of First Lines

H.M.K.

APPENDIX II

DEFEAT, MAY 1940: SUPPLEMENTARY HISTORY. BEFORE, AND AFTER, *LA ROUTE DES FLANDRES*

Several months after *La route des Flandres* appeared, Claude Simon received a letter from a fellow-survivor of the disaster of 1940. The letter came as a considerable surprise to Simon because it was immediately evident that it had been written by an officer whom Simon was convinced he had seen killed, together with the Colonel leading the remnants of his cavalry squadron, when they were ambushed near Sars-Poteries, on the road between Solre-le-Château and Avesnes-sur-Helpe, during the morning of 17 May. The author of the letter, the former Commandant Cuny, now a retired Colonel, was enthusiastic in his praise for the novel, despite an obvious reluctance to engage in a personal correspondence with someone who had been but a humble *brigadier*. However, despite chiding Simon for a minor inaccuracy concerning equestrian terminology, Colonel Cuny had clearly been impressed by the description of the final ambush, and some other scenes. The novel as a whole had caused him to relive a period in his past; he had been literally "stupefied" by it.[1]

When a critic tentatively raised the question of this letter during a discussion following the first paper given at the 1971 colloquium on the *nouveau roman*, alluding to it as evidence of the inadequacy of approaches to Simon's novels which concentrated exclusively upon what the theoretical spokesman for the movement called the "literal dimension" (meaning the text as a space within which material signs are organised), the suggestion was derisively dismissed as further proof of gullible readers' inveterate habit of projecting themselves into what the same theoretician had baptised "the referential illusion".[2] The possibility that certain sequences in *La route des Flandres* "referred" to "quelque chose de réel" having thus been vetoed, the discussion moved on to the consideration of the problems involved in analysing descriptions of more obviously fictional entities, notably the wedding cake in Flaubert's *Madame Bovary*. It was clear from remarks made by Alain Robbe-Grillet, however, that the issues raised by the letter were potentially troublesome for the theoretical camp, for while he maliciously profited from Simon's absence from the first discussion to classify him as a writer who needed the support of "references" of various kinds more than the other writers whose work was to be examined, he also admitted that all were to differing degrees "tempted" by what he called "un certain passé référentialiste".[3] Clearly, not only "referents", but the past in both its collective and personal dimensions were areas with which the "New Novel" should not concern itself, since their evocation would threaten the anti-realist thrust of the new writing, and endanger the ideal of totally "self-referential" fictions to which it seemed, at the time, to be committed.[4] Since the concept of reference employed throughout the Cerisy *décades* – including the one devoted to Simon's novels in 1974 – remained more or less unquestioned, with the result that both autobiographical and historical matters remained largely excluded from consideration, it is worth emphasising that Colonel Cuny's unsolicited letter was prompted not by the naïve reading habits of an old soldier, but by what could be called a "recognition effect" produced by a text which carefully avoids the kind of facile use of references typical of so much historical fiction in the modern period. As I stress in my essay,[5] the incidents depicted are not located (either temporally or spatially) in any precise way, and no mention is made of real personages involved in either the overall "event" or the episodes which served as the models for certain scenes in the novel. The place-names which occur in the text, moreover, connote disorientation rather than pointing to the towns and villages through which Simon's squadron passed during the advance to the Meuse and the subsequent retreat towards the French border. Consequently, while it is obvious that Colonel Cuny perceived that his commanding officer, Colonel de Ray, had been the model for "de Reixach" in the novel, and that he had himself been satirised as "le petit lieutenant", it is far less obvious that his reaction to the text consisted merely in "self-projection". Indeed, in view of the less than flattering portrait of the "petit lieutenant" presented in the closing pages of the book, the tribute to the persuasive power of Simon's writing appears more, rather than less remarkable.

Perhaps, also, those who dismissed Cuny's letter on "theoretical" grounds (which barely concealed an element of class prejudice) should have examined more closely the terms he employs when describing the effect created on him by the reading of *La route des Flandres*, for he speaks neither of having "identified" with a fictional character nor of having "believed" in a fictional reconstruction: "ce qui me frappe plus personnellement sont les scènes si semblables à celles que j'ai vécues en 40", and a little later: "Cet épisode (the ambush) est fidèle jusque dans le moindre détail."[6] These claims in no way prove that Cuny's reading of the novel involved simple-minded self-projection into essentially fictional situations; on the contrary, the officer was acutely aware that parts of the text were "faithful" to what he had witnessed and experienced. Retold as part of a tissue of fictional and autobiographical narratives, in which some of the former are historicised, and some of the latter fictionalised, Simon's version of certain events created a formal and a linguistic configuration such that an unlikely connection was made, between two mens' memories, across a forty-year gap.

It would therefore appear that there is the possibility of overlap between historical narratives proper, fictional narratives involving names of real persons and real places, and fictions devoid of such obvious references, and this must have the effect of bringing immediately into question the meaning of the term "proper" as just employed, just as it introduces a doubt regarding the possibility of radically anti-representational and anhistorical writing.

Certainly, those who stress the ways in which Simon's novel "subverts" historical representation can benefit as much from a clearer awareness of the network of complementary and even competing narratives of which the text is a part as can those inclined to read it within the context of the historical field it specifically calls up. Neither position, I would argue, can be upheld in such a way that it excludes the other entirely. At the very least, it will be appreciated that if, in the fiction/history, the troops cross and re-cross frontiers, so readers should be prepared to transgress generic boundaries and to ask why they are sometimes well defended in one place, but wide open elsewhere.[7]

Whatever history is, as an academic discipline, a profession, or a field of enquiry involving all who wish to understand some feature of the past, it is clear that it still defines itself principally as a practice of *writing*. This presupposition, so often forgotten, or ruled irrelevant by historians themselves, is clearly set out by Paul Ricœur: "'L'écriture de l'histoire' . . . n'est pas extérieure à la conception et à la composition de l'histoire; elle ne constitue pas une opération secondaire, relevant de la seule rhétorique de la communication, et qu'on pourrait négliger comme étant d'ordre simplement rédactionnel. Elle est constitutive du mode historique de compréhension. L'histoire est intrinsèquement historio-graphie, ou, pour le dire d'une façon délibérément provocante, un artifice littéraire."[8] This observation, among other similar ones made by theorists of the "narrativist" persuasion, is not so much "true" as very hard to controvert without recourse to arguments in which historical "facts" are simply taken as given, that is, arguments which do not consider the so-called "temporal paradox" as either relevant or interesting in itself.[9] In a novel such as *La route des Flandres*, however, it is clear from many passages that the paradox of the pastness of the past, and the problems raised by attempts to describe the *traces* it has left in the narrator's consciousness, are of central importance, and not merely the pretext for linguistic virtuosity and compositional experiments. Indeed, the evidence for a powerful attachment not to the past "as such", but to that very quality of "pastness" which the dynamism of poetic language freed from the limitations of a purely pragmatic concept of reference throws into sometimes tragic relief, is precisely the source of the fascination which Simon's novel can exert on it readers. *La route des Flandres* thus complements and supplements conventional histories of the defeat of 1940 not by supplying any new facts, nor by allowing us to "see" an aspect of the disaster any better than we can "see" a total event and all the incidents which might have been part of it when reading other types of narrative. A novel does not "recover" the past, any more than a work of history – indeed, playing on that word, we could say that all texts, to some extent, "recouvrent", or *cover up* the past by adding more and more layers of writing to existing records and testimony. However, when both the "reality effects"[10] and the poetic meanings of the fictional text combine to produce either precise "recognition effects" – as in the case of Colonel Cuny – or an awareness of a network of "referential frames"[11] from which the text has been not so much detached as *distanced*, then it seems reasonable to suggest that we are dealing not with meanings that are wholly enclosed within a text but with meanings set in motion by the interaction of a text and its readers. In other words, *La route des Flandres* obliges its readers, in one way or another, to look back upon their own expectations when reading both histories and fictions, and to re-examine the basis of the "competence"[12] which enables them, in the majority of cases, to make categorial distinctions between narrative genres. As the historiographer and critic Stephen Bann has noted, "the evidence that we have learnt this capacity can be found in our disposition to insert the signified 'it happened' behind each and every instance of the past tense in a historiographic context".[13]

That some *suspend*[14] the signified "it happened" when reading a novel such as *La route des Flandres* is clearly the result both of cultural training and greater or lesser degrees of informedness regarding the overall historical background and the writer's personal experience. Others, convinced that histories in some way "copy" the real,[15] will assimilate the text of an "historical novel" to what they take to be "real history". Still others, making a generic distinction between fiction and history, will perceive a gulf too wide to be bridged, and when Formalist literary theory, based upon the intra-linguistic philosophy of structuralism,[16] makes that gulf into a total epistemological break, then, clearly, it leaves itself somewhat stranded, in a world of fictional mirrors and purely "self-reflective" aesthetic and philosophical values. Largely because of the forcing of distinctions between concepts of the real and the imaginary based upon an opposition between the ideality of linguistic representations and the materiality of a text, the challenges offered by Simon's writing (whether in *La route des Flandres* or any other of his novels, for all allude in one way or another to the events of 1940 and previous disasters) have been to some extent neutralised.

The suggestion that Simon was more attached than the other New Novelists to what Robbe-Grillet called "un certain passé référentialiste" thus not only created the impression that his writing was deficient with respect to certain modernist ideals, but implied that both the role of history in a writer's life, together with his or her historical role, great or small, in major or minor "events", were irrelevant to the aesthetics of the new writing. A question of some importance is thus elided, for it could be argued that the *suppression* of the past, and of overt autobiographical or historical "references" simply begs the question of the historicity of all discourse, and by emphasising blanks or "no-go areas" in fact draws attention to them. Would it not be interesting in itself, for example, to know more about Robbe-Grillet's wartime experiences and the period in which he worked in a German tank factory? We might then be in a better position to answer the question of why that experience is nowhere reflected in his writing, whereas much ink has flowed concerning his subsequent professional interest in the cultivation of bananas.[17]

Perhaps, therefore, it is time to emphasise that even modernist and "postmodernist" writing calls up its readers within the context of the historical dimension of all writing, a dimension from which a certain practice of "self-referential" fiction may wish to be excluded, but which it reflects in both its exclusions and its wilful delusions, since all acts of comprehension require frames of reference even when they can be shown to exist within other frames and to produce not hard and fast meanings but a continuous relaying of signals.

La route des Flandres does not "refer" directly to "history", but the suppression and the transformation of *names* does not abolish all the signposts, for these point to a number of "routes to reference". The most obvious of such signposts is the novel's title itself. The "referent" along that road, moreover, is not just a week in May 1940, but the very dimension of the historical imagination, in which the real and the unreal produce many strange meetings, all of which occur, finally, in *texts*, none of which can claim any exclusive privileges when dealing with the problem of establishing "what happened", let alone why it happened.

The following piece of "supplementary history", generously written by Claude Simon, in response to my request for a short "chronicle" of the events in which he was involved in May 1940, is therefore not offered as a key to *La route des Flandres*, nor does it imply that Claude Simon supports any of the arguments advanced either above or elsewhere. Indeed, as another *narrative*, Simon's text causes many of the issues evoked to rebound, for by its very nature it is full of *gaps*.[18]

Clearly, it remains up to individual readers to decide for themselves how relevant this "petit historique" is to their reading of *La route des Flandres*, but the problems it raises do at least show that when history represses its own theory, and fiction its own history, both are diminished in the process.

A.C.P.

* * *

Paris, le 6 juillet, 1984

Cher Anthony Pugh,

Voici le petit "historique" du 31e Dragons que vous m'avez demandé (Tout au moins du 1er Escadron).

Ainsi "mis à plat", il est difficile de réaliser ce qu'ont été ces sept jours et comment non seulement un régiment mais encore une brigade de cavalerie tout entière s'est pour ainsi dire "volatilisée" (c'est l'impression qu'a dû avoir aussi le général qui la commandait avant de se tirer une balle dans la tête...)[19]

Cela paraît dérisoire. Et pourtant...

Très amicalement,

Claude Simon.

31e Régiment de Dragons.

Garnison en temps de paix: Lunéville (Meurthe et Moselle).

Cavalerie montée. Armement individuel: sabre et mousqueton de cavalerie. Un fusil-mitrailleur par groupe (12 cavaliers). Une mitrailleuse et un canon anti-char de 35 par escadron. Pas de mitrailleuses ni de canons anti-aériens.[20]

Je ne peux vous donner qu'un compte rendu des actions du 1er Escadron dont je faisais partie: un simple brigadier ne sait d'une bataille que ce dont il a été directement témoin.

A la veille de l'offensive allemande du 10 mai 1940, le premier escadron bivouaque depuis environ un mois dans la forêt de Trélon (Départment du Nord), tout près de la frontière belge.[21]

Le 10 mai, ordre d'alerte à 10 heures du matin environ (l'armée allemande a pénétré en Belgique et en Hollande à cinq heures du matin).

L'escadron se met en marche à midi sur un axe Rance – Boussu[22] – Morialmé – Annevoie-Rouillon où la Meuse est franchie le 11 vers midi. La progression continue par Assesse, puis Natoye. A cinq kilomètres environ après cette ville première attaque par l'aviation allemande,[23] suivie peu après d'une seconde.

L'ordre de retraite est donné le 12 au matin sans que le contact ait encore été établi avec l'ennemi. Vers midi l'escadron se fait surprendre près du hameau de Lè Fontaine par des éléments motorisés et est dispersé.[24] Certains cavaliers restés isolés (dont moi) ne parviennent à repasser la Meuse que vers le soir, à Profondeville.[25]

L'escadron se groupe à l'ouest de la Meuse dans le Bois de la Haute Marlagne. Il a perdu dans la journée environ un quart de son effectif. On dit que le 3e Escadron, immédiatement à notre droite, a subi des pertes beaucoup plus sévères par des mitraillages d'avions.

Le 13 et le 14 mai, l'escadron reste en réserve.

Les troupes d'infanterie qui ont pris position sur la Meuse subissent de violents bombardements aériens et sont pratiquement anéanties. L'aviation française semble inexistante.[26] Le soir du 14 des éléments allemands parviennent à franchir la Meuse sur un barrage que l'on a oublié de faire sauter.[27]

Remarque: la Meuse qui, à cet endroit, coule au fond d'une vallée profondément encaissée et aux rives escarpées constitue une "coupure" très difficile à franchir pour un attaquant, et par conséquent très favorable à la défense.[28]

Le 15 mai au matin, l'escadron prend position dans les villages de Cottaprex et de Bossières. Attaque de l'infanterie allemande (mitrailleuses et mortiers de tranchées). Grâce au soutien de l'artillerie française (et de trois chars dont deux sont mis hors de combat) l'attaque est repoussée. Peu de pertes.

16 mai – Décrochage. L'escadron bat en retraite toute la journée.[29] Organise le soir la défense du village de Joncret. Faible bombardement d'artillerie. Contact à la tombée de la nuit avec premiers éléments ennemis. Ordre de décrocher vers environ minuit.

17 mai – Après avoir battu en retraite pendant la nuit, l'escadron à la tête duquel est venu se placer le Colonel Ray tombe vers huit (?) heures du matin (on est, dans ces circonstances, dans un état semi-somnambulique. Je suis bien incapable, à une heure près, de dire l'heure exacte) dans une embuscade tendue par des blindés allemands déjà parvenus dans le village de Cousolre, à la frontière française. L'escadron est pratiquement anéanti.[30]

Vers dix heures (?), le colonel Ray accompagné du chef d'escadron Cuny se dirige (toujours à cheval) vers Avesnes-sur-Helpe par la route Solre-le-Château – Avesnes.[31] Il ne lui reste alors de son régiment que deux cavaliers (dont moi). Des blessés et des réfugiés signalent que des parachutistes allemands sont embusqués derrière les haies.[32] Des avions allemands passent en mitraillant.

A ce moment il n'existe plus de front organisé. Je peux témoigner que la ligne fortifiée française qui longeait la frontière belge (barbelés, fossé anti-chars, nombreux blockhaus en béton) *n'a été occupée à cet endroit* (c'est-à-dire au nord-est de Solre-le-Château) *par aucun défenseur*. (Je suis revenu sur les lieux, il y a une quinzaine d'années: les blockhaus étaient toujours là, intacts.)[33]

Peu après avoir traversé le village de Beugnies, le colonel Ray et le commandant Cuny sont abattus par un parachutiste allemand.[34] Les deux cavaliers survivants errent au hasard dans la campagne, se cachent dans une ferme et sont faits prisonniers le lendemain tandis qu'avec un groupe d'autres soldats coupés de leurs unités ils cherchaient à rejoindre à pied les lignes (?) françaiscs.[35]

Avec le 8e Régiment de Dragons (également en garnison à Lunéville), le 31e faisait partie d'une brigade (quatre régiments) de cavalerie commandée par le général Barbe (qui s'est suicidé). Cette brigade faisait elle-même partie de l'armée Corap qui, *sur l'ordre de Paul Reynaud*, alors président du Conseil, est entrée en Belgique où elle a dû affronter en rase campagne le choc de l'armée allemande au lieu d'attendre celle-ci sur la ligne fortifiée qui protégeait la frontière.[36]

CLAUDE SIMON

NOTES

[1] A photograph of the letter is published in *Entretiens, Claude Simon* (Rodez: Editions Subervie, 1972), between pp.152-3.

[2] *Nouveau roman; hier, aujourd'hui* (Paris: Union Générale d'Editions, 1972), vol.1, pp.83-4. Jean Ricardou defines this concept in *Le Nouveau roman* (Paris: Editions du Seuil, 1973) pp.28-31.

[3] *Nouveau roman; hier, aujourd'hui*, vol.1, p.31.

[4] The concept of "self-referentiality" (or *autoreprésentation*) is debated in a series of articles in *Texte* 1 (1982), and most effectively challenged in "Le Texte littéraire: non-référence, auto-référence, ou référence fictionnelle" by Catherine Kerbrat-Orecchioni (pp.27-49).

[5] Above, pp.59-70.

[6] From Colonel Cuny's letter.

[7] Quite apart from the "deconstruction" of generic frontiers, we could well see Simon's novels as responses to the kinds of questions asked by the historian Lucien Febvre: "Sensibility and history – a new subject! I know of no book that deals with it. . . . please forgive a poor historian for uttering the artist's cry, and yet what a fine subject it is!" From "Sensibility and history: how to reconstruct the emotional life of the past", in *A New Kind of History*, Edited by Peter Burke (London: Routledge & Kegan Paul, 1973).

[8] Paul Ricœur, *Temps et récit*, Tome 1 (Paris: Editions du Seuil, 1983), p.228.

[9] For an example of such an argument, see Maurice Mandelbaum, *The Anatomy of Historical Knowledge* (Baltimore and London: Johns Hopkins University Press, 1977), p.9.

[10] For the already classic definition of this concept, see Roland Barthes, "The Reality Effect", in *French Literary Theory Today*, Ed. Tzvetan Todorov (Cambridge and Paris: Cambridge University Press and Editions de la Maison des Sciences de l'Homme, 1982), pp.11-17.

[11] See Umberto Eco, *The Role of the Reader* (London: Hutchinson & Co. 1979), "Textual levels: A theoretical abstraction", pp.13-15.

[12] A concept developed notably by Jonathan Culler in *Structuralist Poetics* (London: Routledge & Kegan Paul, 1975), pp.113-130.

[13] Stephen Bann, "Analysing the Discourse of History", *Renaissance and Modern Studies*, "Structuralisms", vol.XXVII, p.81.

[14] For a discussion of the concept of "suspended reference", see Paul Ricœur, *The Rule of Metaphor* (London: Routledge & Kegan Paul, 1978), "Metaphor and reference", pp.216-256.

[15] "The fact can only have a linguistic existence, as a term in a discourse, and yet it is exactly as if this existence were merely the 'Copy', purely and simply, of another existence situated in the extra-structural domain of the 'real'. This type of discourse is doubtless the only type in which the referent is aimed for as something external to the discourse, without it ever being possible to attain it outside this discourse. We should therefore ask ourselves in a more searching way what place the 'real' plays in the structure of the discourse." Roland Barthes, "The discourse of history", in *Comparative Criticism, A Yearbook*, vol.3, Ed. E. S. Shaffer (Cambridge University Press, 1981), p.17.

[16] For a critique of this aspect of structuralist theory, see Paul Ricœur, "Structure et herméneutique", *Esprit*, novembre 1963, pp.596-627, and from a different angle, Stephen Gaukroger, "Logic, Language and Literature: the relevance of Frege", *The Oxford Literary Review*, 6, No.1 (1983), 68-96.

[17] Seen, of course, in the historico-sociological context of decolonisation, in, for example, Jacques Leenhardt, *Lecture politique du roman*: *La Jalousie d'Alain Robbe-Grillet* (Paris: Editions de Minuit, 1973).

[18] "... every narrative, however seemingly 'full', is constructed on the basis of a set of events which *might have been included but were left out*; and this is as true of imaginary as it is of realistic narratives. This consideration permits us to ask what kind of notion of reality authorises construction of a narrative account of reality in which continuity rather than discontinuity governs the articulation of the discourse." Hayden White, "The Value of Narrativity on the Representation of Reality", *Critical Inquiry*, Autumn 1980, p.14.

[19] See *La route des Flandres* (Paris: Editions de Minuit, Collection "Double", 1960), pp.200-1, 282. Colonel Cuny, in his letter, names the real General Barbe, and Simon confirms this subsequently.

[20] The inadequate equipment of certain regiments, with particular reference to anti-tank guns and anti-aircraft guns, is discussed in many of the histories of the defeat of 1940. The following are offered as samples: William L. Shirer, *The Collapse of the Third Republic, An Enquiry into the Fall of France in 1940* (London: The Literary Guild, 1970), p.511; Colonel A. Goutard, *The Battle of France* (London: Frederick Muller Ltd., 1958), pp.39-40; Len Deighton, *Blitzkrieg* (London: Jonathan Cape, 1979), pp.192, 199. The general conclusion of historians is that just as the Armée de l'Air failed to take in the lessons of demonstrations of dive-bombers put on by the Luftwaffe before the war, so the French General Staff failed to see the need for adequate air-defence equipment. French-manufactured anti-aircraft weapons were still being sold abroad up until the commencement of hostilities, and no attempt was made to import such weapons when, after the Norwegian campaign, deficiencies in this area were made all too evident.

[21] The locations mentioned can be followed either on the Michelin Tourist Map. No. 53 (1/200,000 scale, Arras; Charleville-Mézières) or on the 1/100,000 scale Tourist Map of the Institute Géographique National, No. 5 (Charleville-Mézières; Maubeuge). Locations beyond the East bank of the Meuse were checked on the map covering the region of Namur, published by the Institut Géographique Militaire (Bruxelles). These, together with the appropriate Cartes d'État-Major, show how Simon's novel avoids the mention of too recognisable place-names, but still provides enough names of towns, villages and *lieux-dits* to situate the novel in a world of real referents as opposed to wholly imagined ones. This does not of course mean that the novel somehow "transports" its readers into geographical reality, but it does show that the fictional narrative leaves open the question of how narratives relate (back) to the real.

[22] Boussu-lez-Walcourt, on the N.36, between Beaumont and Walcourt.

[23] See the fictional treatment of this episode in *Les Géorgiques* (Paris: Editions de Minuit, 1981), pp.176-7.

[24] This episode provides the basis for several scenes in other novels, including *La bataille de Pharsale* (Editions de Minuit, 1969) and *Leçon de choses* (Editions de Minuit, 1975). Simon's account

of his squadron's first encounter with German troops (a short narrative, plus a sketch map) occurs in some correspondence arising out of the "petit historique". I hope to publish it in due course in the context of a study of other works by Simon including scenes based upon his memories of the battle.

[25]See *La corde raide* (Paris: Editions du Saggittaire, 1947) pp.79-88.

[26]See L. Deighton, pp.300-1, Col. A. Goutard, p.34, and W. L. Shirer, pp.301, 332-3, 337, 369-71, 594, 596, for discussion of the accusation that many available French aircraft were not committed to the battle, and Marc Bloch's *L'Etrange défaite* (Paris: Albin Michel, 1957), pp.231-9, for the historian's explanation of how this might have reflected a theory held before the war by the military hierarchy, according to which expensive equipment such as aircraft should be held in reserve for counter-attacks. Most historians now agree that the French airforce could have done much more, although outnumbered, above all against the German dive-bombers, which were particularly vulnerable to fighters.

[27]The weir at Houx, where Rommel's motor-cyclists established a bridgehead (see L. Deighton, p.236).

[28]In *What Happened to France* (London: John Murray, 1940), Gordon Waterfield (Reuter's correspondent with the French Armies) stressed that not only Colonel de Gaulle and Paul Reynaud, but "every army officer who studied topography" knew that the Meuse was not in fact at all easy to defend. He quotes a speech by Paul Reynaud to the senate, prior to the German Attack: "The Meuse has wrongly been considered as a redoubtable obstacle for the enemy. . . . it is difficult to defend, machine-gun fire on the flank is impossible and infiltration is easy for manœuvring troops" (pp.24-5). Together with subsequent historians, Waterfield blames the General Staff for sending a weak and over-stretched army, consisting of mostly reservist troops, to the most vulnerable sector of the front, in forced marches which left them exhausted.

[29]The two "Divertissements" in *Leçon de choses* relate to episodes during this retreat.

[30]The description of an ambush in *La route des Flandres* (pp.146-154) appears to be based upon this incident. An historian at the University of Lille, J. Heuclin, whose family lives in the village of Cousolre, has instituted a local history workshop in order to collate material relating to the war and the Occupation. His groups produce a bulletin called *Memor*. No. 3 (juin 1984) contains many accounts of the German breakthrough in the area. The historian's father, Pierre Heuclin, recalls stories of the ambush just outside Cousolre, and the disposal of the bodies of French Dragoons and dead horses. Another description of the incident occurs in *Les Géorgiques*, pp.44-7.

[31]See *Les Géorgiques*, p.52. The naming of these locations, and retrospective comment on *La route des Flandres* in the later novel, are indicators of Claude Simon's desire, in recent years, to distance himself from the concept of absolute "autoreferentiality". See his comments on the "maximalist" theories associated with the *nouveau roman* movement in the 1970s in "Reflections of the novel", forthcoming in *The Review of Contemporary Fiction* (Spring 1985).

[32]After reading some extracts from *Memor* and Rommel's diaries, Claude Simon commented in a letter (23rd August 1984): "Ainsi donc, les avertissements que nous criaient les blessés et les réfugiés sur la route d'Avesnes (et que cet imbécile de Colonel refusait superbement d'écouter) étaient exacts!: les blindés allemands étaient déjà passés dans la nuit alors que nous étions encore à plusieurs kilomètres de là en Belgique: cependant, en regardant attentivement le croquis de *Memor*, je pense que l'embuscade qui nous a été tendu était le fait d'éléments de la Ve Panzer; la VIIIe, de Rommel, était déjà au-delà d'Avesnes à ce moment. Par ailleurs, je m'explique maintenant pourquoi il n'y avait aucune trace de bataille au N.E. de Solre-le-Château (là où j'ai retrouvé le colonel) et pourquoi, à cet endroit, les blockhaus sont restés intacts. Je me souviens, en effet, qu'en repassant quelques jours plus tard, prisonnier, par Clairfayts [where Rommel broke through the frontier defences], avoir vu un ou deux blockhaus éclatés comme des grenades et noircis par les flammes. Mais ce n'était pas une raison pour abandonner les autres sans combat!"

[33]See Col. A. Goutard, pp.169-170, for some of the explanations for the abandonment of pill-boxes on the fortified frontier line beyond the end of the Maginot line. In the same letter quoted in the previous note, Claude Simon recalls a garage-owner in the region, many years later' claiming that he was given the wrong measurements for the armoured doors and windows he was commissioned to install in such pill-boxes.

[34]This confirms the claims made by Colonel Cuny in his letter, while the circumstances of his escape remain unexplained.

[35]The units which had not already been captured had fled by the time Simon's squadron was ambushed for the last time. Attempts made to regroup the remnants of the 9th Army in this area were unsuccessful.

[36]Reynaud claimed to have opposed the advance into Belgium, but to have been obliged to conform to the wishes of the Conseil de Guerre which drew up the plan shortly after the outbreak of

war in 1939. (See *La France a sauvé l'Europe*, Tome 2, Paris: Ernest Flammarion, 1947, pp.44-7.) The Belgian refusal to allow Allied troops into the country before the German attack on 10 May made it very hard for the units sent ahead to slow up the German vanguard (units such as Simon's Cavalry regiment, and those sent into the Ardennes further south) to be effective. The secret orders given to Belgian troops, unknown to Allied commanders, to retreat behind the Meuse at the beginning of hostilities, had been issued as early as 12 February 1940. (See William L. Shirer, p.606.) The First and the Fourth Light Cavalry Divisions, to which Claude Simon's regiment belonged, were sent, initially, to hold a line running from Havelange to Mont-Gauthier (just north of Rochefort on the east bank of the Meuse). The Germans made rapid progress during the night of the 10-11 May, and turned the flank of Simon's regiment the next morning, his squadron finding itself left defending a railway bridge north of Natoye, when German units had already cut off their line of escape. After being ambushed in the hamlet of Lè Fontaine, survivors tried to get away across the fields in a northerly direction. Simon effected his escape by sliding, with his horse, down a thirty-metre-deep railway embankment. He lost his horse, and ran back up the track towards Assesse. Memories of this incident form the basis of scenes in several novels. For details of troop movements during this and later phases of the battle, see *La Campagne de France*, Lt-Colonel Lugand *et al* (Paris: Presses Universitaires de France, 1953), first published in *Revue d'Histoire de la deuxième guerre mondiale*, Nos. 10-11, June 1953.

QUEEN MARY
COLLEGE
LIBRARY